The Infinity Loop
for Women

The Infinity Loop for Women

Spiritual, Communication & Leadership Development
for Every Woman to Change the World

Krista Vorse

ISBN-13: 9781979047425
ISBN-10: 1979047421

I dedicate this book to
my younger self
and to
the woman being burned at the stake

"I refuse to keep silent about societal expectations
that marginalize women and girls to be
submissive at the expense of their dignity."
- DR. TERERAI TRENT

Acknowledgments

I chose not to footnote or give a list of references. Truths I've come to love are woven together with my work and my personal experience of transformation. My hope is you'll explore these teachers. I don't claim to represent their philosophy, as I synthesize the both/and of these teachers. Complex topics are covered and it may appear I contradict myself; it's the both/and. My prayer is these principles bring you more freedom and that I articulated them with skill and sensitivity. My heart is full with utmost respect and gratitude for these souls. With complete joy, I thank those mentioned and those not.

Richard Rohr, the Franciscan Priest, who's authored so many books I stopped counting after thirty. He has The Center for Action and Contemplation. Rohr has influenced me more than any other in my trajectory into the life of a contemplative. I call him my spiritual father.

James Finley, the clinical psychologist, author, Merton scholar, and so much more.

Cynthia Bourgeault, the author, teacher and scholar who knows how to live from the soul.

Mirabai Starr, and so many others Richard Rohr has introduced me to.

Martha Beck, Byron Katie, Deepak Chopra, Eckhart Tolle, Caroline Myss, Andrew Harvey, Melody Beattie and Karla McLaren. And Kathleen McGowan who shows us, women were always meant to lead in The Way of Love to change the world.

The mystics and teachers who've been gone for decades, hundreds and thousands of years but whose words live on.

Thomas Merton, the author and contemplative of the 20th century, showed me the way into an inner life.

The fathers of Organizational Learning: Chris Argyris, Bill Isaacs, Otto Sharmer, and Peter Senge.

Some other influential teachers have been Clarissa Pinkola Estés, Mark Goulston, Gavin de Becker, Daniel Kahneman, Gary Klein, and the creators of Egonomics. We must not forget good 'ole Socrates if we're talking about inquiry.

My intimate comrades: Kiz Richter, Jennifer Joss, Jennifer Miller Williams, Sean-Riley Burns and Leo Gorcey.

With special gratitude for Ajana Miki. In session after session with her, my vocation was birthed.

To my clients over the years who showed me what's possible in The Infinity Loop. This book exists because of you. I love my work and hold you all with remembrance and love.

To those who've loved and supported me and to those who haven't, you've all been gifts to me in my move toward my soul's compass. Humility has its gifts. We love our enemies because they're our greatest teachers; they show us our wounds and what we truly stand for. Our enemies clean us out to do this work.

Lastly, I honor my Great Wound. It bounced me into my life's work. This book is because of that wound. Mystery has the last word.

Contents

The Set Up

The Down and Dirty

"In the dominator model the pursuit of external
power, the ability to manipulate and control others,
is what matters most. When culture is based on a
dominator model, not only will it be violent but it
will frame all relationships as power struggles."
-BELL HOOKS
THE WILL TO CHANGE: MEN, MASCULINITY, AND LOVE

We're fed up with whatever men do that bugs us and we've decided we've had enough. It's time to lay out what they do wrong. We correct them, act parental, and think that's the right thing. There's no connection, no awareness, and no inquiry. *That's* being a strong woman, we've been told. It may feel right even though it's not the most emotionally intelligent or effective way to communicate. Even if we get compliance, our relationships aren't strengthened.

That's *not* The Infinity Loop.

In The Infinity Loop, we step into a structure that becomes second nature. It's our check-in with ourselves to become centered and aware every time we engage; it's a discipline to retrain our brains. We break habits and cultural taboos as we're open-hearted and vulnerable. We're aware of what's going on under the turbulence. Our truest selves want something better than an ego win where we never ultimately win. Humility and respect guard and direct us in this loop. We honor what serves from our anger but not what doesn't. What we experience is expressed in a way that's open to feedback. Through inquiry, we get feedback on how they experience us.

It's powerful, it's beautiful, and it's love. It takes intention and conviction. It feels so damn good and it's so damn effective!

May You Be Seduced

"Hope is being able to see that there is
light despite all of the darkness."
- DESMOND TUTU

"You are stronger than you believe. You
have greater powers than you know."
- ANTIOPE TO DIANA
WONDER WOMAN

The Infinity Loop reminds us that what we do to another we do to ourselves. When we hurt another, we hurt ourselves. Staying connected to ourselves helps the other to be connected. By being aware it creates the most awareness. True inquiry helps us learn and isn't just a trick to get someone to see what they're not seeing. Divine union is connection to everyone and everything. We have lost that awareness that can't be said enough by all who remind us. My intention is to help you step into The Infinity Loop with more power, grace, and skill.

Women struggle to communicate with men. In our truest selves, we want to be in humility but not false humility; in confidence but not in condescension; in truth but not in competition.

We often feel powerless in our interactions with men. But we don't realize the power we have when we're grounded, heart-centered, and use our ability to connect and lead; we haven't always been taught what true leadership looks like.

Chauvinism is alive in our culture. It's how we've been raised. Companies discriminate against women; a woman will be corrected as a manager if she doesn't show enough empathy, but the same thing would not likely happen to a man.

Millions have been spent on consultants and therapists to try to fix the cultures in our companies and relationships. But these investments have left us with huge gaps between our stated values and our practices; we talk east and walk west. We pretend things aren't happening when they are. Unconsciousness comes at a great cost.

Women's anger toward patriarchal men is appropriate because of men's unconscious bias toward women. We've been dismissed, not listened to, not taken seriously. However, in the grid of emotional intelligence (EQ), it's how we use emotions and feelings to serve, not hurt, that makes the difference. The message of our anger often tells us what needs to be honored and protected. It becomes destructive when we allow it to make us less aware.

It takes the contemplative mind to hold the disturbance about the behavior we see in another and, at the same time, see that person as one who deserves respect.

We think what gives us the ego hit is the only way. But in reality, connection, awareness, and inquiry give women a greater jolt of juice. They help us gain insight and innovate while detecting and correcting error. We're able to attract and retain talent and likely be more effective in our relationships. As we tap into our own abundance, we're able to bring that abundance to our organizations and relationships.

Leadership is the power to influence others, to create a Learning Container, which lifts everyone into a higher level of awareness. Leadership is about structure, direction, and clarity. In The Infinity Loop model, we create structure, direction, and clarity as we move toward deeper connection, awareness and inquiry. Here, all that was lost is found.

The Infinity Loop model comes from over a decade of my work in Training and Development, Organizational Learning, and Culture Change. My coaching work with my private clients (individual, couples, and families with adolescents) also informs this model. My 30 years of study in the psychology of influence, personal growth and development are woven into this loop. I've worked with thousands of people from sales and customer service to management and leadership. My expertise is developing others' ability to shift quickly and think and act on a deeper level of connection, awareness, and inquiry. My personal path and life lessons flow throughout this book.

It's how *we* shift ourselves that creates the shift in our cultures. Shared language and meaning create a safe container that holds everyone accountable without a culture of blame. A Learning Culture is a byproduct of creating safety.

Some may be cynical and don't believe in infinite possibilities. From *Alice in Wonderland*:

> Alice laughed. "There's no use trying," she said; "one can't believe impossible things." "I daresay you haven't had much practice," said the Queen. "When I was your age, I always did it for half-an-hour a day. Why, sometimes I've believed as many as six impossible things before breakfast."

This kind of believing requires us to become childlike - to let go of our smug certitude and be willing to believe in the magical world of The Infinity Loop. There's no other way but through this rabbit hole.

However, The Infinity Loop will not reach someone who is a narcissist, sociopath, or has untreated Borderline Personality Disorder. If someone doesn't show genuine empathy, or cannot transcend their ego, what I teach won't work. This model is a way to turn on someone's empathy, not cater to their ego.

This book contains tools I use to set the container for The Infinity Loop eliminating the need to repeat toxic patterns. Repetition is needed to learn these tools; it takes patience to allow this way of being to sink in and do its work. Every time you come across an Infinity Loop principle, allow it to take you deeper.

I use the terms "false self" and "True Self" the way Thomas Merton used them. Merton used "false self" as our ego construct, our identity, and True Self as the nothingness that transcends our identity. In that nothingness, beyond our stories and accomplishments, is a place where we're greater than we think we are. It's the "me that was before I was born, and the me that will never die," as the Buddhists say. But it's also something beyond that. It's an integration of all that we are in this life. We transcend and include as Ken Wilber teaches.

Our spiritual growth has more to do with becoming who we already are in our True Selves.

I use the word "soul" in the way the sixteenth-century Spanish mystic, Teresa of Avila used it. Teresa believed God dwells in the innermost mansion of our souls which are made in the image and likeness of God.

Throughout this book, you'll read about the many ways I abandoned myself, was driven by my wounds and suffered throughout my life because of certain choices I made. You'll also read about how a Necessary Nemesis can lead us to our greatest liberation from compulsions that seem irresistible. Our Great Falls are covered in mercy. May you learn from my mistakes so you don't find yourself in situations like I did. But if you do or did, there's a fabulous recovery waiting for you. And you and I are forever in sweet solidarity.

This book contains topics that emerged for me in 2017 as I was being healed up in preparation for my work as a leader. My waking up to deeper love and freedom came in layers. I'd think I found my Source, but then it got even better. It was the Great Seduction toward the dying of the small me that gave me greater life. Once it's been done to us, we become the Great Seduction for the world.

I hope you too will resonate with these topics and reflect on them in a way you wouldn't have thought as central to leadership. I've included journal questions for your reflection. Because of the length of this book, I chose to give one page per chapter for questions. I encourage you to use a notebook to journal in depth on each question and see what comes into your awareness. I've found my clients derive considerable value from the journaling process to awaken how this applies to their lives.

I don't believe we'll lead effectively without learning how to love well while practicing elegant and intelligent self-care.

May you be seduced.

For All of Us

"Be the change you want to see in the world."
- Mahatma Gandhi

In this book, I refer to men and women mostly in my use of pro-nouns. My heart is for all genders and gender identifications. In however you identify yourself, I honor you. Times are changing and that's a good thing. I will likely look back a year from now and reflect on how I could have done better. My desire is to be inclusive and not stereotype or marginalize anyone.

This book gives you tools to create the tribe you yearn for. Through shared language and intention, we're able to connect with those hungry to live this way.

You're going to see how to take your weaknesses, your wounds, your shortcoming, your mistakes, your suffering and turn them into superpowers. I'll give you tools, techniques and disciplines to make these powers into a reality in the world, and to show up in your high-est, best, and most powerful self. When we change ourselves, we can change the world around us. As the Nobel prize winning theoreti-cal physicist Max Planck says, "When we change the way we look at things, the things we look at change." All of us have the power to change the world if we're willing to change ourselves. We have to stop being victims and that's what this is about. We are the chore-ographers and orchestrators of our lives. We are co-creators. When we're able to dis-identify with the ego's obsession with unworthi-ness, then we're free to be our most powerful and loving self.

The Infinity Loop shows you how to be the change you want to see in the world. We can start being that change right now.

Bird Set Free

- Sia

Clipped wings, I was a broken thing
Had a voice, had a voice but I could not sing
You would wind me down
I struggled on the ground, oh
So lost, the line had been crossed
Had a voice, had a voice but I could not talk
You held me down
I struggle to fly now, oh
But there's a scream inside that we all try to hide
We hold on so tight, we cannot deny
Eats us alive, oh it eats us alive, oh
Yes, there's a scream inside that we all try to hide
We hold on so tight, but I don't wanna die, no
I don't wanna die, I don't wanna die, yeah
I don't care if I sing off key
I find myself in my melodies
I sing for love, I sing for me
I shout it out like a bird set free
No, I don't care if I sing off key
I find myself in my melodies
I sing for love, I sing for me
I'll shout it out like a bird set free
I'll shout it out like a bird set free
I'll shout it out like a bird set free
Now I fly, hit the high notes
I have a voice, have a voice, hear me roar tonight
You held me down
But I fought back loud

Today I sobbed for all women whose fire has been dampened.

Right before the movie *Wonder Woman* came out, I had a vision of being goo on the pavement, rising up with my roar into who I am - a phoenix from the ashes. I fought back to live. I am alive and a bird set free from all that held me down, including myself. May this be true for you. I hope Sia's song gives you strength when life knocks you down.

Wonder Woman

"Only love can save this world."
- Diana Prince
Wonder Woman

"Here's to the crazy ones. The misfits. The rebels. The troublemakers. The round pegs in the square holes. The ones who see things differently. They're not fond of rules. And they have no respect for the status quo. You can quote them, disagree with them, glorify or vilify them. About the only thing you can't do is ignore them. Because they change things. They push the human race forward. And while some may see them as crazy ones, we see genius. Because the people who are crazy enough to think they can change the world, are the ones who do."
- Steve Jobs

We women need a new way to be in the world that expands our capacity for awareness, and where we neither lose our power nor abuse our power. The old self falls into habits that hinder us. Our desire is to emerge in our new self, free from life-long reactions. Our new self stands in The Infinity Loop, humble, curious, and honest. We are then never the same.

Our biggest challenges to this new way are the old patterns and our egos when they're not in service. We'll go through our own heroine's journey as we die to our identities and are reborn into our Essence. That's what I call The Bounce - taking our weakness and our wounds and making them our strength and our superpower. When we move to Essence, it all transmutes into our superpowers.

It's the truest part of us that we find in The Infinity Loop. We stop being a winner or loser. Love wins.

When we realize we're in this together, we build bridges. We're emotionally honest. We're connected to our hearts that care.

There are those who cannot enter into The Infinity Loop because they will not change. But most aren't beyond hope. Many are trapped by their unconsciousness and how they've learned to protect their egos. That's why they need Wonder Woman to save the day. What The Infinity Loop provides is an understanding that that's why we're here in this life, in this time and place. It's the understanding that we are all Wonder Woman. May this book help you discover that truth deep within yourself.

The Woman Being Burned at the Stake

"I am not afraid. I was born to do this."
- JOAN OF ARC

I write this in honor of all men who don't bully women. Sometimes a man behaves like a bully in one situation but encourages a woman to flourish in another. It's the old, worn out ways that need repair. Men have had power for a long time and haven't always used it well. We need each other in The Infinity Loop.

The brunette beauty gazes at me. A fierce plea pours out of her last minutes. Her wrists are tied above her in an infinity loop. She will not escape but be ushered into infinity. The men who have bound this woman will not escape the fires that burn with the fear, ignorance, and arrogance that have bound them to an internal hell. She's one who wails, who intercedes for all women who've gone before her and for those who come after. Her jaw is clenched with a holy anger, a fire in her womb, that says without words her dying wishes.

I am not her. I honor her powerful sexuality and her strength. She is courageous in suffering. She chose to live in truth and integrity. Underneath all that burns so hot, we are one.

She sees me late in the year 2016, in the time and place where our milieu is on fire, burning what we worked so hard to build, and what needs to burn because we were too comfortable.

This dark haired, fair-skinned woman sees into the future; a prophetess that offends because she sees what others don't. *She's trapped in time*. I have the opportunity she'll never have. I've been summoned... and so have you.

She tells me without words that I have the privilege to live in a time and place where communication tools have been made available to question beliefs, assumptions, and fears. Availing ourselves of these tools and skills could set us all free.

The power of the feminine is in staying in the heart, instructs Martha Beck. We stay in The Infinity Loop, and through connection, awareness, and inquiry become leaders to men who suffer under a patriarchy that needs to burn away.

The healthy masculine and healthy feminine are both needed. The intent is to create a new way that honors the balance and harmony of both.

I'm girded up with a mission. I've been equipped for my work which is as passionate to me as any fire in the belly is.

We *can* reach men who are reachable, who are willing and have a capacity to get free from their unexamined beliefs. They want to be free. We have compassion for them like we do on our sons.

No longer do we have to surrender to their habitual patterns of defending their ego positions. As warriors, we go in and wield the sword of truth with compassion.

There will be a revolution of radical leadership that will set the captives free.

1

The Infinity Loop

"When we change in The Infinity Loop,
what gets mirrored back to us changes."
- KRISTA VORSE

Infinity * Connection * Mystery * Eternal Now *
Binding the Broken-Hearted * Healing People *
Healing Relationships * Dialogue * Feedback Loop *
Thinking Together * Organizational Learning * Communication
* Infinite Possibilities * Oneness

As we move forward, may the words above ground us and set an intention of what it means to live our lives in the presence of The Infinity Loop.

Symbols mean a lot. They ground us and serve as a way into our deepest truth when we've lost our way.

The Infinity Loop logo represents a central theme and framework in which we see and experience the world and our relationship to it.

We believe our options are limited when they're not; we're not able to get past the blocks in our most intimate relationships, and yet, I've seen that when we stay in the loop of connection, awareness, and inquiry, we can help one another heal and transform.

Often, we feel unsafe and separate. However, when we fold into each other in our vulnerability and acknowledge that we feel unsafe and separate, there's a way to have our boundaries and still be in connection.

When we mirror one another in The Infinity Loop, it shows us our limitless potential. When we drop into our True Selves - our Infinite Selves - we tap into an awareness that's limitless. We see a new view of what's possible. Through the lens of The Infinity Loop, we see the world differently.

2

Staying in The Infinity Loop

"As gold is purified in the fire, purify me in the fire of
your love."
- KRISTA VORSE

It takes humility, curiosity, and honesty to stay in The Infinity
Loop. Empathy and our ability to transcend the limitations of our
ego are needed. There's a shift from being non-reflective to being a
learner. We move from winning to creating a Learning Container,
and from Breakdown in Debate to Dialogue. It only happens when
we Re-spect (re-see with new eyes).

In The Infinity Loop, we co-create the interaction and lead
one another to be our best selves. We mirror, listen, and attune to
one another's needs under all the messiness. It's how we love well
while practicing elegant and intelligent self-care.

The Infinity Loop is the reminder of how "even though I'm
not you, I'm not other than you either," as James Finley teaches.
It reminds us how much power we have in every interaction to
lead all participants (and ourselves) to Think Together and explore
what's possible. Most of the time it works. And it's a trip.

The Infinity Loop is how we fold into one another in love,
compassion, and engagement. We don't break connection through
our ego identification that believes "we are our point of view."

And lastly, it's the vision I have of how we see ourselves in one
ring of the loop - the yellow-orange loop being a fire that's solid as
a block of gold - that keeps us safe. We stay in connection with the
other who's in the other loop. The other may appear hard to reach
in their defensiveness and aggressiveness. But we decide to stay in

The Infinity Loop, girded up with the fire of love and truth that comes from the True Self. From our True Self, that's unmoved by the offense of the other, we connect, inquire, and create awareness to bring the other into new possibilities. It's radical, but so is the concept of infinity. We need radically new ways to relate.

3

Clarifying The Infinity Loop

"That which is essential is always an invitation.
The nonessential is always imposing itself."
- James Finley

The Infinity Loop is an invitation for engagement. It's not bondage. Author Brené Brown, who's famous for her work on vulnerability, stresses the importance of discernment. She teaches when to, and when not to, be vulnerable.

In The Infinity Loop, we don't use spiritual or communication models, tools, and principles as weapons against one another. We never say, "You need to get into your True Self." It's how we love and allow another's pain that empowers one to feel safe and bounce into their True Self.

In my not too distant past when I was way too open, I opened my home to a meeting about racism. I had already lost my way in my relationship with the leaders (a couple); I denied my needs and my truth in exchange for a sense of community, thinking I was being supportive and wanting to grow. The meeting was what a meeting about racism shouldn't be; there was no connection, awareness, or inquiry. Later that night, when I shared my feelings about the meeting and that there was neither safety nor boundaries, I was told to take a deep breath and get into my big self. One of the leaders (woman) told me my experience wasn't valid, my feelings, my view, even my expertise in the field of facilitation and Dialogue, was a pathetic delusion. There was neither compassion nor humility to acknowledge she may have contributed to my pain.

This is consistent with her behavior. She decided to set me straight in a condescending email. I forwarded the email thread to my support system and sent her an "F-off." Yep. I did. I continued to be mocked, messaged repeatedly after I told her and her partner to stop the confrontational and mean-spirited messages and to please respect my boundaries. When I did eventually run into her, she looked at me as though I was the most grotesque human-being to walk the earth.

My friend who gave me feedback on this book suggested I needed to add in this story to anchor the principles of The Infinity Loop. I believe everything into my life can be in service of my growth and healing. By having this person in my life and allowing that situation - while ignoring the alarms I had going off in me months prior - I didn't learn that she was correct. I learned that I'm too open. I learned what I wrote in the later chapters, *Lessons in Listening to Myself* and *Supportive Krista Died Tonight*. I learned what I believe about how the topic of racism should be held. I learned all I hold dear about the need to create a safe container with teaching about Dialogue and rules of engagement; without proper facilitation, judgments and games ensue. She woke me up to stop abandoning myself and what I believe is right.

Your discernment may tell you that entering into a confrontation, with someone who isn't aligned with you, will just traumatize the hell out of your nervous system. Sometimes an unproductive confrontation will distract you from what's yours to do or trigger you to respond in a way that isn't helpful for anyone; it may just be a fruitless mess. We don't owe it to anyone to hear their truth if they're an emotionally unsafe person who thinks it's their job to show us the light. There will be ample opportunities for us to see the error of our ways. As James Finley teaches, nothing happens without safety.

I've lost many people in my life and many have lost me. Sometimes relationships end. And they should, because some relationships can't be fixed by a confrontation. We need to step out of engagement in The Infinity Loop. To push past people's "No," because we think they need to hear our truth, isn't loving or effective. If we don't start with the awareness of where we contributed, how in the world do we think the other person will welcome in our unwelcomed critical assessment of them? This is one of the ways we cause trauma. This isn't about a highly skilled intervention for an alcoholic who's destroying her own life. It's about someone we don't agree with and their reactions. And it bugs the hell out of us.

Beside the people we can't stay connected with for a myriad of reasons, there's also a certain segment of the population who cannot see themselves and who will never own their behavior. These are people we can't engage with in The Infinity Loop.

I teach empathy, but that isn't always what's needed. I teach inquiry, awareness, and connection, but all three of those may lead us to the conclusion we no longer want to stay in The Infinity Loop with someone. I teach how to step back from our ego, but we also need a healthy ego (sense of self) to push back and stand for what we believe is right. In life, even if we're off, we can only be where we are. We all respond at the level of consciousness we are in at the time. We behave in line with how we see things through our mental models. Even when we know what is the better way to behave, we sometimes choose to do what "works for us" instead of what is loving, kind and right. So, even in that, we don't have the consciousness and integrity to do what we know to be right. For that, we need compassion.

Concerning the ordeal around the meeting at my house, I didn't respond to every interaction in emotional sobriety (I'll explain later what that means). "F-off" comes out of me in the rarest of situations. However, the intensity of my emotions through the whole ordeal got my attention. The ordeal happened because I stopped listening to the messages of my emotions. My suffering got my attention. Right after that meeting, The Great Love Affair began (the love affair with ourselves). If I had had the self-love prior to that encounter, that self-love would have alerted me to honor myself and not continue with relationships that don't serve.

Someone asked me after reading this, "If you had been in The Infinity Loop, would you have handled the meeting at your house differently?" I was caught in a situation where there was no way it would be okay. I would have been grounded in my integrity and discernment to not have allowed the meeting to occur because I knew it wasn't going to go well based on the dynamics that proceeded. Through connection to myself, through awareness and self-inquiry and hearing my support system's inquiry into why I would participate, I would not have gone forward with the meeting. It was my ego's version of trying to be good and brave. Good and brave would have been canceling the meeting and being honest about what didn't feel right about the relationships. Always wanting to be open to learning isn't helpful without discernment.

Never use tools of communication or spiritual growth as a weapon. Research shows when we're shamed, our brains don't learn well. It doesn't mean the other won't feel appropriate shame for what they did when they hear our truth. It's how we communicate that will more likely help them feel safe enough to face it. Love is the most powerful force to help us learn. How we talk to others is how we most likely talk to ourselves. Our True Selves love us and from there, we're gentle and safe. The other person always has the right to say "No," and in some cases, it's "F-off!". We're free. Let others have their freedom too. The Infinity Loop doesn't work for everyone and every situation. It's beautiful when it does, but we're okay, loved and lovable when it doesn't.

4

The Bounce

"Sometimes our souls co-create what will bring The
Great Death because we know great love and great
suffering are opportunities for deeper transformation."

"The Great Mystery – how our wounds are
used to lead us to deeper healing."
- Krista Vorse

The Bounce is not to be used to be insensitive to one in the midst
of loss. It isn't intended to dismiss our pain nor to fix anything.
You'll sense what The Bounce means in your life. When I say we
may co-create The Great Death, to be clear, I in no way refer to
physical death. The Bounce is about something else and it happens
in different ways and different times. Let us ever be sensitive to
those suffering. This is about the Transformational Path where
what we go through will expand us. In the sacredness of our suffering, we're transformed. In loss, we honor the grief as our love
for what was lost.

We'll all face heartaches. Sometimes we get hit by a grief or
trauma that all but kills us. We may need to escape into the tent to
receive nurture. Others are needed to show up for us in connection, awareness, and inquiry to hear what we need in this despair.
Some of us have to keep going in the midst of the trauma because
that's required of us and because we're able to.

Whether it's how to weather the storms we're in, or how to
transform trauma, my work is about The Bounce. Love holds us

and Life calls our name even when it doesn't look like what we thought. But there's beauty even in that.

The Bounce is also about how when we drop into connection, awareness, and inquiry, infinite possibilities spring back up. When we drop what we think we know, are willing to unlearn, and allow the fall, we bounce back up with a bigger life. We're more than we thought we were. That's true life.

As we enter into The Infinity Loop where we're more vulnerable, we're dislodged from our comfortable place. No one will achieve what's possible if they don't decide to get comfortable with being uncomfortable.

The Bounce is about how our lives are enlarged because of the turbulence. Our hearts enlarge as we let the pain crack us open and dislodge us from our comfortable crevice to go deeper into the great abyss of Love. We see with new eyes in solidarity with suffering. The connection we feel for the rest of humanity bounces us back up into a life of profound meaning. We're transformed. We walk around the earth as having touched the underworld and found the mystery to be our new normal. It's a high we get as our ego dissolves "who" we were to the new "who" that's touched this oneness with the world – this abundance that comes from the True Self.

It's about learning to love well while practicing elegant and intelligent self-care as we bounce back from trauma, abuse, loss, addiction, co-dependency, family crisis, divorce, life changes, etc. These challenges hit us as we do this work.

We allow and move through all emotions and stages. We grieve, honor, learn and heal.

We embrace the gift as we learn to live in each moment. The calm becomes our deepest reality as moment by moment we tend to what's needed of us. We neither project into the future nor get stuck in the past.

We're grateful, less entitled and humbled, as we realize how comfortable we were. The veil is torn and we pass through. Life will never be the same and that's beautiful. We let go and learn to be of service to the world in a healthy way, full of self-love that's poured out onto others. There's always The Bounce and it's no longer about our need to do everything right; mercy and grace are part of the deal now. No need to hide our flaws, and so, we wear them for the world to see; we want our insides to match our outsides. Then others will feel safe to show themselves and we cover their shame with a blanket of love. We look into their eyes and they're transformed too. As Richard Rohr says, "Transformed people transform people." Our life is not our own, but it belongs to Love and we like it that way. We create a life in tune with our deepest truth, gifts, and joys. When we lose our lives, we gain them. And what a bounce it is.

There's something remarkable that happens when we take the Transformational Path as a reflex to what transpires in our lives. When we have wise counsel to guide us, the suffering creates a profound intimacy with ourselves.

If we're able to not believe the lie – that what we go through diminishes us in any way - or believe the lies that were perpetrated upon us, we bounce into the reflex of The Great Love Affair with ourselves. Great suffering is a doorway to great love.

We know that whatever comes against us, whatever knocks us to the ground, we'll rise again. We'll be made greater because of great love and great suffering. Wonder Woman rose again in the power of great love when her Necessary Nemesis knocked her to the ground and out of her anguish, her roar did rise. She knew Love was calling her to rise again. Love is calling us to do the same.

It's The Bounce. Come bounce with us. We'd love to have you in our family.

Part 1: Preparing Ourselves

5

The Inner Work

*"When we desire to be more connected than
separate, when we first go to stillness, we can then
be completely honest and we won't hurt people."*
– MARTHA BECK

The word *leadership* may make you think you literally have to lead…
like in business, or a group. But leadership is being confident, true
to yourself, kissing the leper. You'll know what I mean as you read
on. The word *leadership* can be overwhelming, but leadership in
The Infinity Loop is realizing your inner Wonder Woman. It's
being a contributing member of the tribe. It's the Alpha Woman
(the way I mean it). It's how we influence another.

Leadership has a lot to do with who we are in our deepest selves
and how we show up. We're only able to give away what we have.
A meaningful life comes from our wholeness. This book is about
becoming whole. It's an invitation to prepare ourselves to be leaders.

Have we learned how to observe ourselves and not act out of
our unconsciousness?

Do we know how to work with our anger and empathy in a way
that serves, that doesn't destroy our capacity to influence, or harm
another with our lack of self-control and presence?

Do we know how to not by-pass the messages of our anger and
not turn our anger against ourselves?

Do we know how to work with our empathy in a way that
doesn't take us off course to care-take, excuse bad behavior or
make us ineffectual?

Do we know how to move from a Judger to a Learner?

Do we know how to connect to another versus our need to feel separate, superior/inferior, or important?

Do we know how to tap into our hearts and our guts and speak with honesty and grace?

Do we know how to be humble? (What don't I see? What don't I know?)

Do we know how to be curious? (Use inquiry to learn and create learning versus as veiled judgments in disguise.)

Do we know how to create more awareness within our own beings as we move past our Constricted Awareness, as Deepak Chopra teaches, to an Expanded Awareness?

Do we know how to create more awareness in the other by the way we connect and inquire?

Do we know how to stand in the protection of the golden fire of The Infinity Loop, and not be moved by the push-back, the ego-defenses, the fears and insecurities of another?

Do we know how to tap into our compassion for men like they're our own sons, even when they dominate or are disrespectful?

Do we know how to turn on another's empathy?

Do we know how to love well while practicing elegant and intelligent self-care?

Do we know how to find that inner-well to keep us filled?

Have we entered into The Great Love Affair with ourselves where we know how to treat ourselves and set beautiful boundaries in line with our values?

Have we integrated with our integrity so our inner "No" and inner "Yes" are in line with how we speak and behave in the world?

I'll grow in these skills until the day I die. Some I do better than others. Together we'll create a movement, a tribe, and a Learning Container among ourselves, to change our world. We need it, the world needs it, men need it, and the future needs it.

This book is my process of preparing ourselves to be able to do this work.

Here we go....

6

The Great Love Affair

"I think the reward for conformity is that
everyone likes you except yourself."
- RITA MAE BROWN

The Great Love Affair, that didn't come to me until the second half of my 51st year of life, is a good foundation to begin.

The Great Love Affair is the healthy self-love that's so abundant, it's the game-changer and healer from so much of life's traumas. It heals us from how we bring trauma on ourselves. The Great Love Affair changes how we see ourselves and aligns with how Love sees us. We're then able to lead others to see themselves with that great love. We do this by the way we mirror them and are examples of our self-love. Our speech is filled with truth and kindness in connection, awareness, and inquiry.

Learning how to love well while practicing elegant and intelligent self-care is nuanced and tricky. It's an art form. It may be the most beautiful art form there is. What makes it tricky is the language around all that goes into what love and self-care look like. If we've been abused, shamed and controlled, we may have confusion around this. If we've been raised to be good co-dependents that need to take care of others' feelings, if we've been exposed to some of the unhealthy teachings in both religion and new age spirituality, it's head-spinning to figure it out. I've suffered for decades under that confusion and failure at how to do that sentence well (loving others and myself).

After The Great Love Affair began, I stopped feeling shame that came from me owning others' shameful behavior toward me.

Because others did what they did shamelessly, I would own their disowned shame; I thought it belonged to me. That's what happens when we're abused shamelessly early on and we don't get healed. The self-love in The Great Love Affair is our protection against owning what doesn't belong to us. We know it's not about us. It can't get in. In the silence of my heart, I give it back with the gift of awareness. I'm not the recipient. I want us all to be free from shame that doesn't belong to us.

We can't talk about being in The Infinity Loop unless we address appropriate and wise self-care and discernment. It's how we look out for ourselves and others. To pretend abuse doesn't exist and that we'll change the world without our connection to reality, is not helpful.

7

I Had a Dream

"We have forgotten the age-old fact that God
speaks chiefly through dreams and visions."
- CARL JUNG

I had a dream. As I stood in line to make a deposit in a grand white marble, international bank, I had both of my hands on a baby stroller. My baby girl laid in there. I was in front of the line when I sensed a predator – someone I know in real life that I refer to as my Necessary Nemesis - lurking behind the pillar to my left. From the hem of his garment I could tell who he was. He wore beige linen. Startled, I looked down at my baby and noticed she was completely exposed, without a diaper on. I immediately gasped and turned around and quietly exited the bank in a rapid clip.

As soon as I got outside to the stairs I knew I was safe; I didn't have to continue to run. When I looked down at my baby, I noticed she peed on herself because I never put a diaper on her. My heart ached as I picked her up and held her close and told her I was so sorry and that I loved her more than anyone in the entire world. I cried that I didn't care for her like she needed. To love her more than anyone in the world was new for me. She just smiled, never complained, and beamed love at me, while she enjoyed to both give and receive love. Her love filled me up. How I had forgotten her basic needs! As soon as I knew I loved this baby girl more than anyone in the world, I knew it was Little Krista I held.

The dream also showed me that my injured instincts were now healed. From *Women Who Run with the Wolves,*

I quote Dr. Estés:

"When a woman's instinctual nature is strong, she intuitively recognizes the innate predator by scent, sight, and hearing... anticipates its presence, hears it approaching, and takes steps to turn it away. In the instinct-injured woman, the predator is upon her before she registers its presence, for her listening, her knowing, and her apprehensions are impaired."

I was able to sense this predator from the smallest trace, and he wasn't in his usual attire. From a sliver of his garments, beyond what our natural senses could recognize, I just knew. Making a U-Turn from business at hand, I put my well-being above anything else; without that safety, it doesn't matter what money's in the bank. It showed me I'm able to drive the stroller, I have the power, and it's my job to care for me.

I was able to see as plain as day, the severity of myself neglect. Who doesn't put a diaper on a baby?! Little Krista didn't even complain to alert me that I had forgotten her diaper because she wasn't aware of her needs. My love I felt for her, that wasn't there fully before, would drive me to know how to care and love her. The way I laid down in the stroller was how I took it laying down and didn't complain in regards to this predator. My dream was my Re-do to get to show up this time for Krista.

I've traveled through life, both stateside and abroad, as someone who has been both instinct-injured and as one with extraordinary gifts of discernment, pattern detection, and spiritual sight. I've agonized over this to say the least. I was paralyzed to act on my discernment and instincts and didn't fully honor them. Those days are over.

I held Little Krista as tight and lovingly as I could. I knew I would make amends to her by my love and care for her for the rest of her life. It's my job to do that.

It's so often unconsciously spouted, "You can't love anyone else until you love yourself!" I find it insensitive and untrue. We just told someone they can't love another person because they struggle to love themselves fully. Some of the most loving people I know have neglected themselves. It may be true that we love others more than ourselves. We try so hard to help and support, that we don't love ourselves and care for our basic needs. We permit horrible behavior toward ourselves in part because we love the other person and want to be longsuffering. How many loving mothers get out of balance and don't love and care for themselves? Do we actually say they can't love another? For me, it's the life-long challenge of learning to love well while practicing elegant and intelligent self-care. It's just that when we do love ourselves, we serve others in a healthier way.

My wise friend JJ (Jennifer Joss), who knows about dream analysis from a Jungian perspective, said it's also about my integration with my divine masculine and divine feminine. Since this dream, I've made huge leaps forward in the integration process. When I held Little Krista close to me, she was against my heart and my lower belly. I try to come from these two points in my feminine heart and teach others to do as well. The marble of the bank was the masculine. I left the world of the masculine to tend to my feminine heart.

This dream may speak to you about your life. If we reflect, we recall how we didn't make those U-Turns or we didn't care for ourselves like we could have. We didn't think clearly. We allowed ourselves to be in harm's way. It's one of the ways we inflict trauma on ourselves. In our healing and integration, we become fully present and know how to move through this life. It's a miracle that my instincts are healed after over 50 years of creating brain tracks that didn't honor my discernment like I should have. That's the power of transformational healing which lives in the realm of infinite possibilities. And that's where I live. Come join me on the mystery side where The Bounce is. Together, we experience more and more integration, healing and transformation.

In our wholeness, we're able to create meaningful lives. We're able to lead. May we ever seek deeper connection to ourselves, grow in our awareness and inquire into our beliefs and assumptions. When we experience The Great Love Affair, we lead in The Infinity Loop like never before. We need our power. This work takes courage.

I Had a Dream
<u>Reflection</u>

Is there an area or areas where you've neglected to care for yourself? Is there anywhere you aren't instinctually awake to protect yourself?

What would it look like to make a U-Turn in these areas?

How could it be helpful to see where you've neglected yourself to give yourself the power to change, versus just seeing yourself as a victim?

If you tended to your feminine heart and mothered yourself, how would that serve your life more fully?

8

The Poem and Our Return

"You yourself, as much as anybody in the entire universe, deserve your love and attention."
- BUDDHA

My friend JJ, shared with me one of her favorite poems, written by the late Derek Walcott. Before I heard the poem, I asked JJ why it might be her favorite poem of all time. She said, "Just hear it and you'll understand."

Love After Love

The time will come
when, with elation
you will greet yourself arriving
at your own door, in your own mirror
and each will smile at the other's welcome,

and say, sit here. Eat.
You will love again the stranger who was yourself.
Give wine. Give bread. Give back your heart
to itself, to the stranger who has loved you

all your life, whom you ignored
for another, who knows you by heart.
Take down the love letters from the bookshelf,

the photographs, the desperate notes,
peel your own image from the mirror.
Sit. Feast on your life.

I understand. I felt both elated at each line and sad I lived so long without this poem. What would my life have been like had this lived inside of me? Now it does. And I'll never abandon this poem like I've abandoned myself. I am returning to Love.

I sent this to my former partner, Leo. He wrote, "I wonder, after all we've been through, is it possible to be with another and *not* ignore yourself?" I wonder that too. Our focus is to greet ourselves. Maybe yours is too.

THE POEM AND OUR RETURN
<u>REFLECTION</u>

What would it look like to greet yourself again?

What would it look and feel like to feast on your life?

How have you perhaps ignored yourself? How do you look for love outside of yourself?

How does the awareness that you, know yourself by heart, give you a kind of warmth inside, a kind of containment that feels sturdy?

What would a love letter to yourself say?

9

The Homecoming

"For some of us the biggest source of suffering
hasn't been because of losses outside ourselves but
the loss *of* ourselves. Major Homecoming time!"
- KRISTA VORSE

The arrival of that poem, *Love After Love*, was timely. It came in both Leo and my life during our homecoming to ourselves, which I call The Great Love Affair. Leo meditated on that poem for weeks. And then we chatted about it soon after he returned from his Transformational Road Trip.

(Leo) It's just like that poem by Derek Walcott. It's coming home to yourself. I broke up the stanzas but the crux of the message is:

Give back your heart to itself
To the stranger that has loved you all your life
Whom you ignored for another
Who knows you by heart

Homecoming is about the awareness that you have so allowed yourself to become diminished, you were willing to give your heart to anybody but yourself because you were so estranged from your heart. That's:

the stranger who has loved you all your life.

You have this mystical experience of this flash of insight.

OMG! I have ignored my own heart for another!

(Krista) Because of my recent awareness of this, I just noticed where I've been habituated to not tune into my heart, and allow my heart to hurt, which wants to serve as a beautiful guidance system. It tells me what it wants to be around, what's life-giving, what is loving toward another. Now I'm willing to fully feel my heart and allow the pain because the cost of not feeling it is immense.

(Leo) My experience of what estranges us from our hearts is we compare our insides to others' outsides, which we idealize. What estranges us from our own hearts is our unwillingness to descend into our own shadow and to forgive ourselves for not being perfect. We can love our shadow, have compassion on our shadow, integrate our shadow and all of our parts. As soon as that happens, we're home. We really can't ever then ignore our heart for another. Those days are over, as soon as you experience that homecoming. That's your True Self because the True Self includes all your parts. Then we're free and freedom's what increases our capacity to love; the freer we are, that better we love.

Peel your image from the mirror.
Sit. Feast on your life.

(Leo) You're always at the banquet table after you've come home because to ignore yourself comes from a place of scarcity - I'm not enough. So, I have to ignore myself for another because I'm not enough; I need another to make myself whole.

(Krista) What caused this to happen to you?

(Leo) Time alone. Being on my road trip. Enjoying myself. I greeted myself, arriving at my own door. I sat with myself, warts and all.

(Krista) Me too. Being with myself at such a deeper level at this time in my life.

(Leo) When I started out, I said one theme of my road trip was to face my fear: my fear of being alone which is ultimately the ego's fear of death. Once you stare at the fear long enough, the fear just vanishes and all that's there is love. The problem isn't fear, it's fear of the fear. It takes us away from our home inside ourselves in search of ourselves because we don't think we're enough and we can't face the fear we're not enough. That's because then we'd have to face the ego's fear of death. When we're able to let go of that attachment to the ego's fear of death, indestructible life emerges. You realize you can let go of your identification and let yourself fall into that death and when you come back up you realize that not only am I okay, but I'm bigger now.

Richard Rohr teaches this is level seven of his nine levels of spiritual development: "I'm bigger than I thought I was."

(Krista) This is what I call The Bounce. Welcome home.

When we're home in ourselves our capacity to stand in one loop of The Infinity Loop vastly increases. We know better how to hold our dignity and another's. Our compassion for our weaknesses that we acknowledge makes it easier to have compassion on another's. We have enough within ourselves to validate us without our need to promote bad behavior by how we permit it. We respond in calmness and containment and address what doesn't work for us. Our self-love alerts us we have a healthy right to model what it means for all to be treated well.

THE HOMECOMING
REFLECTION

We don't manage our lives well when we're estranged from our hearts. Can you see where you may be estranged from yourself?

How have you allowed yourself to be diminished because of it?

How will feeling your heart fully, with all the pain and beauty, help you to not be estranged from yourself?

Where do you feel you're not enough as a result of comparing yourself to others?

In what areas can you have compassion for your weaknesses and accept them?

How do you see your fear of being alone, as a fear of your ego's fear of death?

10

Great Compassion

"Suffering ends when compassion shows up."
- James Finley

A few years before The Great Love Affair, Great Compassion showed up. He (masculine energy) began my return.

While deep into my practice of living more from my inner life, one day Great Compassion arrived. I can't recall the first time he appeared. But I remember he came again when I was feeling sorrow over regrets in my life. I was driving in my little town of Ashland, Oregon. As I turned a corner he was there, next to me. We can be wide awake, in the middle of daily life, and if we're paying attention we'll hear and see things that our souls, True Selves, older selves, God, whatever it is, is sending to us. I hear guidance, see and sense things, and see visions.

It was a painful peek to look at my life - the choices I've made and the ways I was in error in not loving well. Before Great Compassion, I experienced that peek with commentary that wasn't seen through truth. What I saw and heard may have been true, but as Caroline Myss teaches, it wasn't the truth. Great Compassion showed up to show me the truth.

What is true are the facts of what happened. The truth is, we don't know why things are the way they are. We don't know why people do what they do. Truth is about the spiritual perspective that transcends what's true. And that's the truth that sets us free. The truth is, all that would condemn us is irrelevant in the presence of such love. That's the message the mystics with their spiritual experiences tell us. In the presence of that kind of love, we are set free.

To my right and in front of me, stands Great Compassion. He's a winged warrior, an angel that crouches down to hold me, but is as tall as an old redwood tree. This masculine presence is my protection from the lies that threaten to name me. He guards me against anything that would tell me to look upon my life without Great Compassion. He's the final word, he's the proclamation of Great Love, and he is the truth.

With him by my side, I look at my life with a tenderness that says, "Only Great Compassion is allowed here." With that safety, I'm able to see anything I've previously feared to see in myself, because of my fear that it has the power to name me, diminish me, or take me out.

He wraps his wings around me in comfort and protection. He takes me with him to the heights he travels. From that view, everything looks different. He creates awareness, Expanded Awareness, and Pure Awareness that rescues me from the constriction that makes my life way too small.

After he showed up, I was able for the first time in my life, to look upon what has happened and cry with a Great Compassion. I never felt the needed and appropriate compassion for myself. It was and still is one of the most beautiful and intimate encounters. We need to have access to Great Compassion to stand in the fires of The Infinity Loop and do this magic.

Great Compassion guards us from the attacks against our freedom that try to imprison us because we aren't aware we roam in this beautiful forest of redwood trees with no prison bars in sight. We need to feel that love and tenderness and realize it's our True Selves loving us. We're so much bigger than we think we are.

Now, Great Compassion is with me always. I feel him right now. All we need is the awareness. We use our imagination to bring Great Compassion to our awareness. He's how we guard our minds. We hold fast to our spiritual experiences that liberate us from our suffering, as James Finley says. It's like once you've been liberated from eating junk food, you don't want to go back to it. I've been liberated from how I used to contribute to my own suffering by believing my faults are the truth; what I've been through makes me damaged goods; what others believe about me is the last word. We are more than that. We're found in the nothingness that is beyond this material plane. The True Self exists in that nothingness.

Great Compassion grounds me in my body. It's sturdy strength like a redwood tree. When we recognize the truth, we're not flailed around by what others think. We become warriors when we have a solid foundation.

Anytime we realize we're living our lives without Great Compassion, we use that awareness to observe ourselves in Witness Consciousness (The Watcher) to notice what we're thinking and what happens to us when we believe those thoughts, like Byron Katie teaches. Then we set an intention to call to mind Great Compassion as our winged angel. His power can shut down what isn't the truth. We allow him to do so.

As I edit on this Dec. 1st morning, I have a new awareness. As I lay in my bed upon waking, I realized that I've become Great Compassion. I'm experiencing him as me in this moment. In the mystery of the True Self, divine union, whatever is occurring that is beyond language, it's the ever-expanding awareness that "Though I'm not God, I'm not other than God either." As I type, I feel my being as this winged warrior. It's strength and gentleness. My body has wings with feathers. It is as the spiritual teachers say: our suffering comes as a result of our illusion of separateness -from God, ourselves, each other, creation. It is an illusion.

May we be wooed to drop into the awareness that not only is Great Compassion by our side, we are Great Compassion. I knew that was the part of me that's in union with God, but now

I experience it. Great Compassion is powerful. May we live with the awareness of how full and sturdy and loving and calm and alert and wise and fast and beautiful we are in our True Selves. Now this intimacy isn't just with Great Compassion loving me, it's the total trip of my form morphing into Great Compassion. It's another gift to help us dis-identify with our passing form and stories. They are the dream. We awake from the dream and decide we like being awake. How deeply we know we are loved and are Love! We step into The Infinity Loop and change the world.

Once Great Compassion arrives, we have that to share with others. Great Compassion is needed for our brokenness and all the ways and times we couldn't do then what we now know how to do. Then we're able to hold it all - the good, the bad, and the ugly. It's not that we don't do things that hurt, it's that we're able to look upon it all with Great Compassion for our brokenness. We bring it in close, hold it, love it and forgive it. There's a choice to hate or have compassion. This doesn't mean we don't carry the gift of aversion for what isn't life-giving; it's that we let go of what constricts our bodies, our minds, and our hearts, and allow ourselves to live from a much higher view.

GREAT COMPASSION
REFLECTION

How will you use your imagination to bring in a reminder of Great Compassion into your life? What's your Great Compassion like?

What will help you experience yourself as Great Compassion? Meditate on being Great Compassion.

How will Great Compassion become a reflex for you when you struggle? Remember: awareness, set an intention, bring him in.

How would regular experience of Great Compassion help you have a tender heart toward yourself and others?

How would the ability to call to mind Great Compassion alter your body, mind, and spirit?

11

It's Time to Kiss the Leper

"If you have forgiven yourself for being imperfect
and falling, you can now do it for just about
everyone else. If you have not done it for yourself,
I am afraid you will likely pass on your sadness,
absurdity, judgment, and futility to others."
- Fr. Richard Rohr

Saint Francis of Assisi, (1182 - 1226) is my hero. He's the star of
Franco Zeffirelli's 1972 film *Brother Sun, Sister Moon*, and the
priest with a bird resting on his hand in the garden statues. He was
a spiritual genius. Francis brought us back to the connection to the
earth and a dignity and connection to all of creation. Franciscan
Spirituality is considered an alternative orthodoxy; Francis saw the
blessing in all, not the curse.

What I recognized as my home in him, which began in my
teen years, was his courageous and contagious love that moved him
to leave his father's house with the wealth that was poor in love,
in joy, and in freedom, to the outskirts where the lepers lived. His
encounter with the leper broke through all his fear and shields and
wooed him to an awakening that made him the person with the
longest bibliography in the Library of Congress (so I've heard).

Francis's brilliant contribution to our evolution in the midst of
middle-age religion was his ability to incorporate the negative –
the leper. What we're so ashamed of, what seems so disfigured and
diseased in us, what we try so hard to push into the shadow, is to
be loved, accepted, even kissed. When we kiss our faults, the leper
who beams right in front of us, we're on our way to getting free,

even someday as free as the birds. When we kiss the ugly situation, loss, shame, shit-storm, we embrace what is, and our disgust turns to love of what is. Then we embrace the leper in another. We kiss even what we most fear, and the kiss transforms us. We're in the flow where Love comes in, and we realize we're greater than fear.

Francis wore his garment covered with patches because he wanted to show what he was on the inside – covered with patches. He wasn't afraid of his faults; they were irrelevant in this encounter with Love and freedom. When one reaches the point where they're who they are, warts and all, they have seen themselves in the leper, and love the sun and the moon as their family. They have kissed a freedom that makes them sing and write poetry.

It's Time to Kiss the Leper
<u>Reflection</u>

What aspect of yourself or your past do you despise or try to run from in shame? How do you run from it?

In what ways have you allowed the leper in you to name who you are as less than fully loved and loveable?

In what ways do you overcompensate for the leper in you to prop yourself up to make yourself feel better about yourself?

Richard Rohr teaches we compare, compete, conflict, conspire, and then condemn. How do you do this to numb the pain of your own leprosy?

How could you love better if you loved the leper in yourself and another?

12

Women Who Run with the Wolves

"Though her soul requires seeing, the culture around
her requires sightlessness. Though her soul wishes
to speak its truth, she is pressured to be silent."
- Clarissa Pinkola Estés
Women Who Run with the Wolves

I have two friends named Jennifer. Both coach and consult, read voraciously, in their early 50s, tall, athletic, have exceptionally high Spiritual Intelligence, and have Labradoodles. One goes by JJ and the other Jen.

This conversation is with Jen. We met when our kids were little. Now all six of ours are in their 20s.

Anyone who reads that much and raised four children has something to say.

(Jen) What's gotten me through difficult times is to have a reason for the difficult times. To go into the myth empowers me, to be the heroine. I then feel okay that I earned my battle scars. Everyone has a different way of how they get through.

(Krista) But what you choose is the Transformational Path as we call it, where the focus is on our inner work and what the struggle teaches us about ourselves, rather than how we're just victims.

(Jen) I'm over the story because I've gotten so many gifts from it, I don't want to be dragged into the drama of it. That doesn't empower me. It's more empowering to me to share the lessons than the story.

I brought up the story of Bluebeard from *Women Who Run with the Wolves* by Clarissa Pinkola Estés. We were in a book club on it years ago. The book remains among my collection, even in the ruthless donation of most of my books. I believe it needs to be combed through over and over throughout my years. Had I actually done that, it may have woken me up to where I was unconscious.

In describing *Women Who Run with the Wolves: Myths and Stories of the Wild Woman Archetype*, it is said: Within every woman lives a powerful force, filled with good instincts, passionate creativity, and ageless knowing. She is the Wild Woman, who represents the instinctual nature of women. But she is an endangered species.

(Jen) Bluebeard resonated with me. It's a lesson of a woman who doesn't have her voice yet. Bluebeard (her husband) tells his wife: Here are the keys. You can go into any room but not this one room. The sisters in the story who represent our female tribe, encourage her to go into this forbidden room.

Dr. Estés: "The sisters also represent our soul's curiosity and our impulse toward consciousness."

(Jen) She hasn't found her power yet so she questions herself and when she finally opens the door, there's the skeletons of all Bluebeard's other wives. Because at this point in the story she doesn't have her power, the sisters call in the brothers who represent the masculine that she hasn't integrated. Once a woman finds that, nothing can stop her; there's nothing more powerful and beautiful than when a woman is grounded in her divine feminine and divine masculine.

Dr. Estés teaches from this story that the captor is the dark man who lives in all women's psyches; it's the voice in us that doesn't want us to honor our soul's impulse to be curious and awake. It wants us to "be nice." To restrain this predator, a woman must keep in possession of all her instincts. We women must "develop a relationship with our wildish nature." Wild women must protect their soulful lives. We are no longer naive. We know how to push the predator back where it belongs. We must "use our wits to do what needs to be done about what we see."

Dr. Estés: "When a woman's instinctual nature is strong, she intuitively recognizes the innate predator by scent, sight, and hearing... anticipates its presence, hears it approaching, and takes steps to turn it away. In the instinct-injured woman, the predator is upon her before she registers its presence, for her listening, her knowing, and her apprehensions are impaired - mainly by introjects which exhort her to be nice, to behave, and especially to be blind to being misused."

The naive or injured woman is in collusion to even her not knowing. She is then lured by things that promise life but only lead to death of her spirit.

Dr. Estés writes, "As long as a woman is forced into believing she is powerless and/or is trained to not consciously register what she knows to be true, the feminine impulses and gifts of her psyche continue to be killed off."

(Jen) I listen to my instincts and if I don't and let anyone overpower them, I suffer. Thankfully I wake up. It's my connection to my higher self. If I don't listen, I'm in big trouble. So, I try to listen to my instincts and soul. My soul is what I feel is my connection to God. Even 29 years ago I was aware of my internal "No!" of my instincts, but I overrode them. Our instinct to listen to our souls weren't supported in society in the era we grew up. Had our culture known how to support women to listen to our instincts, I would have had a very different life. But that wasn't my journey. My journey was to learn this way.

(Krista) Again, you take the Transformational Path. You choose to accept it, not expect life to be any different or that it should be easy. And you move toward wisdom.

(Jen) It's not the life of "being identified with our life" – all these parts, our persona. In reality, when your world is stripped clean by trauma, you soon realize these roles you play, this attachment to your persona, mean absolutely nothing. So, you learn to go deeper. You dive deeper for the gems, going deep into your soul in the underworld. No one is able to take those jewels of wisdom from you. The gifts of wisdom take you out of victim mode to hero mode, because no one can take away the gifts from the experience. And these gifts make our lives richer.

WOMEN WHO RUN WITH THE WOLVES
REFLECTION

In what ways do you see the need to see life's traumas and hardships through the lens of myth and as the opportunity to transform, versus staying trapped in the horrible story?

When in your life have you been uninitiated and innocently fell prey to what wouldn't serve you?

Are there areas you may be instinct-injured and don't see the danger around you?

In what ways will being fully awake to see what you need to see, help you as a leader?

Bluebeard lives in our own psyches – the voice in us that shuts down our intuition - the voice to "be nice" instead of honoring our intuition that's there to keep us safe.
Are there voices in your life that you have internalized, that have told you that you're powerless?

What would it be like to have a regular practice to tell your psyche that you're ready to see what you need to see?

What do you need to see?

13

Women Who Run with the Wolves - Part 2

"What does this wildish intuition do for women?
Like the wolf, intuition has claws that pry things
open and pin things down. It has eyes that can see
through the shields of persona, it has ears that hear
beyond the range of mundane human hearing. With
these formidable psychic tools a woman takes on a
shrewd and even precognitive animal consciousness,
one that deepens her femininity and sharpens her
ability to move confidently in the other world."
- CLARISSA PINKOLA ESTÉS
WOMEN WHO RUN WITH THE WOLVES

Jen gives me her thoughts on how to be a Wolfie Woman, as she calls it.

(Jen) Like I said before, I have to find meaning in what transpires. I need a higher vision that's beyond the victim. The waking up begins when the hardship begins. In my life, there's always gifts in the hardships. I spot manipulation or whatever now. I'm not knee-jerk now with any of my decisions. I weigh things out. That's what wisdom has given me.

Then there's how I learn to climb back into my body, to feel the emotions I need to feel and process them. What do the messages of my emotions and body tell me?

I've learned this through self-awareness - Witness Consciousness – I observe myself, pranayama which is the connection to my breath, and then being aware of where I feel it in my body. I feel it in my throat, chest, anywhere. This tells me intuitively what needs to happen. If it's my throat then I know I need to speak up. If it's in my heart, I practice self-inquiry: Where am I shut down? Hurt? Where do I need to open my heart? If it's in my gut, it's my intuition. That sick to my stomach, nauseous feeling is usually an attack: where do I need to honor myself? If it's in my gut, it's a root - not safe, like primal: home, money, personal relationships, grounding, survival, primal needs.

(Krista) We know from the mind-body connection that even our ailments tell us something, as they represent aspects of ourselves and our relationships. You're the one who introduced me to that so many years ago.

(Jen) What am I'm feeling and where?

I give myself a reality check, try to take ownership if mine, try to let others' business go. I need to know my inner work. I like to embrace inner work as play. It's fun to explore something about myself, versus guilt and shame. My kids call me "Menopause Mom" or "Newport Beach Girl" which makes it more light, compassionate, to give grace to that part of myself and allow it. Once we allow it, we move through it. I like to allow. I like to hold the space for that too. I have to work on that because I try to be perfect. Throughout the day, I'm in Witness Consciousness. Sometimes I want to hang on and be in a specific space, but I'm aware that I choose to do that. Then I'm ready to let it go.

Self-care is frickin' huge! I have learned how to do that pretty damn fast compared to what I used to do.

(Krista) When you allow, you allow yourself to wake up, see what you need to discern, feel what you need to. In self-care, you don't flee from yourself, betray your discernment, your heart, your body, and your needs. Instead, you make yourself number one in the self-care aspect. But not in an imbalanced way where one would say you aren't free from yourself. When done with elegance and intelligence, taking care of ourselves enables us to be more in our True Self versus the small self. When we're hungry, angry, lonely, tired or stressed, it's more difficult to drop into our Abundant Selves. That's why we need to be compassionate with ourselves when we can't, and attune to what we need.

(Jen) There was an adjustment because I used to put my children and husband before me, and now I honestly say l love myself, and I wish every woman loves herself.

(Krista) We're enculturated to care-take and shamed to have boundaries. It's all of it. The being present and observing part because asking myself what I need is observing myself too (self-inquiry). If we don't, we leave ourselves in a bad way and it cuts us off from our instincts, our Wolfie wildish nature that's crucial for our being in the world.

(Jen) Exactly. I had to retrain myself because I served my family so much in the extreme. What I have to ask myself to check in with myself is: "Do I feel like doing this?" I do that now, 99% of the time. My family had to learn and I have to do what feeds me. It's an ongoing lesson for me. You've known me for decades and you know me so well. You recently pointed out to me how I've over-compensated and have been hyper-responsible and I lost some of my "Fun Jen-Jen." Balance in mind, body and spirit is one of the greatest gifts.

(Krista) oh yes! And how that balance in mind, body, and spirit all plays out in lightness and joy. We live high-performance lives, be on our game to live our most courageousness lives, and not be neurotic, (which is defined as unbalanced).

(Jen) Too much restriction or overindulgence isn't the answer. I've taught my kids (all in their 20s) to check in with their own balance instead of me being the one to point it out.

(Krista) Stuck in our idealized self, which is neither self-acceptance nor self-love. It kills some of our aliveness or Wolfie Women nature. Then we're not aware of what serves. It's all part of being awake. It's learning how to love well while practicing elegant and intelligent self-care.

(Jen) What I need is to feed my soul. I'm very selective of what my soul is being fed: food, yoga, what I read, healthy people, sleep. My body is sensitive.

(Krista) The Transformational Path, the awareness of ourselves, the messages our emotions and bodies tell us, our wisdom, instincts, balance and self-care all serve us as Wolfie Women who take the key and unlock the door of what is unconscious. A woman who runs with the wolves is Wonder Woman who stands in The Infinity Loop and changes the world.

WOMEN WHO RUN WITH THE WOLVES - PART 2
REFLECTION

How does the Transformational Path translate to being more conscious?

What does Witness Consciousness seem like to you? How will you observe your thoughts more than just think them?

What practices do you have in place to help yourself pay attention to what your emotions and body tell you?

How would you rate yourself in the area of self-love and self-care that would help you be more alert and present to what needs to be paid attention to?

How can you create a Wolfie Women Wisdom Journal to hold what your life's struggles have given you in terms of wisdom? How will you remind yourself of the precious lessons you've learned and hold fast to them when similar situations arise?

What strategies will you put in place to stay in balance - not too much restriction or indulgence but healthy, life-giving choices?

Have you become aware of what you need to do to feed your soul?

Is there something you're ready to let go of that doesn't feed you?

Is there something you need to be honest about and let go of in terms of care-taking?

14

Loving Well

> "If I speak with human eloquence and angelic
> ecstasy but don't have love, I'm nothing
> but the creaking of a rusty gate."
> - *The Message*

Karla McLaren, whose work is understanding the messages of our emotions and emotional genius, spoke recently about the ineffectiveness of shaming others. She emphasized that shaming is *not* the way to help people tap into their own shame mechanism to change behavior. Karla: "*Emotionally incompetent activism* triggers people's fight, flight or freeze behaviors, and not their shame. It engages their panic. Back off the shame if you want the world to change. Shame needs to come from within the person and be manageable, authentic, and healthy. It doesn't come from the outside. That's just abuse. Real change requires shame to come from the inside. To be people of influence, others have to know you care about them. We know from shaming people for hundreds of years that it doesn't work."

We have an epidemic of shame and abuse; people are so committed to their cause or convictions, that the focus isn't on being loving or effective: The homeless council that's outraged and disrespectful to anyone who doesn't see that things should be handled exactly like they do; the polarized political problem that causes family members to label each other unfairly; the dismissing of others who we think aren't useful in their mission because they need kindness, and to be coached and developed. We see our cause sometimes but don't see each other.

Richard Rohr, who founded The Center for Action and Contemplation, talks of this often. We need to develop a contemplative heart and mind before we do our activism. Without love, what's the point? With a contemplative heart and mind, we're able to still see dualistically what isn't in line with love and care for one another. And then we see the wider view (non-dual) that's whole and calm and holds even the offending person's dignity and humanity, without losing our way. We always run the risk of doing to others what we find most offensive. If we start with that humble awareness, we're in a much better place to not become what we don't like in another. A calm, contemplative heart and mind are energized, enthusiastic, engaged, but we're not in fight or flight where we lose our ability to hear and see one another. We're able to feel the anger at injustice, but it's a grounded fire in our bellies that becomes the fire of love to protect and provide for those who are most vulnerable among us. If we don't move to inquiry to create a Learning Container, we won't change our world. Truth and love, action and contemplation, humility and conviction must kiss.

When we develop the contemplative heart and mind, we're able to witness ourselves and not get entangled in our own stories. With the contemplative heart and mind, we're able to practice Dialogue and transcend our ego. We're able to have Disciplined Decision-Making. It helps us to be respectful and give one another The Second Look that's beyond the critical view. We're able to manage our emotions in a healthy way. This may be what we need to survive as a planet.

Our everyday awareness of where we're rude and disrespectful is a good practice to have. I know I'm rude and disrespectful at times. My True Self doesn't want that. I want to bring change to the world. I want to be a prophetic voice for how soulless policies and practices kill us, but I don't want to be without the fire that burns with love, that cannot help but spill over to those who need it most – those who are disconnected from love within themselves.

Let's look how we can help one another do the work of love in this world that isn't at the expense of love.

Love is the only emotion that expands intelligence because of the parts of the brain in yourself and the other that get activated.

Science confirms it from all different directions. If we think about how safety helps us move to more expanded awareness because of the freedom in our bodies and hearts, we'll use our energy toward our genius versus self-protection. So much is possible for all of us with deeper connection, awareness, and inquiry. And it's so much fun...and a natural chemical explosion in our brains.

Loving Well
Reflection

In what ways do you see how you behave, react, and think similar to the normalized notions of what the world tells us it means to "stand up for what's right"?

In what ways do you desire to become more of the observer of your reactions? In what ways do you see the freedom in being able to be more conscious and not identify yourself in a way to get an ego hit of being superior, separate, or important?

In what ways do you see how if we had an ability to hold both the offense and someone's humanity, we would behave far more patient, humble, and wise?

How will you guard yourself to not behave in self-righteous ways by your choice to not expose yourself to that kind of normalized behavior that can be contagious? How will you create or strengthen your spiritual practice that changes the way you see people? Do you need to re-evaluate who influences you?

How do you shame others, either inwardly or outwardly?

15

What My Losses Gave Me

"For everything you have missed, you have
gained something else, and for everything
you gain, you lose something else."
- RALPH WALDO EMERSON

"We just don't want to gain something
at the cost of losing ourselves."
- KRISTA VORSE

This is about the losses that come from living in integrity. They come because we know in our hearts what gives life and what doesn't, and we no longer want to support what's crazy-making. Many people struggle out of fear of loss if they held fast to their truth. I call that "thinking we need others' love more than living our most courageous lives." We may also believe the lie that we're bad if others walk away from us.

I have empathy for those who struggle. I've spent years in grief for what I've lost in my life. Grief is healthy of course but not the way I was attached to it; my protest to reality and being lost in blame of myself and others wasn't serving me. Precious time was lost that could have been spent living fully and showing up for my life in the most courageous way. I felt stuck. I thought my poor decisions - which are now regrettable - disqualified me from the infinite possibilities of how my life could turn out.

It's understandable why we fear to lose those who are most dear to us if we don't play it right - if we don't look the other way and take the abusive behavior. We'll lose out if we don't give in to another's demands fueled by entitlement and self-pity. We're not wanting to suppress people's emotions that could be telling them what isn't working or what they need to process. We feel compassion for their pain. That can be why we tolerate their lack of self-control. However, tolerating it doesn't help them learn to work with their emotions in a way that serves. We're allowed to have boundaries around how we're treated. Addicts, narcissists, teenagers (or any age) who don't always know how to deal with their pain, frustration, or manipulative patterns, may show up as punitive and unbearable to be around. This can be true whether we give in or not. Sometimes we don't feel ready to take the hit of possibly losing the relationship with all we have on our plates. Denial to feel okay about the current state of affairs becomes a skill. Some of us are quite skilled at anticipating what it takes to keep others from being in a foul mood; we organize our entire lives around this behavior and develop coping skills to crack the code. One day it'll all break down; our bodies will tell us we've lost our way. It's a tough path we're on as we try to navigate this life and not lose the love and connection.

Many of my losses came from living in my integrity. Most of them came because I betrayed my integrity for so long that when I finally did take a stand it was a shit-storm. I walked away from the Evangelical Church because I had no business ever being there in the first place. Unfortunately, my exodus from that branch of Christianity coincided with my exodus from my marriage and was accompanied by an intense custody battle. My mother testified that I had lost touch with reality and needed to be locked up because I set boundaries with her and my stepfather.

My time in the Church was over 20 years of betraying myself. I'm so sorry for the person I was all those years. I did it to myself by not being willing to stand up in the face of fear and shame. It made me weak.

I hold myself responsible for much of the loss my children suffered during those horrible divorces – from their father and from the Church. But to this day I know I could no longer have betrayed myself, my values, and what I held as my deepest truth about parenting. There just wasn't enough Zoloft to deaden me enough to be who others thought I should be. When I finally did set boundaries, those people I set boundaries with had access to my support system, my family, my deepest wounds. They used it against me. I lost a lot.

I share my experience as one who's lost nearly everything at different times. There's another way to look at these dilemmas.

All my losses gave me myself. There's a love affair of all love affairs waiting for us. It's The Great Love Affair with *ourselves*. There's a certain self-containment in it - I came into this world alone and out I will go alone. However, we find that in that aloneness, we're not; we're connected to our True Self that has the whole world in its heart.

From Derek Walcott's beautiful poem, *Love After Love*:
"You will love again the stranger who was yourself."

My experience tells me I don't have to fear what my integrity will cost me because my integrity is my guidance system. And co-dependency makes a poor guide. It's a sneaky thing - to control others' behavior by how we over-adapt, anticipate, manage, and all manner of insanity we humans do to keep from the drama others bring. It's like the dry drunk who hasn't done the work on herself and everyone wishes she'd just take a drink to get "happy" again and stop making everyone miserable. I speak as an "expert" on this as someone who's elevated co-dependency to an art form. We love, we care, we empathize, we want to comfort and help. It just gets out of balance. And balance is really important.

What if your losses gave you yourself that's so strong and powerful, it realizes it could thrive and have a beautiful life no matter what the other person chooses to do? This is the great work of spiritually. With it comes The Great Love Affair. When we honor the wisdom that no one deserves to be treated poorly, we wake up to realize that includes us. It gives the other the opportunity to wake up as well. We don't promote bad behavior by how we permit it.

I feel deeply for you but also say, don't spend years as I did because I thought I couldn't bear the losses. Even when I tried to keep people, the losses came anyway. In those losses, I finally got the love of my life which inhabits me; my best friend lives inside of me and together we feel the abundance of all the love and connection we need. This is also because our integrity draws our tribe to us and they're fabulous!

Support is needed as we set boundaries for our own self-care. We'll often feel the ache, the emptiness, and the reflex to want to play the role we play, just to be a part of the festivities. We need wise support to weather the storm to stand in our integrity, allow the loss to occur if it's what reality brings, and learn to show up for our lives in the most courageous way. Our job is to express the life that wants to be lived through us and let others do the same - even if they're our children, partners, family or whoever. May we learn to love well while practicing elegant and intelligent self-care.

I've been able to experience living from my True Self more and more lately, but The Great Love Affair with myself is brand new. The years of study of self-care, recovery from co-dependency, and doing my work didn't give me what just showed up for me. It all prepared me for The Great Love Affair, but I've waited so long for me to arrive. It changes everything. Decisions become clear and freedom is accessible. The love of others, the love of the Divine Gaze and even my Necessary Nemesis gave me this. It's the mystical path that transforms trauma - the trauma of the estrangement from ourselves.

Caroline Myss says we're always on the path but not always managing it well. We know we're managing it well when we don't have to betray ourselves.

Our joy and lightness or heaviness and suffering will show us how we're managing our path. We need to get still and honest to hear that wisdom that lives inside of us. Our True Self is fierce because it doesn't live from fear. It honors freedom. It knows our losses give us *us*. It doesn't get any better than that.

Our integrity is needed to do this work like nobody's business. That's our center and our power. The more we know ourselves, the more we're able to be in integrity.

What My Losses Gave Me
Reflection

What areas of your life do you think you may over-adapt and not stand fully in truth, out of fear of loss or punishment?

What do you think the cost to yourself, your integrity, your guidance, your growth, your health, or your opportunities is when you come from fear versus fierce trust and surrender of the outcome?

Meditate on how it feels, and the rewards that you could have when you live in integrity. How will you love yourself more fully? Describe what that would feel like and how that would change you and the course of your life.

It takes courage and intention to honor what's loving to ourselves when it very often will lead to loss of comfort and belonging. What would it be like to make that belonging about belonging to you and your soul's path, which will lead to the right kind of belonging to your tribe? Is it worth it to you? If so, what needs to be done for you to move in that direction?

16

Integrity and Honoring Our Aversion

"I prefer to be true to myself, even at the hazard
of incurring the ridicule of others, rather than
be false, and to incur my own abhorrence."
- Frederick Douglass

Integrity has been a tricky one for me my entire life. It's what I valued and longed for but remained elusive. If integrity is defined by how we honor our internal Yes or No, I've been inconsistent, to say the least.

In my desire to avoid suffering (what my integrity would cost me), I didn't manage my path well. I suffered far more than I would have, had I honored my integrity.

I recently woke up to an area of my life where I wasn't in integrity. A family member's choice to stand with someone who doesn't bring good into the world disturbed me. I said to myself, "I'm going to use my DNA to stand for what I believe." At that moment, it hit me where I wasn't in integrity. I was able to turn it around and look at where I stood by someone – my Necessary Nemesis, whom I had begun to call again a friend - who I knew deep down wasn't a good person. My integrity gave me a clarity and a healthy aversion to what isn't in line with my deepest values and life purpose. I had to stop pretending and embrace the cost of living in my integrity. I was beginning to wake up to how I was complicit in a con by protecting this person. It was my life-long tricks of keeping people in my life I had no business being around. I had my own psychic agenda going on in the healing process by being around this man, but it was just plain wrong of me. I tell myself I'm so strong by being able to be around these toxic people, that I'll eventually get my power back, that I'm such a loving person and can help them change, blah, blah, blah. It's me trying to create a re-do; it's my ego's way of trying to heal the trauma. But when I do that I'm really weak. Integrity makes us strong. Standing alone makes us strong. Splitting from truth makes us weak. I'm not wired to look the other way under the guise of acceptance, forgiveness and support. I tried it. I looked the other way and didn't stand in my own truth in favor of the crowd.

An internal war was going on as I tried to suppress my own discernment in favor of politeness, belonging, and "being loving." I thought I needed the love the group brings. And my shame shut down my discernment.

This last time I got a big bounce. I chose integrity and honored my aversion to what wasn't right. My losses didn't feel like losses at all. I experienced energy, joy, lightness and strength. It seems sad and silly that I ever hesitated. My capacity for self-deception humbles me.

Integrity is a body experience that grounds me. I feel it in my body. Just like aversion. When aversion serves, we feel it as a wake-up call. We don't judge ourselves for not being more ooey-gooey toward someone when our intuition tells us something doesn't line up; someone is predatory, lacks empathy or is unsafe. We need to learn what we need to learn, see what we need to see, process what we need to process, to make sure we don't end up in the same situation again.

We still take The Second Look that holds that person with their humanity and divinity, with compassion for where they are and what made them that way. But we don't need to make our bed with them. We don't need to be around people with whom we cannot fully be ourselves. Well, maybe that's not true. Maybe circumstances require us to keep our mouths shut and our heads down to get through the family dinner party. Maybe it's not safe to be that real around those who won't see or hear who we are and what we hold dear. God, do I want to minimize those situations as much as possible!

As I go through the change of life, it's more difficult to just make nice. It feels like if I don't live in my integrity I'll end up with a disease.

It's a strange bounce, this integrity thing. At first, I'm afraid to allow myself to feel my aversion and honor the soundness of it. But then when I jump off the group-think cliff and honor my aversion, I'm able to fly. I see the big view and feel light and strong. Then I feel the gravity of what I didn't want to see before - the dark underbelly which is the reason for the healthy aversion. Under that is my anger that I censored. When I listen to what my anger says to me to be aligned with my integrity I know what action honors truth and love. I feel The Bounce. And that feels really, really good.

We must honor our aversion, what's in line with our internal No or Yes to be women who run with the wolves.

We also have aversion that isn't tied to our instincts or integrity, but comes from what we fear in ourselves that we see in another. That's when our integrity – our deepest Yes to wholeness – woos us that it's time to kiss the leper.

Integrity and Honoring Our Aversion Reflection

In what ways or areas of your life are you able to experience aversion as a message to your integrity?

How will you allow yourself to be more honest with yourself about your aversion and not judge someone in an unhealthy way?

How will you build the reflex to acknowledge aversion and to check in with your integrity, and hear what the message to you might be?

If we constantly check in with our integrity and where we may be off course, we're able to be more awake to our aversions without our need to stuff them or feel hatred toward others. What will help you do that well? How will you experience it as discernment and take action every time?

Are there any situations in your life, like the family dinner party mentioned, where it doesn't feel safe or fruitful to speak up? How will you take steps to have better boundaries and self-care in those situations?

When have you felt aversion toward someone that was a projection of what you don't like in yourself, and an aversion that is telling you something or someone is toxic to you? How do you discern the difference between both kinds of aversion: aversion you should run from and aversion you should kiss?

17

Self-Trust and Self-Distrust

"We need to assume the shadow is always operating.
It's the Spiritual Director's job to assume you're going
to drop the ball. Never leave someone to their own
devices. Our job is to show them their shadow."
- CAROLINE MYSS

Trappist Monk and author Thomas Merton, who helped bring contemplation to the west in the twentieth century, wrote often about healthy self-distrust. I've read nearly every one of his books. Even though I've read, high-lighted, and meditated on the concept, I haven't always integrated healthy self-distrust into my life.

Because of our wounds, weaknesses, blind spots and compulsions, we'll be drawn into situations that exacerbate our suffering (not the good kind of suffering). That's why I'm now committed to having my Accountability Partners close at hand.

Two years ago, I fell headlong into a relationship with my Necessary Nemesis. I was drawn in by my past pain and abuse. The wound was still there and this situation made it quite apparent. I left a loving and soulful long-term relationship to be with someone I just met. I thought I was too old, had worked too hard on myself, too recovered, and too educated to have done such a crazy-ass thing. I knew almost immediately this person fit the profile of every one of my past abusers. There was a crack through it all that never got completely healed. This relationship was destiny with my wound.

Because I developed the bad habit of keeping secrets in my abusive relationships, I didn't tell those closest to me the truth. The situation felt like destiny and so familiar I was lured in and trapped by my own psyche. That's where healthy self-distrust would have helped me care for myself, even when I felt powerless to resist. Had I had my agreement with my Accountability Partners (A.P.s) in place, I would have disclosed to them, "You know my past, my wounds, my patterns. I want to pursue this, and I need you to look out for me." They would have then said, "Alright. We'll talk every week. We want to know how you're treated and how you treat yourself." And even before that, they would have asked me questions that would've broken the spell over me that made my body weak and weird.

My A.P.s are safe, astute, and love me to my death and beyond. They'll always be there for me and nothing will break that bond. I could say they're my Destiny Partners, as they help me stay the course.

Before I understood the value of having A.P.s, when I experienced things that didn't align with my values, my sanity, or my health, I didn't trust my own truth to stop submitting myself to the crazy. I listened to others as they would adore this man even though they didn't have the inside scoop (remember, I was hiding and protecting); I didn't practice healthy self-trust. So, I did the opposite of what I should have: Trusted myself when I shouldn't have and didn't trust myself when I should have. Oops. The suffering finally won out and I got free from the illusions and confusions. Lots of learnings but lots of trauma to heal from.

It was a few of those who helped me recover from the trauma of the abusive situation that became my A.P.s. The idea of having A.P.s came to me during the healing time when I acknowledged to myself what I already knew - just how safe and loving these people are and how I could have disclosed to them the intimate details of how much trouble I was in. They would have been the ones to keep me from the abusive situation, to begin with. The truth is, I pretended and was secretive in part because I was so ashamed. It was also my pride of not wanting to face how I made a mistake. A key piece is my survival instincts were damaged from trauma that occurred before I was old enough to remember. I also didn't know how to break the bond that happens in the cortisol and oxytocin exchange in the body and brain when one is abused and exposed to serious pathology. PTSD does crazy things in our bodies and brains. It's complicated. But my shadow, shame, and wounds led me down a dark path. I should not be left to my own devices. We need each other in a safe way to help us see where we're squandering our divine inheritance.

I try to tell my A.P.s everything. When I feel tempted to do something stupid - so tempted it feels like an alcoholic who wants to drink - I reach out and tell them the thought that took over my brain. I come to my sanity, but it's a scary place until I'm back to my senses. If they're the right A.P.s, you'll never feel shame for your struggles. A.P.s are people who shower unconditional love on you in all the right ways.

I'm beyond grateful I have my A.P.s in my life. I think Carole King sang about A.P.s back in '71 in, *You Got a Friend*. I loved that song when it came out and I wasn't yet six years old. Now when I think of her lyrics, the ache in her voice, she's singing my song like never before.

SELF-TRUST AND SELF-DISTRUST
REFLECTION

Because of our shadow, we'll always miss something and be self-deceived. Where will you practice more healthy self-distrust and allow those who love you well and are wise, to look out for you?

What are some incidences you recall where you were certain you were being led, but found out later you were wrong and suffered as a result?

What relationships do you have that would make excellent A.P.s?

How will you set up the relationships with the humility to make it safe for your A.P.s to speak up and ask the tough questions so you don't lie to yourself?

What causes you to doubt yourself and listen to others' opinions of someone when you know things others don't?

What will help you to stop doing that?

Our mistakes don't name us. How does self-acceptance help strengthen you to humble yourself and get others' help?

How does self-love help you to not split from your truth when the crowd doesn't see what you do?

18

My Commitment to Myself

*"The willingness to circle back around, to
gather up all that is still lost and broken within
myself, is itself the path I discover - the intimate
richness of the oceanic love which is our life."*
- JAMES FINLEY

In my desire to love well while practicing elegant and intelligent self-care, I commit:

To have the right amount of self-love that serves truth and love.

To honor what's sacred. I sovereignly walk in how I was created to be, in my deepest truth, even when it costs me.

To love myself every time I feel less than, excluded, disrespected, or dismissed. To give myself that love and care, and connect to the abundance that lives inside of me.

To walk away from any situation that causes me to split from who I truly am or from my values.

To not enable implicitly or explicitly, to be accepted.

To not engage with those who spew their self-hatred.

To not hang in there with relationships that cause me to doubt my own reality.

To not be with others who use my deepest wounds and shame to manipulate and use me.

To not engage with anyone who believes I'm not spiritual enough, humble enough, or teachable enough when I have boundaries, question what they say, or have a strong reaction to their assertions.

To not engage with anyone who manipulates or says I'm not letting them lead.

To not engage with anyone who claims to know what I really think or feel, against my own reality.

To not engage with anyone who tries to fix me.

To not engage with anyone who repeatedly expresses anger and bullying where there should be empathy.

To be courageous to see what others don't. To own the discernment earned from my life experiences.

To trust The Bounce. When my small self hurts, allow myself to bounce into my True Self. When I'm burnt up, trust I will rise like a Phoenix from the ashes. To trust that the contrast of this situation will bounce me into healing from what drew me to it in the first place. When I feel shameful or am shamefully treated, bounce into deep self-love, self-care, and decide to remove myself from the situation even when it feels like fate to be involved.

To know that when I sense someone's love of power and control over me, that I was made for greater things than being used and misused and know something is deeply wrong. When I speak up from my inner integrity, I'll know based on the person's response how long I should stick around.

To trust that I'm allowed to have high standards for everything in my life. I'll endure a humble situation if it's not abusive. I'll know what's for a season, for my benefit, and what promotes abuse by permitting it.

To look at what I project onto others – both my good and bad qualities. What do I look to that person to give me that I'm able to give to myself and bring into my world?

To not endure abusive or boundary-busting behavior in exchange for a crumb of truth. Our True Selves don't cause us to get in our heads about a situation and try to justify others' bad behavior. When a healthy person hurts us, there's deep remorse on their part and you know it to be authentic and that change is possible.

To know that to speak up for what we need and value is used for good in the other person's life as an opportunity for them to heal, grow, and love.

To acknowledge that any time we face abuse, trauma, addiction, loss, co-dependency or any other life change or growth, it will cost us the relationships that will no longer serve our transformed selves. We bounce into the True Self every time we're tempted to be something we no longer are, to get that old crowd back.

To wake up, have integrity, and love well while practicing elegant an intelligent self-care will always cost us. We love those people from the fullness in our True Selves, kick the dust off our feet and keep on walking. Our new tribe is waiting for us.

MY COMMITMENT TO MYSELF
REFLECTION

Which ones on this list were most personal to you as areas to grow in?

Journal in depth around those areas to get more awareness and to help you commit to the change. Pain helps us change.

How will you focus on The Bounce to not get stuck in hate and rage? How does the focus on our growth in self-love and care keep us focused on doing our own work?

Hope in the Transformational Path helps us focus on our work and not lose our way. How will you keep this list before you to see it's about self-compassion and not being complicit in our own wounding?

How will you be honest in unhealthy situations about what isn't right, and not dismiss anything as "it's all our own stuff, projection and judgments," (as some spiritual teachers tell us, which censors our discernment and keeps us from wisdom and reality)?

19

Making Amends to Ourselves

*"One of the most painful traumas of all is the
constant trauma of self-inflicted betrayal where
you do hear the voice and do nothing about it
and it's your strongest voice of protection."*
- CAROLINE MYSS

When something triggers the memory of what I've been through and how I was a participant in it, I can't help but say, "I'm sorry" to Krista that I abandoned her. Being a willing participant is a complicated thing, but some part of me laid down and took it. Some part of me smothered the fire in me that's given to all of us to guide us on our way. Some part of me decided I wasn't worthy to allow that fire. I didn't allow self-care to weigh heavily in my life decisions. Like a reflex, I put my hand on my chest and hold Krista's heart. My next thought is about how much I want to make it up to her.

There's been a liberation in my clients who see their past through making amends to how they were complicit to their own suffering, versus only being a victim of another's abuse. We realize we didn't rise up and stand in the truth. Even if we were children, we see it was our invitation to be bold enough to do so. It becomes about our inner work.

We have compassion on ourselves. These traumatic events are head-spinning and cause us to doubt our deepest truth. I'm not saying it's our fault. I'm not saying that we should have had the capacity to tell someone to "F-off" in the presence of their invisible dark force. However, we do split from ourselves to survive, even when it betrays us. It served us at the time in our childhoods when it was too much for us.

Caroline Myss and James Finley state the healing of trauma is a mystical one. I am one whose life testifies to that truth. I couldn't heal my traumas, my complicity in re-traumatizing myself, and not heeding my own guidance system, by any of the therapeutic modalities I went through. My survival compass was damaged. I needed to enter the mystical realm where infinite possibilities await. So, deep compassion and reverence are in order. Never self-hatred nor shame. As Thomas Merton said, "Self-loathing *never* works."

We can now speak up and remove ourselves from what harms us. There's no shame in this, only love. Not taking care of ourselves or becoming who we're meant to be can be habit- forming.

The idea of making amends to myself came like this: I felt sorrow that I neglected Krista many times and that I didn't do all I could to rise up and say, "Here I am. What do you need?" The weeks on end I didn't get the exercise that's vital to move energy, heal trauma, and care for my body and soul wasn't good amends-making.

When I abandoned and betrayed Krista, I left my body because it was too painful. I felt so much fear at times in my life, and rightfully so. But now I live here in my body and my heart and never want to leave.

I have fun caring for Krista. I've taught my phrase, "Learning to love well while practicing elegant and intelligent self-care" for years. I admit all the time I have yet to learn what that means and I'm not always good at it.

But when I think of making amends to myself, everything is different. It's clearer, spacious, and beautiful. I love Krista now like never before. Now I'm on The Bounce course - the course where all my failings and falling downs bounce me back up. Like the sun that rises every morning, there's always hope for me and for you.

On The Bounce course, making amends to ourselves is as intrinsic as breathing.

Making amends to ourselves looks different to each of us. Some of us will take every care not to collapse into medicating our pain. For others, it's being mindful not to fall into care-taking. It's creating new habits and brain-tracks to change behavior. It's beautiful boundaries, or getting to know ourselves and be our own best friend and guardian angel.

We keep at it until the big shift happens. Once it happens, making amends to ourselves becomes as natural as breathing. Let's stop holding our breath when the storms come. Just breath.

MAKING AMENDS TO OURSELVES
REFLECTION

How could seeing yourself through the focus of making amends to yourself, help you hold both self-compassion and an energy that helps you use your fire to honor and protect yourself, instead of the constriction that old, unprocessed anger or hatred does to you?

Where do you want to make amends to yourself?

In what areas could you make amends to yourself and bounce into greater self-love, awareness, and sensitivities because of what you went through?

In what ways will making amends empower you to greater self-compassion instead of regret, being stuck in the old story, or wanting to sub-consciously create a Re-do (because you think next time you could do it better and find your voice)?

How does the thought of seeing how we betrayed ourselves out of a survival strategy, strengthen the reflex to turn that into a strength through greater self-care?

How does this level of self-awareness and self-care make you a better leader?

20

Sleeping with the Enemy

"You hear the voice telling you not to do something,
and you do it anyway, then tell yourself you didn't
want to create conflict or be criticized. You have
constantly ended up betraying yourself."
- CAROLINE MYSS

Sometimes something or someone feels like life to us, but in the end, it's the enemy of all we're called to do in this life.

It's tricky because once we go to bed with someone or something that doesn't serve the life that wants to be lived through us, we're kind of screwed. It's tricky to get unscrewed.

Attachments to substances, bad habits, crazy-making relationships that are unfixable, brain tracks that leave us hopeless and helpless, (you fill in who or what you're sleeping with), are not always easy to break off. The attachment may give us "euphoric recall" where we remember the high but forget the low afterward. We adapt to living life on a small scale and call it acceptance or long-suffering. We call it life when it's death. Like the alcoholic who can't wait to get to the bar because it feels like life, the family members know it's only death; often those around us see where we're deceiving ourselves.

I hope I'm done sleeping with the enemy. That's why I have my Accountability Partners (A.P.s) to help me see where I make my bed. We may get out of it disease-free or we may need some intervention to clean up what infected us. Either way, it sobers us to reflect on the concept of where we're sleeping with the enemy.

I make it a regular practice to ask myself, "Are my bedfellows all that terrific after all?"

Sometimes we're so trapped in a one-flesh bond that's at such a low vibrational level, we feel off balance and all we ever learned about self-care is forgotten. We're just trying to figure it out. That has been a pattern of mine.

But with great intention, community, and feeding our souls truth, we're able to get unscrewed and "leave the life we have to get to the life that's waiting for us," as James Hillman said. New life comes with having higher standards. Because we're worth it. Together we'll make our beds with peace.

Sleeping with the Enemy
Reflection

Is there anything that's thrilling, dangerous, euphoric, secretive, or leaves you feeling powerless - 'an enemy'- that you'd like to stop sleeping with, if you believed the bond could be broken?

What are some steps you could take through connection, awareness, and inquiry with yourself, and your A.P.s, that could support you to make that break to stop sleeping with the enemy, and replace that attachment with something that brings empowerment and wisdom?

How would freedom from this enemy make you a better leader?

What power does this enemy take from you? Define your enemy.

In what ways does it feel addictive?

What's the weakest link in you that has allowed you to be seduced (because of an attachment)?

What potential crisis could cause you to be vulnerable to sleeping with the enemy?

How will you protect yourself from that deception?

21

Loving Myself Questions

"It's not your job to like me. It's mine."
- Byron Katie

- What would it look like to love me in this moment?
- What do I need?
- What do I value?
- What kind of people do I want in my life?
- Check in with my body. Do I leak energy to others?
- Do I enable?
- Do I cover for someone out of fear?
- What is the draw to this situation?
- What role do I play in the relationship?
- What feels familiar and why?
- What does that person represent that I disown in myself?
- Am I in my power?
- How am I treated?
- What don't I like?
- With both dualism and non-dualism, what do I see? What do I feel? Where is the disturbance?
- In an elevated psychological aroused state: (energized but not in a fight or flight), how do I speak up instead of shrink?
- How will I be more honest? "I'm struggling with this. I'm not sure how I feel or think about that."
- What is most safe for me?
- What do I tolerate that isn't loving to myself?
- Where do I need to trust The Bounce more?

- What makes me feel bad about myself in an unhealthy way? This is in contrast to feeling sorrow over my not loving well. This is someone's manipulation of me to believe I'm not loving just because I don't agree with their behavior or reality. I acknowledge my contributions to breakdowns in relationships without being treated with distain.
- Who tries to diminish me?
- Where do my thoughts keep me from awareness of what diminishes me and lead me to not take care of myself?

Loving Myself Questions
Reflection

What questions stood out the most for you, as areas you need to pay attention to?

Why did those questions stand out for you?

What would it look like to courageously go deeper and explore what needs to be adjusted in your life? Journaling? Talking with your A.P.s?

What strategies could you come up with to support you to make those changes in yourself or in your circumstances?

What is your greatest fear that may keep you from loving yourself more and honoring love and truth in a healthier way?

22

The Gift of Tears

"Unless we meet the suffering person at the level of their
suffering, we betray their presence in their suffering.
Any kind of romanticized spiritually that tries to speak
from 'up here,' betrays the truth of their experience. The
only authentic response is to get down with them on the
feeling level and say, 'I'm so genuinely sorry you had
to go through that and are going through this now.'"
- JAMES FINLEY

Leo was the loving and soulful long-term relationship I left for
someone I hardly knew, that I refer to in *Self-Trust and Self-Distrust*.
We tried to get back together but we couldn't fix it. He's one of my
greatest losses in this life. And yet, strangely it was supposed to
end. Through my Great Fall, I brought the Great Death to the
relationship. We had outgrown the container that held it. Great
love and great suffering lead to greater transformation. Both of
us wanted to be transformed and our capacity to love grew enormously. It was time to enter the much-needed Great Love Affairs
with ourselves. During the editing of this book, I texted him that it
breaks my heart every day how I hurt him and lost him. He replied,
"I do know you love me. Some things can't be put back the way
they were. As you say in your book (I love saying, "As you say in
your book") it had to get burned up because we were too comfortable. And yet now, because of our trust that everything belongs,
and our love of what is, we are falling into an even brighter future
ahead of us and an even greater love holding us." Paradoxically, we

both bounced into greater life, although we will feel the loss our remaining days. By the time of that text, Leo and I had not been life-partners for a year.

A few months after the end of our 15-year relationship, Leo set out on what we call his Transformational Road Trip to get away and see what would emerge for him.

While Leo was on his Transformational Road Trip in Spring, 2017, he experienced more pain and sadness toward the beginning of the journey. It was the softening, the grieving, the letting go that made way for the joy that sprang up soon after. He wrote to me in the first weeks:

"Embracing brokenness and shadow at the deepest level... many tears and nearly sleepless nights spent in prayer...

(speaking of Richard Rohr - our spiritual father)

Rohr said this about tears:

'The gift of tears helps you embrace the mystery of paradox, of that which can't be fixed, which can't be made right, which can't be controlled, and which doesn't make sense.'

I'm forever thankful for you... for me... for us... and for every moment in the liminal space of groundlessness and emptiness... and for the waterwheel of Kenotic Love.

It's so amazing that when we first got together you talked to me so much about the waterwheel and now that's the image Rohr is using to speak about the emptiness that becomes fullness. We were always mystics."

It is told that St. Francis of Assisi cried every day. Those around him didn't understand (except Clare). I believe Francis was made in those tears.

As we wake up, some of us will cry more. I hope we're all able to cry more. When I see a client cry, I'm happy. We've hit pay dirt; they can't control something anymore. I also believe the tears help us embrace the mystery.

Sometimes what's under our anger is what wants to flow through our tears. Maybe it's our grief, our emptiness that we fear will overtake us. Like a waterwheel, if we let it go, we will be filled again.

I had a vision in '95. It wasn't about tears. It was about a waterwheel. It was an image (according to my concept of the divine at the time) of pure joy and Love laughing while pouring down water from an endlessly-filling watering can from above. The water was hitting the waterwheel and causing it to turn. The sunlight breaking through the falling water created a rainbow. I was dancing under the rainbow. To this day I refer to dancing under the waterwheel as a metaphor for complete joy and trust. It's a celebration of being loved just as we are.

> I will dance for You
> Under Love's waterwheel
> You pour and I leap

Love is pouring down love, and laughing with delight. The water and the light create a rainbow we dance under. If only we remember…what joy and gratitude, lightness and strength would bounce us along.

We're being lavished upon, even when we don't see what's happening around us.

There's a lot about our lives that can't be fixed, made right, controlled or makes sense. Maybe under the waterwheel we will cry and let the water splash all over us. It's almost a scene from a movie: We stand there under the waterwheel and sob, drenched from the water. But just when we least expect it, the sun comes out and we feel it more intensely than ever before. We open our eyes… and there's the rainbow.

Now I cry every day.

The Gift of Tears
<u>Reflection</u>

What's your relationship to tears?

How are you able to experience tears as a letting go of what you can't sometimes fix?

In what situations do you resist the tears and it keeps you stuck in emotions that don't soften you, but armor you?

What would it be like to associate tears with a greater capacity for joy?

How have you experienced that sense of beauty in the midst of the tears?

How have you experienced tears as a better option than when we try to fix or control that which cannot be?

What are the ways you'll embrace tears by staying connected to your heart?

In what ways can you experience the infilling after the letting go, the surrender to be bounced into greater life and freedom, and the emptying of pain that can allow our hearts to be filled with more love and mystery?

23

Emotional Sobriety

"Emotional sobriety: Witnessing what our
emotions say to us and allowing them to move
us where we need to go without needing to hop
on stage and act out all the characters."
- KRISTA VORSE

There comes a moment when you realize you're going to be okay;
you have a True Self that's indestructible. But you can only be in
that place moment by moment; you will only experience that as
you step into the moment. Once I leave the moment, that's when
my false self tells me I'm not going to be okay. It comes out of scarcity. But the True Self always comes out of abundance because it's
in union with the Infinite.

Emotional sobriety is the process of dis-identifying with our
emotions. "I am not my feelings." I don't heighten feelings or wrap
myself around them or give them the power to control my actions.
I don't get drunk on the drama. I step back into the Conscious
Witness or Watcher. Being the Watcher gives us the chance to go
to inquiry or self-inquiry and be in the learning mode.

Emotional sobriety isn't to be used to suppress strong, uncomfortable emotions that can signal what isn't okay or needs to be
processed. It allows, includes, loves, and lets them go after it discerns the message of the emotion and if there's truth behind it.
It discerns whether it's coming from our past, coming from an
untrue assumption, or a too self-referential place. We feel it and
hear the message of the emotions without it causing us to lose our
grounding, our connection, awareness, or inquiry.

Most of what you've already read so far helps us to hone emotional sobriety: *Staying in The Infinity Loop, Great Compassion, The Great Love Affair, Loving Well,* our self-care and self-awareness. I will touch on this more throughout the book. Begin by being aware of your feelings. Name them as you get as still as possible on the inside. This is witnessing your feelings. You have feelings but they do pass if we don't intensify them. This becomes part of our spiritual practice as we grow in it until the day we die.

Emotional sobriety isn't a magic wand; it doesn't take away fear or anxiety or feelings of loss or loneliness or even feelings of abandonment. But it sustains you through these emotional ups and downs. We still feel them, but we don't have to be afraid of our fear or anxious about our anxiety. We're free to witness our feelings, name them, and let them pass. That's meditation. You still have your feelings but they don't have you, as Rohr says. That's emotional sobriety.

EMOTIONAL SOBRIETY
REFLECTION

Emotional sobriety is foundational to be an influencer to those around us. It helps us stay present and aware.
Where are some areas or circumstances when you feel you've lost your emotional sobriety?

In what ways would the practice of witnessing your feelings, (neither denying nor intensifying them), help you hear the message of them - what needs to be paid attention to, what thoughts need to be questioned - and not let those emotions take you off course?

In what ways do you see emotional sobriety as foundational to not collapse into powerlessness when our sturdiness and resolve is what's needed?

In what ways will we feel more empowered to experience equanimity on a regular basis when we make emotional sobriety a serious intention?

How has not having emotional sobriety hurt you in the different areas of your life? What needs to happen in your spiritual practice to get to emotional sobriety regularly? What intentions and habits need to be set?

What other principles in the previous chapters come to mind as other insights that will help you hone emotional sobriety?

24

The Red Pouch

"First pride, then the crash -
the bigger the ego, the harder the fall."
- *THE MESSAGE*

The more we remember our own failings, the greater chance we have to influence another.

One day I recalled something I did earlier in my life that hurt someone. As I looked down at my right hip, it was as though the misdeed was there, with me, never to be forgotten. Something else I'd done that I was sorry for, came to me the next day. It too was there on the outside of the right side of my body. I wanted to remember it. It was a humbling and sobering gift. My sorrow over the hurt I caused signified my greater capacity to love than was there at the time of the offense. I looked again and there was a deep Red Pouch on my waist with a zipper that went around three-quarters of it. It's not a small pouch. It contains all the times and ways I haven't lived in love or truth, all the times and ways I've hurt others, all the wrong things I've done which I never want to forget. What isn't love, is a powerful vision for what is.

Ajana, whom I mention in the Acknowledgments, is the naturopathic physician and acupuncturist who does shamanic healing work. She facilitated the deep work in me that birthed this book. I went to her when Complex PTSD surfaced after a pathological relationship threatened to take me out.

When I told Ajana about The Red Pouch, she said it's over my masculine ovary (the right side signifies the masculine). She liked that. Whatever that means, I like it too. It's outside my body, it doesn't live inside of me, it doesn't have the power to name me, and it's beautiful. This pouch which is invisible to everyone else but myself is now forever with me. It will serve me. I look down and look inside and see and remember that I too have faltered like the person I see before me I'm disturbed about. I look down and remember how I lost my way in a similar situation and perhaps won't again because I remembered. I put my maneuvers that miss the mark in the pouch.

My sister said a wise thing to me recently: "We would be negligent to forget." We'd be negligent to forget what we've discerned or experienced with another that would put us in harm's way; we forget our addictions to substances, behaviors, and people that cause us to keep sleeping with the enemy; we look away from the mirror and forget what we're capable of.

If we feel our hearts in any way besides self-referentially, when we hurt others, we will suffer. Eventually, we will wake up to the error of our ways and gasp. If we know how to work with our own shame, we're able to face it and not decompensate. This is why we project onto others our own undesirable traits - if we faced how horrible we are at times, without something to stabilize us - we'd crack and no one could put Humpty Dumpty back together again. The Red Pouch stabilizes us.

I highly recommend The Red Pouch. It's the color of blood. There's beautiful symbolism in that for me. It's all held in love. Our failings and cruelties are not what we have to push away in disgust out of fear of shame. We wear them, contained in this zippered pouch, carried with awareness. It makes us more connected.

An Alpha Woman is able to carry that Red Pouch. She knows she can hold it all because Love holds her, and all the ways she dances in The Infinity Loop well and not so well. When she's aware of her pouch, no one can use it against her. Humility isn't toxic shame – ("I'm uniquely defective and not enough.") It's a beautiful brokenness that leads to our wholeness.

Humility and confidence. That's The Red Pouch. It's love.

THE RED POUCH
REFLECTION

Meditate on your own Red Pouch. What does it look like? Describe it in detail.

In what ways would The Red Pouch help you to embrace the memories of what you feel sorry for, and not be taken out by shame or wanting to elevate yourself in comparison, to not feel so bad about yourself?

How will you experience the memories in a sweet (because of love), tender hearted way that cracks you open instead of it bringing you down? How do the memories bring you into sweet solidarity with others who don't always love well and live in truth?

In The Infinity Loop model of leadership, we don't hide our weaknesses and failures but honestly share them. Our influence comes from our skill in connection, awareness, and inquiry, our confidence to stand in the truth, and our humility. When we create safety, we foster openness to being influenced. What ways will you feel more comfortable to share how you've struggled as well when you engage with others?

In what situations do you feel your faults have diminished you?

We don't have to drop our standards just because we've done the same, but we'll more likely be in greater awareness and sobriety when we respond if we remember our own weaknesses. When you have a strong reaction to someone's behavior, how will you make it a regular habit to "look into The Red Pouch" and see if you have also done the same behavior?

25

Vulnerability

"This is the great discovery. Once we discover
we're endlessly invincible precisely in the depths
of our vulnerability, then we're paradoxically
free and we can become a healing presence to
ourselves and others, which is our path."
- JAMES FINLEY

The word "vulnerable" comes from the Latin word vulnera, which means "to wound." So, when we're vulnerable, we're likely to get wounded. But the wound is our way out of ourselves and what allows grace to come in. It's most often better to be vulnerable and know you could get wounded. But that's the spiritual practice - to stay open in the presence of pain. We're enlarged and our capacity for love is enlarged when we allow the pattern of death and resurrection (The Bounce) to occur. We allow the True Self to emerge. Our True Self emerges from the death of the ego's attachment to the false self.

That being said, when there's abuse present, there has to be a "No" in there. This isn't the time to be vulnerable but use discernment, connected to our integrity (our inner "No" or "Yes") and walk away if need be. We're sovereign over ourselves. We're free to always say, "I do want this. I don't want this." It's our choice to always walk away. To not be able to have this choice, is nothing short of a cult and abuse. The late Gerald May wrote in *The Awakened Heart*, "Love may be patient, forgiving and bearing all things, but it does not stifle life."

Our ability to handle pain, to allow ourselves to hurt and be uncomfortable, to be vulnerable, makes us strong. We develop resilience and a sobriety in the midst of all that enters our lives. We then don't need to medicate our pain or spew it onto another. Our capacity to be courageously vulnerable, helps us love well. We can stand in The Infinity Loop and change the world. Our world is in crisis right now in a large part because we aren't good at staying open in the presence of pain. When we realize the pain won't take us out but is the doorway into deeper transformation and liberation, we humbly commit our lives to learn how to transform our pain so we don't transmit our pain onto others. When we know our pain can be transformed, we more likely stay open and vulnerable to the risk of pain.

Vulnerability
<u>Reflection</u>

To stay open in the presence of pain, is courageous. To be vulnerable is to be courageous. Are there patterns where you don't stay open at the risk of being wounded?

Feeling uncomfortable and feeling unsafe are two very different things. In what ways do you struggle to hold both: being vulnerable and risk being wounded, but made better for it, and knowing when it's unwise to be vulnerable in certain unsafe situations?

What does it mean to you that to stay open in the presence of pain brings a kind of death to the false self (our identities) and helps you resurrect – bounce – into your True Self who's beyond your identity or your wounding?

In what ways does vulnerability serve you in your spiritual development? Anything that causes you to be cracked open and made bigger (not your ego, but your awareness of your Abundant Self), serves you. Paradoxically, your wounding leads to your freedom from your small self.

How will you help yourself embrace being more vulnerable as the doorway to more liberation from yourself? What cues will you give yourself to stay open?

26

Making Peace with Our Inner Landscape

"Spiritual healing occurs as we learn to live in an abiding
peace in the presence of all that life might bring."
- JAMES FINLEY

In Spring, 2017 I was able to go to another level with my inner stillness. I've been graced with a power in this silence. It may just be the coolest thing ever.

By humbling accepting life as life is, by living in peace with the ordinary, by staying in silence and simplicity as much as possible, we go deeper. I noticed my sturdiness increasing as I remained still more often - internally and externally still when I'm able. I felt I was moving in slow motion. We do the work on ourselves but then it's done to us. It's all grace. But we keep showing up. It's an ok-ness - all is well at the deepest level with life. Emotional sobriety gives us this gift. Since I first wrote this, I've been given the gift of non-resistance to what is. I don't need things to be any other than this moment. Just this month (now late Nov.), I'm aware I under-stand what it means to live surrendered to Divine Providence. I don't have that capacity all the time, but I know what it feels like and it's far better than wanting to flee *what is*. I still acknowledge what isn't in line with my values or vision, but I move toward that sweet spot in peace. I am peace.

There's such a stillness as we move past the Watcher to being the Watcher of the Watcher. It's a power source, 100% alive, present to respond to whatever emerges. It's my most embodied, smart brain, peaceful being. I don't want to leave home without her. I've needed her with me all my life so now that I've found her, I'm addicted to whatever is needed to keep her around. And if that means sitting in the emptiness, the blah, to resist to fix the moment, I'll choose inner stillness to court her to come around more often until she agrees to cohabitate with me.

I stay in my emptiness and don't deny or intensify it. It's true that we become strong and resilient as we choose to grow through our times of emptiness.

I chose not to run for community or connection with another human. I just stayed in my inner stillness that's as sturdy as a redwood tree and hung in the quiet of that private place. What happened next was an intimacy with myself and the sacredness of my own journey that became instantly full of mystery and sweetness and love. It's the awareness of being held by Love in each and every moment. Had I gone for the positive fix, I would have missed the unique expression of "God giving Herself to me as my life" in that moment, as James Finley says.

I've found that to go through the drop of aloneness and emptiness is worth the fall. Until I die, I want to use my sales skills to sell the value of the surrender to the drop. It's the awareness that we're sturdy and powerful in our inner stillness because we become the Watcher of all the things that float down the river of our stories that aren't even us. In that inner stillness, we experience we're bigger than we thought we were, and beyond the power of our moments. When we're present in the Now, we're brought into happiness, beyond what momentary emotional discomfort we're experiencing. Our True Selves live in the spaciousness.

The intimacy I had with myself came shortly after I allowed the drop into the blah, the quiet, the "not exciting" thing. It became the most exciting thing. In many ways society has taught us to run from our blah moments and that we should be scared of them. What if we didn't intensify them, tell ourselves a miserable story about them, but just got still on the inside and found a power source that's more interesting than anything on the outside of us?

That would bounce us into the Now which is ever full of love and life and happiness. It may be the greatest paradox there is.

For this moment, nothing compares to the sacredness of my journey with the emptiness as well as the fullness. It's a powerful thing to embrace it all in inner stillness. Therein lies the peace.

Making Peace with Our Inner Landscape
Reflection

In The Infinity Loop model, we're Alpha Women in an Alpha brain state. We need access to our inner stillness.

The Alpha brain state is attributed to deep relaxation of body and mind, higher levels of creativity, improved problem-solving abilities, improved mood and stability of emotions, peak performance and being in the *zone* or *flow*, super learning and genius states, enhanced immune system and healthy levels of serotonin. How will you bring these benefits to your remembrance when you want to run from inner stillness and flail around?

What practices will you do to honor more inner stillness?

In what ways do you run from the inner stillness out of fear of the emptiness and blah feelings?

What do you think the benefits would be if you tolerated the inner stillness more? Not just in a yoga class but in the bare and lonely moments?

How will our tolerance of the emptiness create more calm, self-control and emotional sobriety in us when we're in a room full of chaos and charged emotions?

What practice would you like to implement that will help you live in the most aware, grounded, unshakeable place, no matter what comes at you?

27

Self-Compassion Vs. Hatred

"I imagine one of the reasons people cling to their
hates so stubbornly is because they sense, once hate
is gone, they will be forced to deal with pain."
- James Baldwin

I believe in the wisdom of our emotions and what they say about us, what needs to be paid attention to, and what we've pushed into the shadow. I don't explain the complexity of how to skillfully work around emotions. Karla McLaren is an excellent resource for that. I synthesize her wisdom with contemplation that helps us "transcend and include," (Ken Wilbur).

I do believe I've found a healthy way to work with our emotions without losing connection, awareness, and inquiry.

We're able to let go of hate when we have self-compassion to handle our pain. Self-compassion does the work that hatred can never do.

James Baldwin's quote gives us compassion why others behave so hateful at times; they're terrified of the pain that lies beneath. We know what that feels like because we've transmitted our pain onto others as well.

Self-compassion has been the game changer for myself and my clients. It creates awareness, boundaries, and truth in a powerful healing and transformation process for ourselves and our relationships. I've seen clients find the ability to change life-long relationship patterns by speaking up from a place of self-compassion and the tools in this book. They practice speaking up until it becomes a strength. It's strong and gentle.

Under all our pain for what is lost, and the abuses we've endured from others' unconsciousness, is our dire need for self-compassion. That self-love and self-care carry truth and wisdom that changes everything. It has a protective fire as it holds our hearts in love.

Anytime we've been hurt, we have a choice to go to hate or self-compassion. Maybe we can hold both, but it's tricky and often the hatred takes us away from the self-compassion that can give us what we need. I'm talking about pushing on the pedal of deep, reverent self-compassion that holds the grief, the life-long pain, and gives us all we need in tender acknowledgment. Hatred creates a constriction in our bodies which limits our awareness. Witness Consciousness and emotional sobriety help us create awareness. Hate may arise to get us to face what we've suppressed. It's important to be aware of what set off the alarm in us now or may come from our past. Sometimes we become skilled at dissociating because of our childhood coping that served us when it was too much for us to bear. Acknowledging the strong emotion helps us come into our bodies and get out of a dangerous or unhealthy situation. We may have developed hyper-empathy that feels empathy for the offender at the exclusion of what's healthy. Rage (boundaries with daggers) - as Karla McLaren calls it - may also come up.

See if you move through hatred and rage when you go to self-compassion. Self-compassion honors the truth. Hate isn't how we heal. It's dangerous to us and others if not worked with skillfully. Hate isn't something we want to linger, nor do we send hate to others who have hurt us. Our world suffers because of what hate has done. Self-compassion gives us a connection to our truth, grounding, and wisdom to take care of ourselves. Self-compassion is the welcome necessary reflex.

We honor our discernment of what's toxic, we might need to remember what transpired, but we don't stroke or coddle the trauma or memory which isn't healthy and re-traumatizes us. Filling our bodies, minds, and hearts with hate to protect ourselves isn't necessary. If anger arises for us, let it drop deep into our bellies and out of our chests. Alert to anger's message in terms of what needs to be honored or protected, we then love ourselves. It's aversion without hate. That's discernment. We don't talk ourselves out of it. The person who offended us isn't less than us and we're not separate, superior, and important. Compassion may arise in us for them and the human dilemma we all share. I have compassion they didn't choose better because of whatever's unconscious in them. I know I can be unconscious. We're able to keep our boundaries because in our self-compassion we love ourselves enough not to be in harm's way. The anger doesn't linger beyond what serves a healthy process.

Connected to our hearts, we fully feel them with the benefit of self-soothing. Sadness, grief, and anger are all appropriate. We have edges but not hatred. If we allow hatred to fill our hearts, we lose our way and our self-control.

Sometimes anger stays in there and we need to go through an awareness process to learn, look at something, grieve and prepare our hearts to let go. There are those who hold bitterness and resentment to their detriment.

Forgiveness is letting go of revenge and all that holds something over someone. It's trusting things will take their course. The truth will come to the light. Hatred isn't justice. We'll know when we're ready to no longer protect someone's dangerous behavior. The pain we carry in our bodies, minds, and hearts is released. We may feel nothing. Forgiveness isn't forced on ourselves or another that would cause us to bypass the messages our emotions want to send us. We don't do forgiveness to censor out painful emotions, seem spiritually enlightened, make others comfortable, or to not have to do the necessary work around what occurred. Even though forgiveness springs from the True Self, we don't ignore what wants to arise - "the ugly" of the situation. When we see things from a whole perspective, we're able to forgive. It's a process and a choice.

Love and healing are sent to them. We don't send them daggers, disgust and contempt when we run into them. Nor do we try to win and crush them. We speak truth from that place. Some believe forgiveness happens after we confront someone and they ask for our forgiveness. I can forgive without needing them to see it; they know not what they do. Reconciliation is another matter.

I believe a whole view forgives all of life and all the humans involved. When we see from that level of awareness, forgiveness becomes what *just is*. We do the forgiveness process with elegance and intelligence that is real, profound and rooted in truth.

Forgiveness is something that comes easy to me. Sadly, it has contained an unhealthy element of forgetting what was done to me almost instantaneously that kept me in harm's way. I call it faulty wiring from abuse that has now been rewired. In that rewiring is self-compassion. That missing piece would have kept me in my body and awake because it would have helped me feel fully. I could have tolerated all the pain that feeling would entail because I can feel in the presence of compassion. With my anger that's grounded and not diffuse, I would have set boundaries as the only sane option in the circumstances. Knowing how to dance the dance of self-compassion, anger, forgiveness, and emotional sobriety, is one of the most beautiful dances there is. The ache in my heart is that you know that dance long before I did.

In my life, it's hard for me to feel I need to forgive anyone because I don't know if I think these people did these things to me as much as I let them (except in early childhood abuse that taught me how to dissociate). I abandoned and betrayed Krista time and time again. If only I rose up and said, "I understand you're in pain, blah, blah, blah, but this is so not okay." It has always been my invitation to my inner work.

I never want to hate anybody. It feels awful to me and like bondage. But I need to love myself through self-compassion and allow anger to move me where I need to be. Loving the world and having a lot of empathy must not come at the cost of caring for our needs and living in integrity.

When we forgive all of life for being what it is, when we surrender our hearts to be conformed to love, we're able to forgive and hate never takes hold of our hearts. We're left with beautiful self-compassion that becomes compassion for all those who suffer, even the offender.

Every time what we went through with that person comes to our remembrance, we hold the necessary boundary if a change hasn't occurred on their part. No matter what, respond with deep and reverent self-compassion. We don't need to hate.

SELF-COMPASSION VS. HATRED
REFLECTION

Describe the areas of your life where you could have more self-compassion?

Is there someone that stirs up hatred? Write about it.

What are you aware of when you turn that around to self-compassion? What does your body feel like?

Are there any areas you have hatred for yourself - any incident or flaw you have?

By acknowledging our short-comings, while not making excuses, what would a committed practice to only have self-compassion look like?

Is there something or someone you're willing to forgive?

Is there something or someone you're not yet ready to forgive?

28

"It's None of Your Concern"

"To get some people to like me, I'd have to sell my soul."
- KRISTA VORSE

For us to be liberated from ourselves to be leaders who change the world, it's helpful to have mantras that protect our minds from going awry.

We can't be telling ourselves stories as to whether or not someone likes us or likes what we do.

I don't mean the Human Resources Director who says, "I'm not here to make friends." I'm talking about our preoccupation with what others think.

For some, this looks a little different. Some are plagued with thoughts that they've let everyone down and it makes them want to move away and start over.

If you check in with yourself, you may have a thought that isn't helpful but habitual. It has to do with how you're seen or experienced by others. It doesn't make you more emotionally intelligent; it causes you to be pre-occupied with thoughts that keep you from being present. It's not about your need to take inventory of what you may have contributed to someone being harmed. This is a bad loop that keeps you bound.

I stood in yoga class. From the right side of the back of my head forward, my soul spoke, "It's none of your concern." That was the instruction to me while I was concerned about someone's reaction to me. They weren't their usual warm self. It wouldn't have been appropriate to ask them. Needless to say, I wasn't being a present yogi. That sentence, "It's none of your concern," came to set me free. It was a directive to be able to serve more effectively and get out of my own way. It was to liberate me from how I contribute to my own suffering. I just don't want to contribute to my suffering anymore.

Since then, I have that instruction as a guard around my mind. It's become so obvious that it's none of my concern what others think, it's expanded to, 'It doesn't matter" and "I don't care."

With 7.6 billion people on the planet, combined with the history of civilization, it just doesn't matter. There's a lot that matters that we should be concerned with, but what someone may think, say, or write about us, must not have the power to take us from being present. We don't need others' approval. It's not usually personal; others have their own filters they experience us through. What they say may be true about us. In that case, we humbly accept it. If it's not, we let it float on by.

We need to be present to do this work. Our concern is whether we love well and not what others think of us. It may sound extreme but I don't think so. If we need to see something about ourselves, we will, without twisting ourselves into a pretzel, as we wonder what we did wrong or how to get others to like or approve of us.

Some of us will find it easier than others based on our personalities; some temperaments are more focused on how they're perceived, while others don't seem to care that much. Whatever the case, this is the call of the soul that's beyond temperament. This is the call of a leader.

"It's None of Your Concern"
<u>Reflection</u>

In what situations do you find yourself concerned with what others think of you?

In what situations do you hear your thoughts that you let others down or something else that's tied to how others may perceive you?

Is there something you need to clean up if you've been in the wrong?

What will you do to replace the habit of being concerned with what others think?

What would it look like to replace the concerns with thoughts of love for others alone?

What practice will you put into place to help yourself detach from thoughts about others' opinions of you?

How does the mantra "It's none of my concern" help you put a guard around your mind to minimize your contribution to your own suffering?

29

We Row Our Way Home

"In our vulnerability is manifested true invincibility in the world. Childlike yet truly mature. Knowing nothing yet manifesting the source of wisdom. That's transformation."
- JAMES FINLEY

"We must never underestimate the need to tell the truth."
- THOMAS MERTON

We're in a constant dance between our false self and True Self. The false self is our identity we've formed from our accomplishments/failures, our personality and all that goes into our ego construct. It's not bad. The True Self is our Essence that really isn't anything. It's hard for many to want that because it feels like nothing. It feels like freefall. The great mystery is, in that nothingness is everything. It's liberation.

Recently I've been focused on the move away from my identity to my Essence.

I walked up to my usual rowing machine at the gym. As I approached it, I recognized a woman I knew of but never met, who's twenty-one years my junior. She was on the stair climber to my left. With the few words we exchanged, it was clear she already had a story about me and it wasn't good. Later I was told she'd been warned about me. She knew I wanted to speak with her in regards to someone she'd been intimate with and still endorsed. Through my inner work, I had become clear that I was complicit in a con by my protection of my Necessary Nemesis; I gave people the impression that who I protected was a good guy as I led lambs to the slaughter. She was certain that what she knew and saw of this person was all there is. The experts in decision-making and thinking models say this faulty assumption ("What I see is all there is") is what causes us to miss important discoveries about people, data, and all that we don't know. Persona isn't all there is.

As I began to row I could feel my utter vulnerability. My intention is for women to look out for women and want to hear the truth. We always have the choice to inquire deeper or discard it. I knew I still had an open heart for her and that openness allowed me to feel it all. Ajana taught me to go bigger when I encounter what comes against me. I breathed in and exhaled in an expansion of my being. I was aware I felt the love inside but it didn't protect me from what I felt came toward me. I was vulnerable in the presence of pain.

As I moved forward on the machine with my legs pulled in, I brought in Great Compassion to put his wings around me and hold me in my utter vulnerability; my humanness needed to be cared for. I would not put on armor and return the disdain.

When I pulled back, I moved from my identity of me that is being spewed upon by her story of me; she didn't have the power to name me, my heart, my truth. I moved past the Watcher (observe myself vs. held hostage by my feelings) to being The Watcher of The Watcher. It was like a cream-colored field behind me. It was also like a protection. Pure Awareness holds it all in love.

I'm not dissociating. I feel it fully, uncomfortable in my false self which identifies with my story. When I choose to move out of that place of suffering to my Essence, the nothingness - the cream-colored field that's beyond that Krista – I'm filled with an abundance that's untouchable. In that death to my small self, I can't be touched.

Like I work my body, I row between feeling fully and allowing, and letting it go. I honor the human condition in that young woman and in me.

The week that followed I ran into someone else who I wrote about in this book. When I saw her, I was again utterly vulnerable in my humanness. My heart wasn't armored but full of love. She had so much hatred for me, I felt totally laid bare. I was clear what I discerned about her energy, her expression, and why we would not be friends. When I walked away, I looked down and my body was filled with love like electricity. But my heart pounded and I wasn't protected. She still stood in the vicinity with an intensity of cold hatred. I began to row in my imagination. Again, I immediately pulled in Great Compassion to put his wings around me and hold me in love.

It was an invitation to pull back from small Krista and be The Watcher and then The Watcher of the Watcher. Essence is there all along. When we find ourselves in situations like this, we row our way home.

WE ROW OUR WAY HOME
REFLECTION

How does this metaphor of intentional self-compassion (pull in Great Compassion, versus being numb or defend), help you keep your heart open in the presence of pain in a way that serves?

How does this metaphor to intentionally observe yourself (The Watcher) and then move past that to Essence (The Watcher of The Watcher), help you to gain emotional sobriety and detach from your story and others' stories of you?

How will you integrate this tool into your life as you encounter that which comes against you?

Rowing Meditation: As the Watcher, see yourself as you row between the two realms – the small self suffering, and the cream-colored field that holds nothing but Pure Awareness, while Great Compassion stands to protect, holding it all in love.

30

The Infinity Loop of Numinous Love

Numinous: The presence of the divine, the
divine nod, a spiritual force or influence.

"The eye in which I see God is the eye in which, God
sees me."
- MEISTER ECKHART

"My own me is God!"
– ST. CATHERINE OF GENOA

St. Catherine of Genoa isn't saying we're God, but saying we're
not other than God either. She speaks as one who has experienced
divine union. Richard Rohr says divine union is, "union with what
is, with the moment, with yourself, with the divine, which means
with everything."

Through the process of this book, I encountered Numinous
Love like I never had before. I found my soul hidden in this love.
My soul spoke to me from the union with Numinous Love.

At my August 1st visit with Ajana, she asked me what that third
presence was in the room. She was aware of it before I was. She said
all she could call it was Consciousness. Was Consciousness showing up as I was moving out of the way? I began to get a glimpse of
what was emerging for me. Everything led me toward this move
through the veil, in a seduction to a liberation I've longed for, as
long as I remember. I fought it of course for many years, because I
didn't know how to die a good death. Until now.

The gift of the encounter on the rowing machine was moving me along. There's something so right about rowing between self-compassion and moving back as The Watcher of The Watcher into Essence for me, and has been a source of freedom and comfort for those with whom I've shared it. We don't get liberated by telling ourselves we should be more like Byron Katie; we get there through our humanity, in honoring our hearts, but without giving our pain the power to tell us we're nothing more than our feelings, stories, and imperfections. We do The Work as Katie calls it - and practice self-inquiry into our stories that cause us to suffer - but we don't get there by pretending. Some things need deep self-compassion and having compassion for ourselves when we don't do it perfectly. It's the allowing it before letting it go.

There were some things going on in my world that bid me to go to Essence to stop identifying with me. I needed to become nothing.

During this time, I was going through a dark night of the soul. There are not the feel-good feelings, spiritual comforts, or exciting things going on to give me that umpth. But I was patient in it because I could tell it was doing a very deep work in me. It was quite a humbling time.

I stayed in the calm, in that blah, like in *Making Peace with My Inner Landscape*, as I watered the backyard this mid-September day. I sensed this cream-colored field right behind me, like a protection, like an angel with me. It's the most real, powerful force of Wholeness, Love and Eternal Awareness. It followed me into the house and at that moment, all that cost me to get this was worth it; it's the greatest gift I've ever been given. It was the awareness of never being alone and freedom from myself and my stories. It felt like it was mine.

I noticed that it was no longer me loving me, like my reflex of self-compassion or self-care; Numinous Love was doing it all. I'm not able to explain it well because it's all part of us, but it was awareness of "the Other" and this "Other" is the best thing in the whole world.

I didn't get this because I was being a good contemplative. I was struggling at the time to stay present. My spiritual progress seemed to have fallen away. I found my way back by reading this book I was writing and the stories of my lessons fed me deeply.

My new mantra to bring me into the present moment is, "My soul," because my soul exists in divine union. My racing mind, my flip-flopping from past to future, vanished. It was the awareness: like I wrote in *"It's None of Your Concern"* - with 7.6 billion people on the planet, along with the history of civilization, things I was thinking about didn't matter. I was only concerned with this presence. And this presence is focused on what matters. It's eternal to me and exists beyond all this.

I had nights where I sensed Numinous Love bridging a gap between stories and limitations that were keeping me from the leader I longed to be. I don't have a Bucket List, but I want to do what's mine to do to give expression to what's in my heart.

Then it got better. I was in the gym again and I became aware Numinous Love was intimately with me behind me. If anyone saw my face, they'd think I was moved by the song in my earphones. It was beyond what I knew of Love before that encounter. It was, "Ah, that's what Love is!" And it was love for Krista. It was beyond the human love I felt for baby Krista in *I had a Dream*. It's how much Love loves us. Call it whatever you want that resonates with you. I could call it a lot of things that are all so, so very good.

As I edit this, I sense Numinous Love right behind me. It's the awareness of Presence.

I'd been dealing with the reality that getting a message like this out would require me to rise to a new level. The thought of marketing myself online was overwhelming. Love said, "Do it for Krista." Numinous Love would help me show up for my life in the most courageous way, step into the field where I'm more than I thought I was, and become what I write about from my encounters with Spirit. At that moment, I *was* Numinous Love, showing up for Krista. I am both aware of "the Other" and "the Other" being me.

I wept in the gym when I experienced that intensely personal love for me. If I never experience that again, it will stay with me. This encounter and the now ubiquitous awareness is causing the biggest transformational change in me. It's not our ego. It's the opposite of it. It marches to the beat of a different drum. It's here for another reason. It's energized by that reason. It knows everything it needs will be provided for. It fears nothing and loves everyone.

"My Deepest me is God!" - St. Catherine of Genoa

Call it our deepest us, our True Selves, Consciousness, Pure Awareness, God, the Numinous, whatever. I know it wasn't a coun-terfeit because the fruit of how I see, feel and behave toward others and myself is also qualitatively different. Now I could not imagine looking upon myself unlovingly.

While in yoga class the other night, my mind wandered. Then I heard Numinous Love say, "I love you." I recognize the quality of which She speaks. It permeates everything. The awareness is the great interrupter and shifter of consciousness. It instantly centered me into the present moment and all the distractions vanished. I stayed in each moment with this awareness, which is interested in the present, not in the things that distract me. I heard it repeat-edly. I could follow the instruction of the teacher, along with the centering power of Her Love. When I did veer away from the pres-ent moment later on in the class when the "I love yous" subsided, I felt the response in me saying, "I love you" automatically rise up. I said it back to Presence, God, Infinite Love, or whatever one calls that which one cannot help but love. My saying, "I love you" had the same effect. Being loved so intimately, and being Love so intimately back, became The Infinity Loop of love and fullness that makes all things possible. Hearing the way "I love you" went through me, it was a love I knew for the first time. Love is loving every inch of who I am.

The next morning in yoga I did the "I love you" to Numinous Love. I became aware of what happens with that now and happened the night before. It doesn't feel as though I'm giving love to God as though God is separate from me; it's as though the love is looping back to me, like an infinity loop. It's truly as James Finley says, "Even though I'm not God, I'm not other than God either." The way of the mystic is the experience of divine union. It's the contemplative heart that also experiences others with the awareness of oneness. It sees others' beauty.

The same way I use the mantra "My soul," I now use "I love you." Before when I'd say "I love you" in meditation, it was me doing the centering and working it. Now, there's a grace that brings the depth of the reality of being loved and being Love, as something that *just is.*

I now experience Love looking through my eyes at myself all the time. Love is loving me tenderly as I pull a sticker off a folder, as I wash my body, eat my food, and as I fumble through life. It's the "Other" who's presence is not just me.

May I see the world with the tenderness of Numinous Love, even as I hold my discernment.

It's not a good comparison but this did come to mind. I experience an almost overwhelming infilling when I coach and connect because the brain's reward system with the neurotransmitters is through the roof for me. I feel like I'm walking around on drugs to a delightful degree. In this way, I'm a drug pusher; I try to sell people how to unleash their own brain's chemicals that give them what they seek on the outside. When I love and "see people" I get filled. Pouring into others feels like I'm pouring into me – we're looped together in The Infinity Loop. For the past 10+ years, most of the time, when I coach someone, it fills like everything I do to the other, I do to myself. It's very much like we're one in our connection. That's why it doesn't drain me but keeps filling me up more and more. I'm addicted to the connection and all that happens when we enter into The Infinity Loop. We gain access through our hearts that desire to love. We know love is who we are. We want to play in that world of being who we truly are. Giving and receiving love feels like the same in that world. Going down this rabbit hole is worth it; we land in this magical field in Wonderland.

May I never lose the awareness or forget how much we're all loved, even as I go through other dark nights of the soul. When we're stripped, let us remember that the absence of those feelings is also Love, doing a deeper work in us, as we surrender to not knowing. We get used to being dislodged and that's okay because we let go to be filled with more love. Tim Farrington says the dark night of the soul is "about a kind of unconditional love that wakes us up and affirms our deepest humanity." We love and honor our vulnerability with tenderness, humility, and solidarity. What a beautiful dance it is to love and embrace our heartaches, along with the grace to transcend our struggles.

To live our most courageous lives and be the best we can be in what matters to us, isn't about being special. Caroline Myss says none of us are special, but all that's special lives inside of us. My experiences do not make me special, but they help me be more in service. Thomas Merton, like Caroline Myss, was a big fan of accepting we are ordinary and saw the freedom in that. Let us make peace with being ordinary and enjoy the sweet solidarity of our ordinariness. Spiritual experiences aren't about making us feel special. The cult leader I knew over 30 years ago thought all her counterfeit experiences made her special. They just fed her raging ego. Spiritual experiences are for us to learn to love and see others from the fullness we experience. They woo us to give our lives away.

The more we experience the Real, the Love, the utter acceptance, we have that to give from, lead from, and keep us from needing others to give us what we already have.

My desire is to help others find this Love that lives inside. We go through the veil into another realm. We drop into each moment more frequently when you don't feel we're the one who has to hold it all; Numinous Love is looking out for us.

Make stillness your friend, remove yourself from distractions and sensory overload, and be alone with yourself. Don't run from the humbling. It's worth it. We find our deepest Love there. And what lives inside can never be taken from us.

THE INFINITY LOOP OF NUMINOUS LOVE
REFLECTION

What does Numinous Love mean to you?

In what ways do you see your persona or false self as different than this Love?

What is your experience of being so deeply and passionately loved by Love, by yourself, by Mystery or God?

What do you think your soul's purpose or focus is?

What tools, mantras, practices will you employ to access your soul more often, be aware of it, or have it as your driving force?

How does knowing we experience Numinous Love as we go through dark nights, as we let go of our persona and concerns with it, as we embrace a death to the small self, bring you comfort and acceptance when you suffer in the annihilation process?

31

The Alpha Woman

"When she entered the room, everyone could
feel everything was going to be okay."
-KRISTA VORSE

"As Rudyard Kipling said,
'A big part of success is keeping your
head when no one around you is.'"
- MARTHA BECK

An Alpha Man means different things to different people, so I'll express the concepts in different language when it comes to men. However, the term Alpha Woman is clear enough to explore. I've decided to claim Alpha Woman for what I mean.

I think of Alpha also in terms of being in an Alpha brain state. Just like an Alpha Woman brings calm into the room because of her peace and alertness, in an Alpha brain state we're both calm and alert. We have the highest chance to solve problems, be creative, be at peak performance, control our emotions, focus and not shoot cortisol through our systems. It's a wakeful meditation where we connect, create awareness, and use inquiry.

In astrology, the female Leo is the most independent of all types. I identify with my lioness nature and it has served me. When I let others shame my Leo assertive confidence, I've suffered and abandoned myself. Now in my early 50s, I celebrate my lioness as regal. I don't apologize for being a lioness. Or an Alpha Woman.

30 years with men have given me children, partnership, love of men, joy, adventure and an education in relationships. But I've struggled to not betray myself in how I've over-adapted to men. In some situations, my brain had to be shut down, my light had to be dimmed, my fire had to be smothered, and shame somehow made it all acceptable. Now I push on another pedal. How will I fully be an Alpha Woman in a relationship with a strong, secure man?

If you spend any time with me, you'll feel my fire, my lioness, my alpha-ness. I've come to appreciate my last name, which means *force*. I don't want to force, but be a force for love. Now that I'm not concerned to know my place (behind a man, I've been told), I'm not concerned to keep my mouth shut.

As a woman in the second half of her life - not just chronologically but spiritually - it feels beautiful to me to give my heart away to the whole world and not to a relationship.

The Alpha Woman is not always well-behaved. She joins the table with the men, she's unintimidated by the roles men play. She challenges them in all the right ways for all the right reasons. Her goal is that the men walk away as better brothers, friends, and partners to the women and men in their lives. She encourages men to be better fathers, leaders and businessmen, better communicators, and more connected to their hearts. She's not afraid to liberate men from what they may not even be aware they want to be liberated from. An Alpha Woman loves men. She's not there to compete but to be the leader in every interaction (not by dominance but by influence) with connection, awareness, and inquiry. And advocacy when that's what's needed. She's not afraid.

An Alpha Woman especially enjoys her sense of humor. She doesn't apologize for it and knows there are great power and intelligence in the play and wit. She laughs at herself.

An Alpha Woman doesn't behave like a man in the business world. She doesn't take counsel from men who tell her she should make decisions like a man. A man can overpower a woman so she abandons her feminine heart that knows when she's procrastinating and when she's letting things flow and not pushing the river.

Both the masculine and feminine in us are needed at the table. It's necessary to have all our parts integrated and available to us.

Some of us have been in hiding. It's time to be the jeweled elephant that cannot hide. We are Ganesha.

In the Hindu tradition, Ganesha is known as the remover obstacles and the god of beginnings. As Ganesha in The Infinity Loop, we remove obstacles and make all things new.

Ganesha
Perfect equilibrium
between force and kindness, power and beauty.
Discriminative capacities which provide the ability to perceive
distinctions between truth and illusion, the real and the unreal.

The Alpha Woman
Reflection

How will you embrace this definition of being an Alpha Woman and step into it, versus how an Alpha Woman has been portrayed as dominating, over-achieving, or not heart-centered?

What images come to your mind that serve you as an Alpha Woman?

By this definition of an Alpha Woman in an Alpha brain state, is there anything you need to grow in to fit this definition: Gentle, kind, wise, strong, sturdy, balanced, powerful, discerning, respectful, influential, curious, humble, confident, empathetic, alert ....?

What do you need to incorporate into your life to help you develop these qualities?

32

Yoga and The Infinity Loop
My conversation with my friend, Jen.

"When you speak, it should be as if Infinity is speaking."
- YOGI BHAJAN

Master Kundalini teacher, Paramatma Siri Sadhana is the source for this yoga wisdom. If you are drawn to this, I recommend you explore how to get access to her teachings.

After years developing an advanced Ashtanga Yoga practice, Jen fell in love with Kundalini Yoga. Clients and friends deep into Yoga philosophy have told me my work is very yogic.

(Jen) After 18 months of practice with master Kundalini teachers, I learned that my power as a woman comes from my navel center. It needs to be really strong. That's where we come into a room and we're radiant beings as women because that's where our power comes from. After 14 years of an intense Ashtanga practice and all my other athletics, I thought I was pretty strong. But I realized I wasn't as strong as I thought! Kundalini does a lot of different breath work called Kriyas. It's the posture, breath, and sound that is so transformational. Breath of Fire is one of them.

One powerful way to do Breath of Fire is to lay on your back with your feet six inches off the floor and your hands parallel to your legs. Your head is six inches off the ground as well while you do Breath of Fire for 3-5 min. After a minute, I had my aha moment that Kundalini isn't just light and easy! After this strength work, you feel this complete calm. After you do each Kriya, you do a complete relaxation for an entire minute and your whole being changes. Your physiology. This calmness, this centeredness, this knowingness - your confidence completely changes. It changes your aura. So, when you go out into the world, your aura mirrors yourself and attracts that energy.

That's when I started to do The Smile Experiment. I came up with that name. That's how we see people, as you talk about, Krista. Every single person that I encountered I would look into their eyes, if they would look at me, I would smile. I got incredible, receptive people. I've done this Smile Experiment for over a month now. Some people it took by surprise. I always naturally did this in my life, but now I more consciously do it. Now I don't look at the phone while I walk. I'm more present and look into everybody's eyes and make the point to make that connection. Some people will look and smile and others won't. I did realize the people who wouldn't give me eye contact also wouldn't smile. The people who gave me eye contact, most of the time, they would smile at me. This was a really good experiment.

In Kundalini, a strong navel center comes from the inside out. It's not like doing 500 sit-ups. I felt like I was too young on my journey when I was first introduced to Kundalini at age 18 to grasp it. I thought it was too woo-woo out there. So later in life when I got into Yoga, I started with the physical practice of Yoga. Now that I'm officially Menopause Momma, I like the calming practice of Kundalini. I need it for my nervous system. It's been life-changing.

Kundalini teachers taught me what it means to be a woman in her power.

Yogi Bhajan started it all with how he honored women. What an incredible practice to honor the feminine. I didn't feel that with Ashtanga. Although Ashtanga has taught me many lessons in each posture within myself (self-realization), Kundalini is extremely empowering to women. The stage that I'm in now, I really resonate with that. Yogi Bhajan started with women's camps where women supported women, versus the competitiveness you see around us.

Kundalini is so much in the heart center. What you teach, Krista, in The Infinity Loop, is what they teach in Yoga – how we show up in our power. Even the love letters to ourselves. All the self-inquiry these master teachers teach for self-mastery to create more awareness. Connection, awareness, and inquiry are at the heart of Kundalini Yoga. The Breath of Fire connects to me what you teach about letting our fire (anger) drop into our bellies (navel center), out of our chests or diffuse in the body, where our awareness gets constricted. You teach to come from that navel center and heart center. This practice is how to experience love in this life: self, others, nature, and beauty. What you teach is about loving well. These master teachers call it self-psychology. Kundalini teaches about the Sound Book, which is a written record of our Sound Current - what we say to ourselves throughout the day; it's the process of becoming aware of our thoughts and words. By writing them down in our Sound Book, we become aware, and intentional, to live in love. The practice of the Sound Book comes from the Tibetan monks. This is their practice to focus on bringing love into the world; the monks carry around their Sound Book and the goal is to stay in love. The teachers say to use mantras every day. Mantras become what we choose to say to ourselves that bring us into our highest selves. The teachers call this "getting mantras into your Sound Current." So many phrases, truths, and principles you teach, Krista, are mantras. Kundalini Yoga is about the Radiant Body – the field of energy that extends nine feet around us - and how we give that out into the world. Being centered, being heart-centered, it's coming from the gut. This is the way we influence. Martha Beck talks about this when she talks about the brain state – Entrainment; whoever has the strongest brain state is able to pull every single person to the level. That's the philosophy of Kundalini. You pull a whole room into that energy so when you walk in, and you're in your power in your feminine power, you're able to change the chemistry of a whole entire room.

Every woman is a leader because they lead others to a higher vibration, greater awareness, greater connection. By my choice to make eye contact and smile, to a great percentage, I pulled that out of other people who may not have done it otherwise. There's always those who don't, but for those that did, they followed my lead.

Our vibration is at a higher level where it's our duty as spiritual beings on this planet to lift others up. By the time you've gotten into your 50s, life has kicked you around somewhat. If you're able to go out into this world with a wonderful attitude and lift others up, that's our duty. That's what we're here to do on this planet.

(Krista) Deepak Chopra and Eckhart Tolle talked about how sad it is right now that people cannot get past the polarities in politics. They communicate with such lack of consciousness, that they only fight. It's the same thing Brené Brown talks about. Deepak and Eckhart said the greatest thing you can do in the world is raise your consciousness. If you have the most awareness, even what happens in you physically, because what we learned from Deepak about Constricted Awareness and Expanded Awareness (you'll read later about it in this book under Awareness), that literally changes the world. If you have a bunch of women who have the spaciousness in their bodies that come from such a deep heart connection, where they don't try to compete, compare, conflict, conspire, or condemn, but literally connect, and then anything they speak out of curiosity, in awareness - we change our world. I see as a principle in Yoga, this curiosity, this inquiry, a kind of playfulness.

(Jen) Definitely, the spiritual thinkers, leaders that I follow today, all have this childlike playfulness. All the mystics - St. Francis of Assisi - all of them, have this playful curiosity. Their joy and childlike lightness makes you want to giggle and laugh. It's beautiful to see especially with the heaviness that's going on around. I don't understand how there's such a great divide when there's so much love. That's why I did the Smile Experiment.

That's what I give back and it amazes me what your world looks like at the end of the day because I get that energy back.

Also, our bodies are temples so it's crucial what we feed them. Energetically, who we surround ourselves with, what we listen to, what we read, what we eat, what we drink. To be at this level, you must care about everything you put in your system. And I enjoy what I enjoy. If I'm going to enjoy a glass of wine, I'm going to take it in as lovingkindness and I also want to enjoy life. That's where the balance comes in. I think we can go too extreme on that area too. I enjoy good food. But I eat and drink healthy, and especially at this phase of life at menopause, I feel the consequences if I don't. I have to be very connected in mind, body, and spirit. Noise levels, too much social media, computers, too much artificial lights. I need that calm environment. What's so beautiful is at this age, I know what I need.

When I think of what makes for a powerful woman, I'd say it's three things: stay present, stay in your power, stay in your truth.

Yoga and The Infinity Loop
<u>Reflection</u>

What would you like to develop more in your life to connect you to your body as a spiritual center?

What is your relationship to your navel center now in terms of from where you speak, your fire in your belly, your truth, holding your own?

What would be in your Sound Book – Book of your Sound Current (what you're putting out into the world by what you think and speak)? What mantras would you like to implement to change your Sound Current and make it more about love?

33

The Infinity Loop of Our
Masculine & Feminine

"I can be a warrior and a flower fairy at the same time."
- KRISTA VORSE

I lay on the table of my healer Ajana. I'm not the person I was a year ago. The old Krista didn't have the integration of all her parts. Now she gives the welcome embrace to her masculine that she had been told to forget about and wasn't necessary. Without the beautiful integration, we'll be used, controlled, left without the balance and skill to be an Alpha Woman who stands in The Infinity Loop and changes the world. Ajana doesn't believe we should be out in the world without our integration. She works with me to love that masculine part that saved my life.

Ajana faces my right side. My left arm has been bothering me. Our bodies, even our injuries, alert us to what we should pay attention to. We've worked with some relationships my left arm (the feminine side) represents. She sees The Infinity Loop between the outside edges of my ribs on both sides. Ajana invites me to completely integrate my masculine and feminine in The Infinity Loop that lays across my body.

Divine feminine is unconditional love, healing, tenderness, gentleness, beauty, wisdom, patience, kindness, acceptance, compassion, flexibility, fertility, and intuition. She's welcoming, nurturing, forgiving, and accessible. Through the feminine we midwife our dreams.

The divine masculine is logical, resilient, fearless, courageous, adventurous, and a protector with very clear boundaries for himself and those he protects. He speaks out for the voiceless. This gentle strength brings peace to conflict. His inner power comes from knowing who he is and that if his actions line up with his intentions, he will accomplish what he sets out to do. Power isn't taken from another nor does he use tricks to gain it. A leader, he's not afraid to speak the truth no matter the consequences. He welcomes uncertainty. He's a provider and brings in material abundance.

When our sacred masculine and feminine are whole and integrated, we're able to create anything. Some call this new sacred feminine "the fierce feminine" that embodies and incorporates these masculine qualities. I love that too.

THE INFINITY LOOP OF OUR MASCULINE & FEMININE REFLECTION

When you read the list of qualities in the divine masculine and divine feminine (or use the word "healthy" for divine), which qualities stood out to you as ones you value the most or seek to integrate?

Write about the contrast between the healthy feminine and masculine and qualities in yourself or in society that are the out of balance or unhealthy.

In what ways have you received messages that have told you not to embrace your healthy masculine or feminine?

When you read that when we're fully integrated into our divine masculine and divine feminine, we can create anything, how does that empower you? We're in The Infinity Loop where anything is possible.

34

Discernment - Part 1

"Denial is a save now, pay later scheme."
- GAVIN DE BECKER

"I will love you, embrace you, and get so
still to hear your sweet messages to me, oh
Discernment, my trustworthy friend."
- KRISTA VORSE

James Finley, a Merton Scholar (as in Thomas Merton), and clinical psychologist is regarded by Caroline Myss as the finest in the spiritual healing of trauma. His words have set me free. "We must be fierce protectors of ours and others' wholeness."

To be able to do that, we must be skilled with discernment. We cannot walk through life open-hearted without discerning who we walk with.

I've always been at war with my discernment; I cherished it as a huge gift and resented it for the disturbance to my positive outlook. An incredibly high positive mental attitude (PMA) has been a grace that has carried me through rough seas where the shore was nowhere in sight. But it has its liabilities; discernment requires we face the sad, difficult, and painful.

A couple of years ago I saw something in a man who is close friends with someone I know. I had heard amazing things about him and was excited to meet him. When we finally met he appeared loving and caring, but I knew something wasn't right. He has a huge halo (The Halo Effect). He's known to contribute positively to lives. Maybe that's true. But each time I was around him it caused dissonance in me that he could be so gifted and equipped. To attribute to him these positive traits that I personally didn't experience, would be me coming under his halo. Although I didn't know him well, I always felt unsafe and uncomfortable around him. I did get to know him 'well enough' to confirm my early hits of intuition. But I was at war with myself to not acknowledge my discernment because he wasn't only those negative things either.

When I registered my discernment, my voice came at me as though Krista stood to my right. She threatened me, "How dare you see that!" Well, that got my attention! I stood up to her, (basically telling her to f*@k off) and immediately this fierceness came over me. Then this rush of life force went through my body and positioned me forward. I had integrated 50 years of lost integrity and energy that I could have used to live my life. I was the one who shut me down all these years. I knew at that moment I would never be the same.

I've shut down my discernment in part because of shame and abuse in my past. I have also used energy to shut down my discernment when I felt I was the only one who saw it. But we are never the only one. Our tribe sees it, or they'll get on board immediately when we share what we experienced. Now, if someone tries to shut down my discernment as though my reality doesn't exist, my new phrase is, "My discernment isn't aligned with yours." I don't apologize for seeing what I do. I don't promote their unconscious behavior by permitting it. When I realize someone isn't part of my tribe, I tell myself one of Leo's father's famous malaprops (where he humorously misuses words) "They're not of my *elk!*"

But it's a skill to see dualistically and see and love non-dualistically - the contemplative mind that holds both: we see where someone talks east and walks west, and hold their dignity and divinity at the same time. We hold both and we need to be honest with those around us with what we experience, even if it doesn't go with the company line.

Gavin de Becker, known by some as the foremost authority on violence prevention, wrote the book, *The Gift of Fear*. He explains the phenomenon of our intuition that often signals to us in our bodies things our minds aren't able to process because the data points come at us too quickly. We know something isn't right. And we better not shut it down if we're to be fierce protectors or ours and others' wholeness.

I knew when I had my epic integration moment with my split parts, it was a game changer. Because of all I've been through in life, I have scary good radar. I see things in people's faces, their voices, their bodies that tell me something isn't in the light or in line with love. I also see things mystically that represent to me what I should run from. De Becker warns us when we are deeply intrigued and curious, we should run. I missed that part in his book when I read it over fifteen years ago and have reread over the years. Now I get it.

You wouldn't always know I have sharp discernment by some of the scoundrels I've been entangled with. But I always knew and I knew in a big way. I find that true with some of my friends. They have fabulous discernment but shame or wounds interfered with their ability to stand in it. It was the shaming voice of the other Krista that shut me down.

Since I took Shaming Krista down, I'm ready to climb the mountain and look out from the precipice as a watchtower for what awaits us. And with my commitment to my Accountability Partners, who I honestly voice what I experience, I'm convinced if I have to trust one person in the world to look out for me, I'd pick me. That me is the part that lives deep in my body. She's a redwood tree, a blackbird, an eagle. The other part is just a temptation that floats outside my body above my head on the right side and talks in an annoyingly, airy high voice. She doesn't want me to be present. She isn't my integrity or my True Self. She's just my coping mechanism I developed to survive my crazy life. Now I've come home to myself, I don't need that group whose membership requires I listen to Shaming Krista who tries to seduce me to look the other way. I think I scared her off with my fierceness so she may not come around again. Our discernment is there to show us who is our tribe in the first place! My experience tells me there's no loss when we lose what costs us our discernment.

The Infinity Loop is what heals our trauma and allows us to trust ourselves again. Because The Infinity Loop is what makes us aware of what's really going on in our bodies, our minds and the world, it wakes us up to *what really is*; it allows us to see the true nature of things and that underneath *what really is*, is goodness. When we can see the goodness in our self, that's what sets us free. What keeps us from the goodness is fear. Fear is what causes us to make up stories that aren't true. "I can't stand up to this person." "I can't say no." "I'm not allowed." When we see *what really is* - the goodness - we can register what isn't good. When we see our True Self, our Wonder Woman, our Alpha Woman, we wake up to that and see that's our real self. Our real self isn't that person who lives in fear and scarcity and needs to please other people to have a sense of self. The Infinity Loop allows us to come home to our self and trust our deepest intuition. It sets us free from illusion; we see differently and put on a different mind. That's discernment.

Now, I quickly respond to my discernment – like an obedience to it - because now I trust it fully. The Great Love Affair gave me the foundation because it showed me I'm worth protecting and that I don't need to split from my truth for anything outside of myself.

I walk through life now honoring my fire, my anger, my boundaries, my wholeness within myself, and my full embodiment that senses and sees. I celebrate my discernment as the gift it is. That celebration is my amends to myself that I will no longer betray myself. This guidance is front and center every single day. My discernment is my homecoming.

The world that awaits me honors my discernment and where it's always my welcome friend.

If we don't use our discernment, love it like the friend it is, we'll invite more trauma into our lives that could have been avoided. Today, I will be a fierce protector of mine and others' wholeness.

DISCERNMENT - PART 1
REFLECTION

Do you have an annoying voice that tries to shut down your discernment? Do you ever leave your body awareness because the discernment coming into your body is making you feel so uncomfortable?

Discernment is a great interrupter of business as usual. In what ways and for what reasons do you ever censor your discernment and make it bad?

Do you ever feel bad about yourself for discerning something that others aren't and feel you're not a team player or loving enough?

If you hold the both/and - contemplative mind - that holds your disturbances and love at the same time, how will that help you embrace what you're discerning?

35

Discernment - Part 2

*"Intuition is always right in at least two important
ways; it is always in response to something, it
always has your best interest at heart."*
- Gavin de Becker

I have clear discernment that cuts through everything. I see and know that I know; my experience and expertise all lineup. It'll come at a mystical awareness as well. But then it's as though I forget it when I come under the spell of the person's normal behavior. It's not that others don't have enjoyable qualities, it's that of the things that are non-negotiable to me, I cannot hang with what's intolerable to my integrity. My discernment is screaming.

Just like we need to hold fast to our moments that transcend our fear and powerlessness, and liberate us from our suffering, we must hold fast to our discernment. There's an awareness that comes from our instincts that's given to us as a gift. We must not squander the gift.

Jen's teaching in the *Women Who Run with the Wolves* chapters about how we take the key and unlock the door of what's unconscious in us, or what is hidden but needs to be explored, helps us listen to our intuition. It may come as a body reaction, an emotional reaction, something you "hear," something that you hear yourself saying, a vision or dream, or a familiar pattern you see. You may see things in people's eyes, face, body parts, or discern something is off with their emotional reactions or speech patterns. It can be as though you hear a snap and you say to yourself, "That's not true." You see something in someone and because you've been around someone else with the same pathology, you recognize it; they all use the same playbook.

I once consulted with a company helping them build their culture and their sales team. It was working beautifully. They then brought some new young buck in with a big ego and a small man's complex. When he walked in, before he opened his mouth, I saw him holding a fire hose, extinguishing the fire that was burning in the hearts, bellies, and culture, and all the work that had been laid out. We built a culture of love and inspiration. He was going to turn it into the military. I tried to get the CEO's attention but he wouldn't listen. He was getting off "mentoring" him. Plus, he liked the military attitude, even though the fruit of this young man's impact wasn't helping the company nor their bottom line. I knew from Gavin de Becker's work on violence prevention, that we need to be careful how we treat people and not trigger their shame. No one would listen. When I saw the way he and his cohorts treated people, fired people, bullied people, I said, "Someday someone is going to come into this company and shoot someone." I parted ways with the company after that. The young man was eventually fired for the reasons I had pointed out to the CEO. But it was too late. The culture had already been created and a disaster was waiting to happen. Three and a half years later someone came in and shot and killed the CEO.

Why I would ever doubt my discernment after that is beyond me. We must do the work on ourselves to let die all the parts of us that kill off our discernment. All the pleasing, all the leaving our bodies and hearts when they hurt to get our attention. All the ways we allow another to make us a caged bird. When I told a relative about the struggle I was having with the young man destroying the work, she shamed me and told me it was just my ego. After that, I regrettably lost it with the young man in "not my finest moment." It wasn't my healthy ego (sense of self) that stood in my discernment that was my problem - as my relative tried to say; it was my unskillful, ego-driven delivery when I was triggered with this man, that was the problem. I will do anything and everything since that event nine years ago to never lose my cool again like that. One can use one's ego strength to give pushback and give a damn how people are treated, or if someone is a pathological liar or dangerous. Our being afraid that someone will think we have a big ego when we stand up to abuse of power, will not serve anyone. We need to be okay being judged. We just don't confront people without emotional sobriety or out of an ego position that's separate, superior, or important. But we don't let others shut down our discernment. Ultimately, we do it to ourselves when we split from our deepest truth.

I have not acted on my discernment when the situation is tied in with a wound. I'm clearer when it comes to my work because my personal issues aren't usually triggered. However, in my personal life, I've ignored my discernment because my compulsions were more seductive than my most trusted friend, Discernment.

A few years ago I saw the website of the man who I left Leo for. When I looked through his site, I got the strong hit, "Charlatan." I actually said that word to myself. I felt a strong aversion and was turned off. After a few months, this man's name came up again and it was suggested I meet him because it appeared we had a lot to talk about as we were both coaches. Being too open at the time, I went ahead and met. My not holding fast to the bad sense I got regarding this man, along with my curiosity, got the best of me. I even liked the emojis he sent back to me when we confirmed our meeting. Leo didn't want to go with me. That first meeting was right out of a text book on pathological encounters; I was under his spell. All my issues were activated. Four-and-a-half months later I witnessed him doing the exact same seduction/speech to someone else. I was too afraid to confront him. Someone else's praise of this man threw me off my intuition as well. Through the next four visits with him, I had both strong hits of discernment that something wasn't right that contrasted with warm and fuzzy, familiar feelings. I had an almost irresistible pull toward sexual bonding. He puts out that energy widely I quickly realized. Since I've only felt sexual attraction to a handful in my life, I thought it meant something; it did, but not in a healthy way. Between the time I met this man and the 5th visit, (three-week span) my petite body had lost seven pounds. I was in a total spin. We met those five times, to explore working together and him coaching me. I wanted to bond with this man just to end the total body freak-out I was going through. I thought what was happening in my body was moving me toward uniting with this man. Clearly, I was so confused. The sexual pull that felt like life was as counterfeit as everything else was. The 5th meeting, I told him I felt I wasn't supposed to be there. I felt like I couldn't talk. I couldn't get words out because I wasn't supposed to talk. I told him I wasn't going to have any further contact with him and thought I should leave it at that. Something was very, very wrong. He, being a coach, told me I should speak. He didn't support my guidance system that was giving me a 'No.' That went against what I know a coach should do. I ignored that. He told me later he knew exactly what I was going to say – that I had feelings for him. Once I did tell him, I felt even more creepy. I told him it didn't make sense and couldn't be right. Something else was tripping me up. I can't remember the exact words but it was something to the effect that I should take the thought that we can't be together off the table. Of course, for the next six months (the length of the relationship) I would tell the story without any of the discernment parts; it was a match made in heaven and I was so responsive to being led. How cute and magical it was all going to be. My life's work was going to be connected with this man.

After that 5th meeting I told Leo that I had to pursue this and figure out what it all meant. It was an intense pull that felt like destiny. This man told me later that he saw what I did for Leo and wanted it for himself. I abandoned a man I love to be used by a man who never loved me.

His rage, lust, control, greed, and megalomania came up immediately in the relationship. I saw it all but shame shut it down, and deep trauma in the face of such pathology, ensued. I told Leo about the shaming and controlling way this man spoke to me during a "coaching session" and how I thought it was good for me. He was speechless. I thought I deserved the way he treated me. Only someone doing something so wrong (me) would be treated so horribly by an esteemed coach. I owned his disowned shame for his behavior even though it was against everything I believe to be right. It hit every lie that I was bad and needed fixing. The sexual relationship was shameful, debasing, abusive, using, and horrifying. I feel the need to make amends to all women for allowing myself to be treated that way. This book is part of my amends. Our relationship was on the brink of ending about every three days. I was paying a very high price for ignoring my discernment.

But mercy had the last word. I went through a miraculous recovery and healed my life-long wounds and faced my shadow that caused me to ignore my discernment. I knew even when I was in it, this was going to be the abuse to end all abuse; I was going to figure this out, wrestle with the angel and come out renamed. I was going to come out more whole and I was going to get healed.

I needed to tell this story because thousands of women will read this and feel where they too have ignored their guidance system. Being so damn vague to protect myself and my pride, to protect someone else who shouldn't be protected, or to avoid being criticized by those who don't agree, doesn't serve truth.

There's a time and place to question ourselves. One is when we've selected only certain data to tell ourselves a story about the situation. And we're calling it 'intuition' when it's not necessarily so. I'm not talking about that kind of certitude that isn't receptive to disconfirming data. I'm talking about true discernment that sees the inconsistencies or "what comes out of the heart the mouth speaks," and you're not okay with what's in their heart, and they're not interested in having a change of heart. It's when we sense one has guile and we just don't trust them. Proceed with caution if you have to proceed. We must not drop those moments just because it's hard for our brains to reconcile the red flags with their like-ability in other areas. Hold fast to the truth. We've earned our discernment from the hard lessons we've had to endure. We need to be kind to ourselves and have concern for those that need our protection, and not for those that may be the ones who use, abuse, and deceive for their own gain.

Women have a lifetime of being told, coached, berated into not paying attention to discernment. We as women have ignored this gift for so long, we no longer recognize it. This is a key part of Dr. Estés work in *Women Who Run with the Wolves*. We must hold onto our 'women's intuition,' listen and trust it. We women feel shame because we know something is wrong and we let it happen anyway. But we need to turn that shame into power and use it to stoke the fire in our bellies. The enlightenment that happens when we listen and do something about it is pretty cool. Discernment is a life-long skill that helps keep us on the right path with the right travel buddies by our side.

DISCERNMENT - PART 2
REFLECTION

Recall a time when you forgot your discernment about someone because you came under their spell of like-ability. How did that end up hurting you, your ability to be in your integrity, or your ability to stand in your truth?

In what ways will you use your Accountability Partners (A.P.s) to process your discernment, to keep you from forgetting it once you get "all warm and fuzzy" for someone again?

How does discernment show up for you? Messages in your head? Body? Emotions?

What do I need to see/discern/wake up to in my world?

36

Discernment - Part 3

"You have the gift of a brilliant internal guardian
that stands ready to warn you of hazards and
guide you through risky situations."
- GAVIN DE BECKER

Waking up is a fascinating process; from one day to the next we see things differently. One day everything is fun and light; the next day we see how we've enabled someone and gotten in the way of their growth. I'm not sure how that ties into discernment, (I guess it's all discernment), but the thought is about how we continually gain insight as we grow.

We're enormously complex human beings. I cringe at any counsel that tries to fit our human experience into a little box. "You did that because...". We do things for a myriad of reasons.

I wrote a few pages ago about how I've shut down my discernment my entire life because it interfered with thinking the best of people. But this morning I realized Krista's shaming voice didn't originate from her; I just repeated what I've heard my entire life. The truth is: I wasn't allowed to have my discernment and I was shamed for it. I think my lifelong struggle has been that I'm too sensitive (I'm a damn empath!), and I'm not allowed to have my discernment and my boundaries. That all falls under discernment.

It comes in the form of being bullied or being the recipient of elder's advice that has outlived the evolution of growing consciousness (i.e. - staying in relationships that are insane, keeping in contact with parents who want to crush you, forgiveness means protecting an abuser and letting them deceive others). If you've been shamed, blamed, and told all that's wrong with you and how bad you are on a continuous basis, it's a monumental feat to stand in your discernment and be able to say, "No, it's not me, it's you."

My parents divorced when I was eight. I immediately got a step-father figure in my life. He was 14 years younger than my mother and 14 years older than me. In the 3rd grade, I remember standing in my school cafeteria reading a card he wrote to me. On the envelope, he called me a wild woman. (He didn't mean it in the way Dr. Estés writes of a wild woman who runs with the wolves.) I've had this mane for a long time. I knew based on all that had gone on and all that I sensed, that once I opened the card I was going to feel sick in the pit of my stomach. When I read it, everything went into slow motion. I was as solid in knowing the truth as the linoleum I stood on. I said to myself, "My childhood is over."

My life became learning how to leave my body, how to pretend, how to keep secrets. When I turned 14 the many elaborate love letters from him would come. On my pillow, on the lid of the toilet. He told me he fantasized about making love to me and wanted to leave my mother for me. It was a trauma that set a course for my life.

I tried to tell myself he didn't mean it the way he said it. I had the courage one day to show it to my friends who were completely freaked out. The dozens of other letters he wrote, my mother found and took. She said she read them and would take care of it. I've been blamed throughout the years for it all; I was the seductress all the years he was in my life. She said I was the problem and she was going to send me off to a boarding school but wouldn't allow me to move back to California to live with my father. That one letter I showed to my friends was used by my father to get custody. I had to escape and leave everything I owned behind because my mother said she was going to have the police at the airports. She always thought she owned me. For the next 35 years, I would escape again and again from situations and leave everything behind in my life.

I didn't get my mother and step-father out of my life. I went back. I was told by a few of my elders, "She's your mother." When I turned eighteen, I joined a cult. The leader either hit me or beat me regularly in her insane rages for one of the two years I was with her. After that first year, I escaped this woman. She promised me she would stop, and so after only one day, I returned to my abuser. I always went back to my abusers. The physical violence did stop, but the spiritual, emotional, intellectual, and psychological abuse only intensified that second year I was in the cult. I went back to things throughout my life and pretended to reconcile what was irreconcilable. All in the name of love, forgiveness, healing, family, spirituality, God. I believed the best of people with no connection to discernment or reality. My wounds, shame, and estrangement from myself caused my standards to be frightfully low. I went back again to my mother and step-father after the cult when I wanted a family so badly. I spent thousands on therapists and no one told me I should get them out of my life. Although friends were shocked throughout the years I had them in my life. I told people I was fine now. I let them have access to my children. I never thought my stepfather would touch my children and I was told by them they have never had anything like that happen to them. We talked a lot about sexual abuse in our home. Both my kids know how to protect themselves in a lot of ways. But they alienated my children from me. Having my mother and my step-father in my life in some ways cost me everything. I had to abandon myself and deaden my discernment to be around my mother and stepfather. I wanted a family and a mother who loved me. I didn't know how to be my own mother. They came against me in a custody battle because I waited 20 years to listen to my discernment and get them out of my life. When I set that boundary, they would do all they could in the name of love and concern to destroy me.

I let them back in one last time. I got sucked in. That one cost me dearly. After a 35 + year relationship, my mother and step-father parted ways. His lies and lust continue. I hold it all with reverence and love like Love holds it.

My story is a taste of all the ways and reasons we ignore our discernment. May the lessons in this book help you reconnect with your guidance system if there's been any damage along the way.

To show up for our lives in the most courageous way is about that monumental feat to stand in our discernment and be able to say, "No, it's not me, it's you." It's the knowing that comes from the silence deep within us. It's willing to stand in it, no matter the cost. It's laying down our lives for the truth. It's living so open and free that it doesn't cling to the outcome or the cost (hence, it's laying down our lives as we know it and control it). It wants truth. And we do it from a place of peace. We may feel anger (what needs to be honored or protected). We let that anger drop deep into our bellies, like a cannonball where it will serve us. We don't need it to get diffuse where we can't think clearly. From there we take action. We know our True Selves abundantly supply us with all the presence we need to take our stand. It contains the presence of the whole world.

You may have had your discernment shut down by others and have internalized those voices as your own. Have Great Compassion for yourself, for others who have had that experience and even for those who have shut it down. We all do what we do until we don't.

Maybe this is how to find what our life-long struggles/themes have been and what can shift for us in a transformational way. The interior journey is the most exciting life there is. We face our wounds and traumas and the untruths that have held us back from letting Life express itself through us. Because the truth really does set us free. No matter what messages we've received in life, we have compassion for ourselves and know we're precious in our humanity. We give the love and be the love we are and walk in our discernment, our sensitivities, and boundaries.

Ralph Waldo Emerson wrote, "All the mistakes I make arise from forsaking my own station and trying to see the object from another's point of view." It's a necessary skill to suspend our point of view to hear another, but we lose our way when we abandon ourselves. Today, I honor my sensitivities, my discernment, and the necessary loving boundaries that protect the precious gift of life.

Discernment - Part 3
Reflection

What messages do you recall receiving that shut down your discernment?

In what ways have those messages been replayed with other characters in your life?

Write about the situation where you had discernment, but then "forgot it" when you came under the spell of someone's charm or good qualities? What caused you to forget?

When you tell yourself something that shuts you down, do you recognize that the message didn't originate from you and to question it? What would that process look like for you?

What are your life-long struggles/themes that can shift in a transformational way when you hold fast to your discernment?

37

Living Out Loud

*"You cannot hold on to the clenched fear and anger
of who you think you are and at the same time open
your arms wide to experience all that you are."*
- JAMES FINLEY

Someone who has known me intimately for years commented to me, "I feel closer to you in some way reading these chapters on Discernment." How I share my journey, the paradoxes and contradictions which flow into the transformation process are powerful for him. He encouraged me by saying, "I see my journey reflected in yours." I'll keep doing this then, living out loud, naked and unashamed.

The late Franciscan Priest, Brennan Manning, said we should be professional lovers - that good at loving people. One way I love people is by showing my warts, my patched-up places, my struggles and the way I got through, so others feel more safe and okay in this world. So often we feel shame. "This is who I am, warts and all. I stand before you naked and unashamed." But I can't do that safely if I'm afraid of your reaction. I do that better from my True Self that's so abundant, your rejection of me won't affect me. I'm probably going to agree with whatever flaw you see. After my awareness of the consequences of my flaw and express sorrow over hurt it caused, my response will be, "Isn't it wonderful that we're endlessly loved and lovable in all our flaws?!"

Thomas Merton, the great contemplative of the 20th century, was transparent and shared his journey intimately with his readers. Merton revealed his agonies and ecstasies, and his contradictions that he would go out with. He taught the contemplative way by living out loud.

As I was beginning this journey of writing, I had an experience of being a jeweled elephant in a Trance Dance. (You can Google Trance Dance.) Someone who was with me in the experience said, "A jeweled elephant can't hide." My days of hiding are over. I am Ganesha. The masculine, the feminine, the balance. The jeweled elephant is the Alpha Woman.

People who share that vulnerably, without the PR version, are who I trust. They're also who I find most interesting. Today, let us taste the freedom of living out loud, naked and unashamed. May it be an offering to our fellow travelers. They too will see that they're loved and lovable in all their imperfections.

LIVING OUT LOUD
REFLECTION

What is your greatest fear that may be holding you back from living out loud?

Is there anything in your current life or past that keeps you from being more transparent?

In what ways do you over-compensate for your shame?

What would it look like to be a jeweled elephant in your life?

38

I'm Not a Mistake

"To believe we need someone to fix us is one of the
most dangerous beliefs there is. Mentoring isn't
shaming, bullying or criticizing. Mentoring is
empowering, developing and loving.
Mentoring is love."
- Krista Vorse

This is me, living out loud, showing you some of my warts and all.
I wrote the following song, *I'm Not a Mistake*, right after I got with
Leo in 2001. We met almost 20 years prior. The moment I saw
Leo walk across the street in Spring of '82, I said to myself, "He's
just like me." That proved to be true in dozens of delightful ways.
The love I felt from him made me believe to a great degree I wasn't
a mistake; the mirroring I received from him healed me in many
ways. But I wasn't all the way healed. I still did believe I was a mistake and I needed to be shown how to behave, how to think, how
to feel. I needed to be tamed. There was still toxic shame in there.

I let the man who I left Leo for tell me that I "needed to be
refined." He criticized me relentlessly. I needed just the opposite; I needed to be more fully me. I needed to dance under
the waterwheel. The Great Love Affair hadn't happened yet,
even though I had experienced God's love for me. If it had, this
book would have been very different. Much of what's in this
book I already knew, but I couldn't stand in it. Everything I
worked so damn hard to heal from wasn't healed. All my shit
was still there. The estrangement from myself was enormous. I
pretended it wasn't so.

My great fall was because of believing I was a mistake. I already had Great Compassion by my side and I still fell.

All the reasons I was pulled in, all the patterns from when I got in a cult 32 ½ years prior, were still there. Once we get pulled in, the exposure to an abuser's pathology does a number on our brains and we lose our way.

My fall also happened because I took the ego's route in my attempt to heal my wound by thinking I could prove I wasn't a mistake. I took matters into my own unconscious hands by creating a re-do; this time I was going to do everything right at my wise age to keep this man from abusing me. Not only was I going to not make mistakes, I was going to show I wasn't a mistake. By being so loving and longsuffering, I would be the one to heal his heart and soul. These are aspects of my wound that mystically merged with what ultimately became my liberation. My wound drove me to meet my soul and follow her compass to the land flowing with milk and honey. Mercy took what was my compulsion (a re-do) and bounced me into a wholeness and strength that will never seek a re-do again.

We keep doing the work, falling down and getting back up. I will be humbled by this last one for the rest of my days. My desire is to give my life away to others in a way that will serve them that they may learn from my mistakes. And that none of us are mistakes. I have deep and reverent compassion for myself and others for our brokenness. We're beautiful in our brokenness. That's how Love sees us. And that is enough. That is enough.

The transformational process from this great fall also turned me into the strongest person I know. I discovered I'm Wonder Woman. I just wasn't conscious of it.

Now let's go change the world.

I'm Not a Mistake
- Krista Vorse

Too many years, so many tears to get to this place
The long and jagged road I've traveled on, too long
The sharp tongues that crept out
and gashed my heart open
Oh brother, where art thou?
It was my brothers all along
Those to hurt me but you to heal me
I needed to be shown how to behave
How to think, feel and they said
But don't feel so deeply
Don't be so wild, so passionate, so free
You need to be more like me
Before you, I believed the day I was
made was not His best day
That He made a mistake
And I needed everyone to set it right
I was trying to learn the rules of the game
I thought I would be safe in their huddle of love
I'm not a mistake
The reflection I see
Being with you
Makes me believe
He didn't make a mistake by makin' me
So now I'm free
I'm wild, I feel, I think
I behave, not like them
But like me
I've got the joy and the peace
I'm not a mistake
But they made the mistake
By trying to tame me

I'm Not a Mistake
REFLECTION

What part of *I'm Not a Mistake* could you relate to? Is there anything you could be ignoring about shame like I was?

What work needs to be done to accept how beautiful you are? Is there anything you need to forgive? Any shame, self-hatred, lack of boundaries, honoring ourselves, that needs your attention?

What pattern do you need to focus on to change?

Who do you know could use some mirroring that they're not a mistake?

I feel the sweetness and safety of being humbled by my great fall. How do you view being humbled?

39

The Spell-Casters

"Owning your own story is the *bravest*
thing you will ever do."
- BRENÉ BROWN

"A woman who runs with the wolves will question
what she's doing at the circus, to begin with."
- KRISTA VORSE

As I was editing this book my friend Kiz challenged me to stop protecting people and tell my story. She sent me that Brené Brown quote. Kiz told me we need my stories to anchor us in the principles and to see ourselves in my story. As I began to type more of my story I connected with a life force that I tend to dampen in myself. The more vulnerable I was, not worrying about the consequences of telling the truth, the more lightness and energy I felt. It just felt right. Then I experienced Numinous Love loving me with utter acceptance and delight as I shared my story. I feel no shame because I experience my weaknesses through the eyes of that Infinite Love. My prayer is that you too will sense it's all held in love as you tell your story. Now, Spell-Casters...

In *Life's Golden Ticket*, author Brendon Burchard teaches us about awareness in the chapter where the protagonist witnesses a hypnotist at work on the crowd. The secret technique is revealed.

The hypnotist is able to hypnotize the crowd by stripping the volunteers of their self-awareness; they're prevented from being able to answer the question, "Who am I right now?"

This is done by taking away the three reference points every person needs to be self-aware. The stripping away of our much-needed defenses is done when we:

* Stop paying attention to our thoughts and feelings
* Stop paying attention to feedback from the outside world
* Have someone else tell us who we are (no ability to see "Who am I right now?")

We need to know who we are and how we want to show up in the world.

Those on the outside give us feedback on what they see happening in us. The feedback may also be about our behavior. That's one way we grow in our emotional intelligence and our ability to love others. It raises our self-awareness.

The Spell-Casters in society are those who do their fancy hypnotist mumbo-jumbo, seduce us to put our brains in hock, and violate our sovereignty over ourselves and what's true for us. Any system in society that wants to manipulate us for its own gain does this.

It's really damn scary when it comes under the guise of guidance or development and someone creeps in through our shame and vulnerability and tells us our reality. Sadly, the "helping community" is contaminated with those whose egos are stroked by getting others to accept their reality and beliefs, or by transferring their own shame. Some of these "helpers" are in those positions for the thrill of controlling and manipulating others. I see highly intelligent and well-educated people accept The Spell-Caster's coaching because the teacher possesses a spiritual power that hypnotizes them; charming people charm. It's eerie and something I'd like to figure out how to break over people. I found out the hard way there's a reason Jesus asked the man who was lame if he wanted to be healed; not everyone wants to be woken up from the spell. I've been the victim and the witness to people with enormous spiritual power that come as an Angel of Light; they deceive others, and it's quite devilish. There was just enough truth to get those with the open hearts to not see the techniques used. The Spell-Caster creates The Halo Effect, which is the tendency to like everything about a person, including things we haven't observed; they're just so darn likable, it's as if it creates a halo over their whole being and we give them way too much benefit of the doubt. Sometimes the volunteers fall in love with the hypnotist and don't see the dark deeds done behind the curtain by the showman or show-woman. That's part of the seduction too - how they sneak into the most intimate place in us. In one situation, many years ago, it was a show-woman who cast a two-year spell over me to use and abuse me. Since then I've seen Spell-Casters in every arena. They roam among us in companies, churches, and communities.

The show-woman was a charismatic and deranged cult leader who was esteemed in the Charismatic Evangelical church I belonged to. Some dynamics in my childhood made me the perfect candidate for a cult. Besides those dynamics, as a young woman of 18 who wasn't listening to herself, I didn't believe my own self was enough, my own truth was enough, and so I needed someone to fix me. I sabotaged opportunities and ran from living my most courageous life to cater to a pathological woman who would point out everything that was wrong with me according to her insane need to be served. All the abusers in my life up to that point were shameless in what they did. I took on the unowned shame and carried it within myself. My hope was this "spiritual teacher" would be the one to teach me how to have boundaries because I couldn't understand how I kept disconnecting from my power (dissociating) to protect myself when someone violated who I was. As a young mystic who saw and knew things but didn't know how to navigate those waters - I was going to be mentored. My life was going to be useful in serving someone who had gifts that would serve the world and God. I was trying to heal from all the abuse up to that point. I was a sitting duck.

For 30 years I worked on myself to recover from the devastation of those two years. But I continued to have pathological people in my life. Arsenic was in my cereal, as I say. Leo was a gift as we grew through our brokenness. We caused each other pain but our hearts broke for one another when we did. When I met the last Spell-Caster, I thought I was more healed than I was.

When I fell under the spell of my Necessary Nemesis, it had similar themes: I didn't know how to live my most courageous life; toxic shame lived in me and I thought I needed to be fixed. Coaching isn't about fixing. Coaching is about supporting, giving skills, loving, guidance, helping someone find their own well within them and their own North Star. The way we help someone see their shadow isn't by dismantling them and taking away their sovereignty over their truth. We neither control nor bully. It's not about rage, gas-lighting, lying, projecting, manipulating, cruelty, using and abusing. A coach doesn't do things to intentionally trigger an emotional reaction to feed off. That's pathology. I knew all of that but I couldn't break the trauma bond.

Besides all the reasons one gets sucked in by an abuser/Spell-Caster, my ego of believing I was this loving, giving, and supernaturally gifted coach who could reach the unreachable was activated. And nearly every time I felt able to break off this addictive relationship, he'd beg me to not give up on him in his quest to find spiritual freedom. In his twisted and monstrous rage, he shamed me that I would be embarrassing him and accused me of lying - and in turn forcing him to lie - when I wanted to leave even for a few days. Ironically, a liar for him I did become. You would never know from reading this how much power I had prior to meeting this man. I was stripped of it quickly. He found both my shame and my deepest yearning to be purified, and used "coaching me" to have cultic control over me. It was the most head-spinning experience I've yet to endure. A supernatural dark force to say the least. Believing I did love that man more than anyone has ever loved him, I would have done anything to help him. Therein lies the problem.

Addicted to the moments he was nice to me, they became over-the-top highpoints in my brain and body. Only one whose been in a relationship with an abuser knows that desperate addiction. My birthday celebration with this man and a group of friends associated with him felt like the happiest day of my life. Because he was kind to me I thought maybe everything was going to be different and I wasn't a total screw-up for being in this relationship. Now accustomed to eating pig food, I was grateful for any scrap of what I thought would nourish my soul. In two days, his usual treatment of me resumed. Within the month the relationship ended and that day of liberation was the happiest day of my life. I think of what the therapist said to Nicole Kidman's character who was in an abusive marriage in *Big, Little Lies*: she told her that her husband wasn't well but neither was she. I had become unwell.

My much-needed fire was smothered. The times when I did feel that fire, it was more powerful than the PTSD that would make me collapse and crawl back into his arms to feel safe. I needed to fan the flame of my fire and let it move me out of the dangerous situation. That holy fire is more powerful than the dark force of shame, spells, and abuse.

My beautiful qualities of empathy, high-relationship invest-ment, adaptability, wanting to look at my own contribution, wanting to grow, as well as my shadow aspects, went into the pot that made this diabolical stew. All those things were in me. This Necessary Nemesis served me well by triggering them so I could heal.

Most Spell-Casters just deceive through their personas so people stop paying attention to what's right in front of them. Their words cast a spell. They have like-ability, charm, and false light.

Although they hide who they really are and act normal, I believe if we're awake and learn how they work, we'll sense a counterfeit; we'll sense the dark force and power that renders people powerless if they don't know how to resist. We are women who run with the wolves.

But we have to want to be awake. And that will cost us.

If we pay attention to our thoughts and feelings and witness them without censoring them, if we allow others to speak and inquire into our lives in a respectful, non-manipulative way that creates learning, and if we know who we are in our deepest truth that cannot be twisted by shame or abuse, we will be able to resist the hypnotists among us.

In our deepest truth lives our True Self that's abundant. From our awareness to our internal abundance, we stand alone from the crowd. We know we have all we need inside of us. We don't have to buy what The Spell-Casters are selling to be okay. We don't have to participate in the circus.

That's being conscious.

THE SPELL-CASTERS
REFLECTION

Recall a Spell-Caster you've had interactions with. In what ways were they able to take away your awareness?

What was the cost to your integrity, your sovereignty over yourself, or your guidance system?

In what ways are you aware how ungrounded you felt in the head-spinning trance?

If we pay attention to our thoughts and feelings and witness them without censoring them, if we allow others to speak and inquire into our lives in a respectful, non-manipulative way that creates learning, and if we know who we are in our deepest truth that cannot be twisted by shame or abuse, we will be able to resist the hypnotists among us.
What parts of the above paragraph do you feel you could use support?

40

Holding on in the Strongest Winds

"Fear not is not dependent on our ability
to navigate the situation."
- JAMES FINLEY

We're often unaware we're directed by our traumas. It's not just "the wounded one" whom trauma is an issue for; we could all use some encouragement around it. The more we let go - instead of trying to control what cannot be controlled - the better everything is. We lead better when we realize we can't hold on.

Trauma will kick your ass. It needs care and caution, wisdom and patience. It makes for damn stimulating conversations – how we really heal. I've known trauma as a frequent shipmate.

You're in the boat. The storm comes suddenly and so violently that holding on isn't possible. You lose your grip and get tossed out. Surely, you'll keep sinking and drown. You do keep sinking as you accept the inevitable. You're no match for these waters.

You finally hit the ocean floor. You've never seen this view before – not where you get to touch it. You think you must have died but you realize you're breathing under water. And you have changed form. The old form wouldn't allow you to survive. And so, you've become a mermaid - blue and green to match the décor of your new furnishings.

Healing of trauma takes what lies deep below the surface, the dark current that drew us down, to provide the new form to trans-figure into something beautiful and able to survive and thrive. We need to be able to breathe under water. But that comes after we let go and die to what won't survive this new landscape.

Trauma brings up what needs to be transformed in us, in our deepest yearning for freedom.

Falling to the bottom of the ocean is the ultimate letting go. It's not that we give up – it wasn't an option to do anything other. We were sunk. Resisting would have made us waste our breath, gasping instead of calmly watching the deep, dark mystery unfold all around us as we fall deeper and deeper.

Healing of trauma involves death. We break our connection to the contracts we made subconsciously, the rules we created that we thought would help us survive. Healing involves a dissolution of the form that carried it in the body and mind. It's a mythical merging with an underworld that turns drowning people into mermaids.

I want to be more healed. I want to be tossed out of the boat, beyond my own strength to hold on, thrust into the deepest of seas, where only mystery holds me and make me into something that's beautiful and transformed; the bumps on the way down rearrange me in preparation for a death and resurrection of a spectacular display. I want to swim with the dolphins and wear seashells in my hair. I want to get to know my brothers and sisters who live in these waters.

So again, I'm saying yes. I'm saying yes to all the commotion that brought me to the bottom of the ocean. Sometimes we're wearing the proper life preserver and we still drown. Sometimes we just aren't thinking we'll need it. But it doesn't matter. Because if we don't live in a world where grace is, where we're made into mermaids, I would rather just drown in the bottom of the sea and call it a day.

But we do live in that world. Even in the falling, we're being prepared for our new forms. We don't see it coming – that we're going to be mermaids - but that's why we need other mermaids to tell us it's going to be okay. Your life will never be the same, but anyone who wants life to stay the same or believes it's anything we're able to control isn't interesting enough to become a mermaid. Mystery belongs to those willing to be at sea to begin with.

So, don't lose heart when you realize you can't hold on. Something else more interesting is about to happen. Accept it and enjoy the view on the way down.

We're all waiting for when you come up again in your transformed self. Darryl Hannah was looking pretty good in *Splash*.

Holding on in the Strongest Winds
Reflection

What sentence stood out to you the most as true for you and why?

What stood out as something you never thought of before?

What event in your life was something you couldn't hold on in the strongest of winds?

Looking back, how did you fair? Have you experienced grace stepping in to transform you in this mythical merging with the underworld?

41

The Necessary Nemesis

"A wound is a sacred force, but only through
mystical eyes. Leave it to the ego and the ego will
use it for personal gain. So, I emphasize, turn your
wound over to your soul and it gets elevated to
where it belongs – which is to shatter it open."
- CAROLINE MYSS

Antiope: Hippolyta, I love her as you do. But
this is the only way to truly protect her.
Hippolyta: You will train her harder than any Amazon
before her, until she's better than even you.
WONDER WOMAN

I'm somewhat annoyed with the quote, "Whatever doesn't kill you makes you stronger." I don't think it's accurate. Absolutes aren't absolutely true in every case. I think it should be edited to, "Whatever doesn't kill you *can* make you stronger, or give you a shitload of PTSD." Along with PTSD that I accumulated after many experiences that almost took me out, I was often left with a gaping wound that predators scoped out and accessed in order to rape and pillage the tender terrain of my soul. In retrospect maybe I was stronger, but I was limping, wounded, left with a compromised immune system and fragile. But that state isn't the end of my story, and doesn't have to be.

While typing this I realize I am stronger in many ways after these storms. Maybe the word is resilient. I see it like going through natural child-birth. Pain is relative to that. I was able to surrender while going through labor with my first child who was a couple pounds bigger than made sense to my tiny body. I was able to relax in the midst of it, thanks to my beautiful and compassionate labor coach. Strong, skillful, empathetic support is a key ingredient to getting through it without losing it, whether labor or life. And after conquering natural childbirth twice and not dying, I think pain seems pretty minor to me now. And I gained the life-long skill of doing Bradley birth breathing through almost anything.

Things that freak other people out are just no big deal to me because it's happened in my life before. But the trauma that many of those events left behind feels anything but stronger to me. PTSD, shame, abuse, lack of self-love, coping skills that don't serve us, psychological struggles, vulnerabilities to people who don't have love as their highest aim in life, and defenses, just don't feel like "stronger" to me.

But then something happens. The Necessary Nemesis shows up and everything changes. **NN** shows up after we've worked our asses off to do all we can to transform our pain and not transmit it to others. **NN** shows when we've tasted our power and know how to walk in it in a regal way. **NN** appears when we're a rugged warrior, humbled many times over from the repeated attempts on our lives.

But we're not quite there. We're still not healed. Our wound is still there down deep, that only the craftiest find and poke with a sharp stick. The pain is so great, even Bradley breathing won't help us.

I heard Martha Beck talking recently about her book and the nemesis that arrives to come against the heroine, Diana. It's a necessary confrontation for the heroine to wake up to her power, creativity, and self-love. It tries to kill her but doesn't. That got me writing this. I owe a lot to Martha.

The Necessary Nemesis came and woke me up. It showed me my wound, my shadow, things I was ignoring in my life and heart.

I had been kicked down one too many times. I didn't have it in me to realize what needed to happen to create a life that required me to be both courageous, and aligned with all the ways I've been made and remade in these traumatic storms.

My life was preparing me for the life that wanted to be lived, but I needed to be poked with a sharp stick to wake up to it.

Our Necessary Nemesis is the storm that threatens to leave us maimed. We need strong, skillful, empathetic support. We need Infinity to whisper in our ear and to find the deeper well that lives inside us. We need to rise up and say, "I was made for this!" In that realm, myth, mystery and all that may appear like madness, transforms us; our wounds heal. Like the lame man who was healed when Jesus told him, "Get up, take your bedroll, and start walking," we too, take up our beds and walk. We become the messengers who are strong, skillful, empathetic and supportive, that look in the eyes of the lame man lying there, and say, "Take up your bed and walk."

That's how The Bounce works. Life is more fun this way. The Bounce is better than we ever hoped or imagined. And then we get to say, "Yes, what didn't kill me made me stronger."

THE NECESSARY NEMESIS
<u>REFLECTION</u>

Describe who or what has been your Necessary Nemesis in your life?

In what ways does calling the person/situation an **NN** help empower you, instead of seeing it through eyes of regret, bitterness, victimhood?

What lessons, gifts, transformations did the **NN** awaken in you?

How are you stronger – not more self-protected, armored, or defensive – because of your **NN**?

42

Honoring Our Journeys

"First the fall, then the recovery from the
fall, both are the mercy of God."
JULIAN OF NORWICH

Yesterday I wailed most of the day. I wished for nothing more than
I had never met my Necessary Nemesis and had a relationship with
him. If only I made the U-Turn and ran away at what was the obvious choice every day I was in contact with him. I wept over the
losses that came from all I went through and put others through.
The fallout is still present. Laying there, I grieved over what was
now gone.

Broken and humbled, I sobbed. And yet, I'm in touch with
Love like I've never been before. I've been purified by my brokenness. The one who held me and wept with me told me that
I was more whole, lovely and alive because of my great fall; the
suffering had done a most magnificent work in me and prepared
me for my work in the world. It had also done a death and resurrection in him – The Bounce – for which he was forever grateful.
We held the loss and sadness and the bright hope that we came
out with a greater capacity for love, truth, and awareness because
of my great fall.

I wish it could be different. I wish I could have gotten free from
what was stuck in there without my Necessary Nemesis; I wish
I could have figured it out through shadow work in the comfort
of my own home. But I wouldn't be who I am today without that
encounter. It brought what was hidden but hurting me into the
light where love and truth and The Bounce could bring new life.

We must honor our journeys that brought us here. So often there's no other way. It's all mercy in the economy of this great Love that holds it all. It humbles us and gives us compassion and wisdom. The fall doesn't have the last word when we embrace the recovery – The Bounce. We're made and remade more beautiful and full of love. We no longer forsake ourselves.

May the lies that cause us to despair because of our bad choices, never have the power to take us off course. May we honor our journeys that brought us here. May even our losses and pain rip us open from the self to which we once did cling to a spaciousness that holds so much more.

Mystery has the last word, not our brokenness. When we know this, we're who we are, warts and all, and we never have to pretend otherwise. Humility and confidence make us a powerful influencer to change the world.

"It is through our coming to know the truest self
that we are transformed into something divine."
- MICHAEL DEMKOVICH, A DOMINICAN PRIEST AND SCHOLAR

Honoring Our Journeys
Reflection

What "fall" or event outside your control needs to be honored in you because it brought you here?

In what ways do humility and brokenness feel different than regret and wishing you hadn't done that which seemed irresistible, or gone through what was done to you? Is the former life-giving and connects you to others, while the latter clings to an idealized version of yourself or life? How will you train yourself to go to the former?

> "First the fall, then the recovery from the
> fall, both are the mercy of God."

In what ways do you still not trust The Bounce - that our wounds that lead us astray, will be transformed into our greatest healings, if we take the Transformational Path? "It is through our coming to know the truest self that we are transformed into something divine."

Because we end up knowing ourselves and the truest part of us that isn't even named by what we've done, do you see how we tap into what is divine in us, all because of our painful journeys? Write about it.

43

Language Beyond Abstractions

"One of the ways we traumatize one another is through
the unskillful and abusive way we use abstractions,
absolutes, and generalizations. We all deserve the extra
effort it takes to clarify beyond bumper sticker living."
- KRISTA VORSE

On one of my hikes with JJ and Charlie, (her labradoodle), we were discussing the problem with language.

I've benefitted from JJ's input. Language matters: the *yeah/but*, the *both/and*, and *we need to clarify* moments of how we communicate; she sharpens me.

I pride myself as one who explains the exceptions. I hear things through the filter of the exceptions because as someone intimately acquainted with abuse, I think: how would someone without healthy defenses hear that? How would someone who struggles in this or that way hear this? Where's that a dangerous statement and unskillfully delivered? What?! They didn't just say that, did they? That's so co-dependent! Are you flippin' kidding me?! One of the many things I love about my spiritual father Richard Rohr, is he uses language like: *tends to*, *often*, *most likely* versus "always" and "never" as regular fare. I welcome any opportunity to sharpen my skills in communicating the nuances.

JJ and I were talking about anger and how it's a God-given response to having a boundary violated. We then said in unison, "Unless someone's angry because they have a problem with anger." No boundary was crossed but they're still angry because they're easily offended.

The thinking models I teach show us how we often feel anger because of our unquestioned assumptions and the data we choose to select. If we were more skilled at going to inquiry to verify what we're assuming, and being transparent about our thought processes, we'd see how silly our anger so often is; we decided to take offense when it wasn't what was going on in the circumstances or for the other person. We must interrupt our habituated way of relating that does this, and learn the skills of connection, awareness, and inquiry.

Just the other day I got angry at someone close to me because I assumed what someone else was telling me - who claimed to be an expert - was correct. I didn't bother to verify the facts. The anger I was getting in touch with wasn't even about the issue at hand. But it got my attention where I wasn't honoring my needs and values. I was heart-broken at how I responded. These skills are a life-long practice.

For the problem of language, JJ and I talked about how in Organizational Development, it's emphasized that all language is considered an abstraction: it doesn't necessarily have a set definition because words mean different things to different people, and the spiritual psychology field has conflicted definitions as well. Then there's the confusion over ego, the big Self vs. small self, vulnerability and healthy boundaries, healthy anger and anger coming from being too offended and self-referential, and the ever-present grid of dualism - either/or thinking. With a contemplative mind, we hear the both/and.

I wrote *Clarifying The Infinity Loop* because someone was critical of me that I don't "walk my talk" because I talk about being open and receptive but I'm not willing to be that for her. If you read my other chapters, it's clear there's a both/and; we need our aversion and our inclusion, our anger and our empathy, we need our boundaries and our openness, we need self-love and selfless love. It takes clarifying language to handle the both/and world of our growth.

My intention is to grow in my communication skills. I teach what I need to learn most, and have never been able to do these ideals without error. None of that diminishes me as being loved and lovable. Or you. We celebrate that we're ever in the process of learning how to love well while practicing elegant and intelligent self-care. We fumble along in finding the right language, but that's where connection, awareness, and inquiry come in. If we all get better at that, we'll help each other get back on our feet.

LANGUAGE BEYOND ABSTRACTIONS
REFLECTION

Where do you have the habit of reacting to certain language instead of the habit of asking, "When you say that, what does that mean to you?" If someone acts miffed like we should know what they mean, we can say, "Words and concepts mean different things to different people, so I want to hear how you experience that."

Where do you have a reaction when spiritual teachers, psychologists or coaches use statements that sound like "always" and "never"? How's it unhelpful? How does it put yokes on people and shut down inquiry?

How will you be more mindful of language and create more both/and as a bridge-builder, learner, and leader?

Is there a way you will speak and help lead the conversations away from abstractions to more curiosity, humility, and honesty?

44

Ideas, Not Identity

"We are not our point of view."
- BILL ISAACS

Three and a half months after my relationship with my Necessary Nemesis ended, we reconnected on the chairlift. Because of my recent and dramatic healing from the PTSD, I was high as a kite to feel safe and in my power, being around him. I was one big, red bouncy ball of love and happiness. That concerned nearly everyone who knew what happened in the relationship. Obviously, I wasn't finished with my healing yet, to be "okay and happy" being around someone who isn't safe. I was trying to be open to any possibility that there was a miracle out there that he could change. It was as though I had forgotten all I went through - things that should have still disturbed the hell out of me. I was still disconnected from my anger that I needed to set that appropriate boundary.

While we rode the chairlift, he told me he was aware that his identity had been wrapped up in being right his entire life, and anyone who disagreed with him threatened him to his very core; being questioned meant there was something wrong with him. That made for some intense defenses and constructing his life so he couldn't be challenged on anything of any consequence. He was in the power position. Anger and rage were at hand at any second to protect that ego. It's a scary world to be in or around. He'd become addicted to shutting others down by telling them they were the ones who were defended and protected if they didn't take everything he said as "The Truth."

That man wept out loud with what appeared at the time as a deep grief over the losses in his life because of it. There's the loss of his own freedom and the hurt and pain caused to others. If the pain is able to create in us a hunger and commitment to love better, it's the sorrow that brings growth; under it is a longing for freedom from our ego that doesn't serve us, a longing to love well, and a soberness over what's lost that will never be recovered. That makes us more aware of the preciousness of those who come into our lives and those still around. It's a dying that brings life. It's The Bounce.

Not everyone is able to transcend the limitations of their egos. There are those with certain personality disorders and pathologies that are essentially all ego and can't get past it. They may even be aware of losses but aren't able to change. No amount of trying to help them or love them will break through. We may love them and care for them, but we won't make the magic happen. That man roped me back in for a short period of time from that encounter, questioning that there was a crack in him with a capacity to change. I soon discovered that those tears and words were a performance. I'm not sure he knew he was acting. The awareness wasn't real to drive him to change. The death of his attachment to his ego that love would require of him, wasn't worth it; not when he had people he paid to tell him he was "a good man."

There are also those who aren't interested in growth. Being controlled and held captive by their egos their whole life seems more appealing than dying to the small self.

It reminds me of my Instagram quote that explains the feeling to me.

> "There's an energy I get from thoughts that make
> me feel separate, superior, or important. And there's
> an energy I get from connection. One makes my
> world small, and one lets me touch infinity."

I'm aware when I'm in the former energy. I feel the charge, but it's become a yucky charge to me now and rather disgusting.

Those who don't want to let go of their attachment to their egos that don't serve haven't been convinced of the good news that there's a True Self that's more powerful, indestructible, and ever abundant already there. It's who we really are. There's nothing wrong with our small selves, it's just not the whole picture.

In Dialogue, it's taught in the concept of realizing we're talking about ideas, not identity. We do a lot of work around where the ego serves and doesn't. When we transcend the limitations of our egos, we're able to suspend our point of view to hear and learn from another. We get to keep our point of view if we decide to, but we're able to be in Expanded Awareness without the constriction of feeling threatened that someone sees things differently. It's having a Learning Container for our communication.

Some people love to educate themselves, but in terms of communication, they're certain of their beliefs and are self-sealed. It takes intention on the part of those around them to see what need is behind that person's communication style, and connect with them through inquiry.

If we all normalized the concept, "We're talking about ideas, not identity," we'd be closer to Dialogue and discussing the "undiscussables." We'd experience a spaciousness in our bodies, minds, and spirits that would be habit-forming. We'd discover that the loss of our attachment to our identities based on our ego constructs isn't that scary after all. Once we let go, we find we are held. We meet who we really are and it's enough.

There's a time to weep when we realize holding onto our identities hurts us and those around us. But joy comes in the morning. It's a "bright sadness" that's aware of our shortcomings, but full of the hope that every new day brings our ever-growing desire to learn to love well, Think Together, and see each other in a powerful way. That's the kind of power we want to get addicted to.

IDEAS, NOT IDENTITY
REFLECTION

Is there an area or relationship that trips you up and you get triggered by your identity (we are not our point of view), and you struggle to detach and see you're just talking about ideas?

In what ways is your ability to love, lead, hear, learn, show respect and be respected hindered when you think your ideas, your identity, your convictions, or your directions, are you?

How will you come up with a strategy to influence the conversation when someone starts to think their ideas are them and they get angry, defensive, bullying, controlling, hurt, condescending, or making assumptions? What would connection, awareness, and inquiry look like in these situations? (You may want to revisit this question after you've learned about Dialogue and how to get from Debate to Inquiry, and see how you will naturally teach it to others.)

45

When Our Egos Serve Vs. Serving Our Egos

"Even though we're ego, we're not just ego. There's a
need to tend to the confusion of the still broken ego. In
the futility of trying to be itself without Infinite Love, it's
confused. It needs compassion for the ego's confusion."
- James Finley

A benefit of learning to live from the True Self, is we don't have to organize our lives to serve our egos. We realize we're something greater. We use our egos as a fire to stand for truth, to hold our ground, and to command the room (in a good way, of course). We use our egos so we don't split from our intelligence and power. We own it because it's needed. When we're able to experience watching ourselves from the Watcher that's more aware and "bigger" than our ego-identified selves, we're on our way. An Alpha Woman openly laughs at herself. She's childlike in her wonder and freedom. There's no need to appear all great and powerful. She has her ego and uses it to stand in the fires of The Infinity Loop.

Some Would Say…
Some would say I'm a great mother. Some would not.
Some would say I'm a great friend. Some would not.
Some would say I'm a great coach. Some would not.
Some would say I'm a great consultant. Some would not.
Some would say I'm a great daughter. Some would not.
Some would say I'm smart. Some would not.
Some would say I'm beautiful. Some would not.
Some would say I'm a loving person. Some would not.

Some would say I'm a great cook. Some would not.
Some would say I write well. Some would not.
Some would say I'm humble. Some would not.
Some would say I'm a great partner. Some would not.

A client was worrying that he may not be as good as he thought he was in his vocation. I reminded him he's both brilliant and he's not.

When our egos are in a healthy place that will serve what is needed, we're aware we're all these things and we're not. And we're okay with that. Our identities aren't wrapped up in being those things.

As soon as we're declaring how we're a great neighbor, we stumble over the incidences when we're not.

It's been said that the highest level of spiritual development is realizing and accepting who we are, warts and all. Though we work on ourselves all our lives, we don't cling to an identity that we're "a great" anything. We may not be all that great when we think we are. Even being a great mother is up for interpretation. So why do we use such language?

It has its place - to recognize we're great at something. But then we let it go and be happy both loving and accepting ourselves and others in our less-than-greatness. There's a sense of humor, light-ness, and humility in being secure enough to see and hear where we aren't so great.

I believe in seeking to be the greatest we can be in what matters to us, but there's humility and freedom in that. It's done in service of our souls, not at the cost of them.

It's humility and confidence. We stand up for what we believe but we don't have to grandstand our brilliance. We don't need oth-ers to validate us to feel okay. It just doesn't matter.

Paradoxically, when we don't have to use our energy to protect, prove or promote ourselves, we use our energy toward our genius. From there we tap into some greatness.

WHEN OUR EGOS SERVE VS. SERVING OUR EGOS
<u>REFLECTION</u>

In what ways are you aware of the difference in you when your ego serves versus serving your ego?

In what ways do you anchor yourself in your True Self and "enoughness" so you don't fall prey to serving your ego out of scarcity, or being separate, superior/inferior or important?

In what ways do you see the value of embracing the ego as not all bad in this Alpha Woman and The Infinity Loop model? In what ways do you see how the ego (our fire) is in service of what is beautiful and true, in boundaries for ourselves and others? This isn't done by running over others but by the grace and wisdom and strength of our wholeness.

46

Our Stories Made Transparent

I heard Brené Brown recently
say something like this:

"This is the story I'm telling myself and this is
how I got there. Tell me where I'm wrong."
This is connection, awareness, and inquiry.

Byron Katie teaches us that we often tell a story to ourselves about others, and others tell a story to themselves about us. It's unavoidable.

I was talking about this to my son. Our discussion was about his friend, Steve (not his real name) who told himself a story about my son. The story Steve told himself was self-sealed and he was unwilling to make his thinking processes transparent. The thought that we asked Steve to open up his story for feedback and confirmation, made him livid. His truth was "The Truth." There was no feedback loop.

This was a pattern in Steve's life. His assuming led to his hurt and anger, which took him out of learning. Steve also wasn't wanting to face his own agenda so he projected it onto my son. He needed to make my son bad because he was the one who pointed it out. Steve's own wounds of not being enough got covered up by his ego. He used his anger to hang on to his own truth at the cost of seeing what could be truer. There was no connection, awareness, or inquiry. This is my observations from speaking with him.

That pattern will cause problems in Steve's life if he doesn't figure out it doesn't serve relationships or decision-making. I was sad about the situation because the young man thought of me like a mother, but wouldn't let me coach him. The good thing was my son was able to see that his friend was just believing the story he told himself. My son didn't take it personally and was able to wish him well. He was also able to acknowledge that he does the same.

The Latin root of the word *arrogance* is "arrogo." It means "I ask no questions." Arrogance also means making assumptions, having excessive pride and disrespect for others. Respect by definition is taking The Second Look (re-spect), as in spectacles we see through. It's willing to see if the assumptions we're making are wrong. And making assumptions is what we all do, all day long, whether we like it or not; it's how our brains work. The safety for that is how we create a new habit of making our assumptions known and asking for verification.

My son piped in, "If we make our stories transparent, that's being more evolved." I like that. We all have stories. We acknowledge we're telling ourselves a story, that may not be true, that leads to suffering. How wonderful life is when we're willing to be courageous and humble to tell the person what's going on in our brain, be transparent, and ask for feedback. We can't be attached to our point of view and do this.

Our stories made transparent. It's called getting down The Ladder of Inference, coined by Chris Argyris. We infer things and go up a Ladder of assumptions. By being transparent about the data we select and the story we tell ourselves and then inquire where we may be off, we make our way down the Ladder. I will go into more detail about our Ladders later in the book.

Ladders aren't anything we want to hang out on for long periods of time. We've all heard horror stories with ladders. It's no different with our Ladders of assumptions. Both have caused injury and death to relationships, opportunities and our evolution. When we make our stories transparent, we grow in connection, awareness, and inquiry – three things that give us a stable surface to stand on.

OUR STORIES MADE TRANSPARENT
<u>REFLECTION</u>

In what ways is this skill of making our stories transparent to others different from the way society teaches us to advocate our point of view or express our emotional charge, based on the stories we tell ourselves that we're so certain are true?

Write about situations where the breakdown in the relationship came as a result of not making stories transparent to each other?

In what ways is this approach full of connection, awareness, and inquiry? Where is it full of humility, learning and honesty?

In what ways are you the leader by being teachable and modeling "not knowing," vulnerability, honesty, curiosity, and safety?

In what ways does this approach challenge the held belief that "My truth is The Truth"?

47

Downloader Vs. Learner

Downloading: Talking without thinking,
regurgitating facts, opinions, judgments we've
read or heard from someone else. It leaves no
space in the conversation for inquiry.

"One cannot begin to learn that which
one thinks one already knows."
- EPICTETUS

The Futurist Alvin Toffler wrote, "The illiterate of the 21st century will not be those who cannot read and write but those who cannot learn, unlearn and re-learn."

What Epictetus and my heroes in Organizational Learning have in common is knowing what's needed: We must get past our defensiveness and open ourselves up to realize our certitude and assumptions, and how we select data, may not be the whole truth; if we think we already know, one cannot begin to learn.

Contrast the dinner party of Downloaders with the table full of participants who Dialogue and Think Together. The Downloaders come to persuade another with the best argument (or pat each other on the back in group-think). The Dialoguers come to deeply listen, inquire, connect and be aware from a humility that knows they don't know everything and their smug certitude just isn't all that interesting to them anymore; they want to be challenged on their biases, limited experiences, and even how they've been enculturated to think and behave. The Dialoguers Think Together. The Downloaders fall into group-think.

This is where The Infinity Loop is my constant reminder of how I want to be in the world. We stay in connection to another, to build a bridge if possible, and to help the other learn as well. What do we have to teach and learn from each other as we sit in The Infinity Loop? We give each other The Second Look (Re-spect) to see into a realm the Downloader will never see.

I'm all for Speech and Debate in school, but what we need are classes on skilled Dialogue where one learns how to listen in an open-hearted way. Even those of us who coach, counsel, and mentor fall into advice-giving. We have a certitude about what we think someone should do. But what if we're wrong? What if we ignore a key piece of data that makes all our expertise what trips us up? In that situation, the outcome will be skewed from what our experience and expertise biased us toward; it felt so good to be the expert, we missed out on how good it would feel to stay in connection. There's a surrender to the unknowable, the Great Mystery that interrupts our plans and knows what we don't. It takes skill, humility, and presence to ride this fine line.

Downloading is defined as conversation where we take turns speaking and then waiting for our turn to talk. It's non-reflective. This leads to where we Deliberate - weigh likes and dislikes, which devolves into Debate.

In Dialogue, we Suspend what we think, relax our grip, and stay open, which leads us to Reflect on what we've done but don't notice. This leads us to explore our thinking through Inquiry, which moves us to Generative Dialogue where we invent unprecedented possibilities and new insights - a collective flow from which many new ideas are free to emerge. I'll explain it further later in the book.

Dialogue is the grid I experience the world through and weighs heavily as to whether or not I want to spend all that much time with someone. Does this person want to impress me with what they know, or is he someone with whom we can both learn and grow?

I'm tired of Downloading. I know I have my biases (it's impossible not to). But I want to connect so deeply, with inquiry and awareness, that I'm able to Think Together with someone where both of us will never be the same. And to do that, I must admit I don't already know.

DOWNLOADER VS. LEARNER
REFLECTION

What relationships do you have where people are downloading – going to Debate or just being agreeable and polite? Which relationships do you think stimulate true learning?

What new habits could you form to influence the interactions with more curiosity, honesty, and humility?

What new habits could you form to influence the interactions to more connection, awareness, and inquiry? What will you do as a leader to encourage Thinking Together?

48

Respect

"Intellectual boundaries: Being respected for my
views. We give the safety by honoring and protecting,
and not being passively in collusion with anyone who
would compromise or violate those boundaries."
- JAMES FINLEY

The definitions I work with for respect aren't how someone has to earn it. Here are some definitions of respect to consider.

Unconditional Positive Regard - (UPR) means everyone is worthy of respect and capable of contribution. Even when others have broken trust, they still deserve respect as human beings.

Re-spect (to look again). Spect as in spectacles – glasses we see through. To re-see one another. I think we need that definition to be able to do the others. We don't dismiss one another because we respect one another. Because we're able to see each other through that lens, we hear and see what we have to say to each other. We don't have to take it as truth, but we take The Second Look to see and hear what they have to say.

"I see you (and your view) and hold a space for you within myself."

Recognize one another's legitimacy - the opposite of judging and blaming. See people for the potential they carry with them. Treat each person as a teacher. What is it this person has to teach me that I don't already know? Looking for what is the highest and best in each person. Treat each person as a mystery I will never fully comprehend. Treat each person as part of the whole - part of us. Respect is the opposite of seeing people as objects in a mechanical world marked by a preoccupation with mechanism, prediction, and control.

I try not to use the phrase, "I don't respect them." I like to say, "I don't admire that in them." When I say I don't respect someone, that doesn't feel right to me - knowing these definitions. I feel separate, superior, and important when I make that judgment. But I'll say they display behaviors I don't admire and am not aligned with.

Respect is foundational to changing the world.

RESPECT
REFLECTION

Which relationships could benefit from more of these definitions of respect?

What causes you to not practice respect (to hold a space for them within yourself)?

Describe the difference between respectful encounters and disrespectful encounters in your life (those that take the Second Look and those that dismiss in disgust).

What part of the definitions hits you as something you haven't thought of before or is most needed in your life?

49

Our Strength is Our Weakness

"It's part of our humble shadow work to hold the tension that our strength is our weakness. 'What am I missing?'"
- KRISTA VORSE

The familiar saying "Our strength is our weakness," is used by Richard Rohr who teaches spiritual development. Rohr's educated in possibly every stream of developmental learning. My friend JJ, who has expertise in this and the Enneagram confirmed it: our strength is our weakness. Let's make peace with it and let it make us more aware of our blind spots so we're not so blind. Rohr explains it as being two sides of the coin; if you try to eliminate one side, you lose the other. Knowing that dilemma, we need compassion and acceptance.

Nearly every day I'm faced with how our strength is our weakness. I see patterns in my behavior and others' that come as fallout of our strengths: some people who have high empathy and develop people because they build enormous safety and trust, may in their personal lives, not check-in with what nurtures them; they may be able to see another's point of view and want to be supportive, but they don't support themselves fully and aren't honest or aware of themselves. Those skilled at adaption are often prone to over-adaptation. One with a high set point for happiness often ignores what isn't okay. Our care becomes care-taking and desire to manage others' feelings; fast-paced decision-making censors out data that more slow-paced skeptical thinkers would catch. Being open becomes too open. Those who support can support bad behavior.

We benefit from this reminder to take a regular sober inventory and invite others to look out for us. We then operate at what's called Thinking Together. We need each other and to know where we're prone to miss things. "What am I not seeing?" "Where does my strength cause me to lose my discernment?"

If we acknowledge how the aspect of everyone's temperament that bugs us does have a strength behind it, we hold it respectfully and look again at what this person has to teach us.

We must make peace with this two-sided coin and not think that if only we had the latest tool we could successfully divide it without losing any value. Instead, if we embrace that we can't divide it, we'll be more aware of ourselves. We take that awareness, connect with others who are able to help us think through things, and inquire into what we may be missing or dismissing out of our strength.

Richard Rohr says the highest level of spiritual development in his estimation is what he calls level nine: "I am who I am, warts and all."

We hold it all: strengths and weaknesses, and with awareness, be present to what we learn. It's humbling, freeing and frustrating all at the same time. However, it bounces us into our need for connection, awareness, and inquiry that makes our dilemma worth it.

Our Strength is Our Weakness
Reflection

What are your strengths that are also your weaknesses?

What is your current awareness around the two-sided coin we all have to contend with? Can you be more compassionate to yourself because of it? How can you be more compassionate to others?

What do you do now to help yourself deal with the weaknesses that come from your strengths?

What would you like to implement to help you be 'not so blind' to your weaknesses?

50

Anger

"Feelings have feelings, and they know when
they're unwanted and will cooperate by going
underground. Anger cooperates by pretending it
doesn't exist. It's impossible to accept an unwanted
feeling, and until you simply allow and acknowledge
a feeling, it will persist. That's all you need to do.
Tell your feeling, "I see you. You belong to me."
- Deepak Chopra

When our physical, emotional, sexual, intellectual
and spiritual boundaries are violated: "Anger is the
God-given emotion that restores the boundary
that was violated. Anger is not rage. Anger is not
vindictiveness. Anger is the angel with the sword of
truth, "I will not let you treat this child this way."
- James Finley

I want to hear what my anger wants to say. It's there because I'm
waking up to the years I allowed horrendous things to be said and
done to me.

"Enough is enough."

The anger I refer to here is as our guidance because we're in a
toxic relationship or something needs to be protected or honored.

Throughout my life, if I allowed myself to feel, to love and care
for myself, I would've heard four sentences (in my vernacular) that
would've helped me make a U-Turn.

+ "This is flippin' ridiculous!"
+ "This is disturbing!"
+ "This is disgusting!"
  And if the offender wasn't willing to look at the situation,
+ "F*@k off!"

The F*@k off! is to the unwelcome behavior. It's the walk-away (not usually saying F---off, but the fierceness of the phrase - said to myself - keeps me moving), with a fierceness that doesn't collapse or acquiesce to the crazy-making, head-spinning, and gas-lighting. It calls bullshit on the bullshit. It knows what's in line with truth and love and won't be sold that what it needs isn't valid. It knows it's able to go elsewhere (7.6 billion and counting), to find it. It finds it also within itself.

Everyone processes anger differently to move through it in a healthy way. For me, my anger doesn't need a punching bag. And no one needs to take it out on someone. I don't need to scream in a padded room. The remedy for my anger isn't to transmit it or even get it out of my body in the same way as other traumas.

I allow it, include it, love it, let it go. (Richard Rohr) The anger flows out of my body and all my cells because I'm 99.9% air and my cells turn over constantly. I embrace it, love and transcend into my Indestructible Self that isn't wounded or violated. I don't spiritually bypass; I witness and learn from my feelings.

A great deal of my suffering has come from not honoring my anger. The patriarchal system, being bullied, being shamed for my needs and emotions, unskillful teaching that makes all anger bad, my own denial of my feelings, my desire to be a loving person and not knowing how to have my anger and still love well, all contributed to my not allowing myself to fully acknowledge that something wasn't okay. But I allowed all of that to happen. I make amends to myself if I betrayed myself. I put balm on my wounds and Great Compassion wraps his wings around me and together we help me bounce into my True Self.

I recently noticed that my deepest truth comes out of my mouth when I'm alone. It's my boundary, my integrity, my internal "No" or "Yes" that blurts out. That's how I came up with my four sentences to alert me and give me permission to feel my feelings. I realize I always heard those sentences, but didn't know how to act on them. That mechanism was broken. Now I really hear those sentences. It's the fire I need to create my life in line with Life.

When I was in the relationship with my Necessary Nemesis for that short period of time, my anger was so shut down by his shaming of my emotions and needs, I lost the fire I needed to move me out of the situation. Five months after the relationship finally ended (and six weeks after I reconnected with him on the ski hill that I refer to in *Ideas, Not Identity*) I gently shared with him the serious trauma I experienced from his abuse. He completely dismissed it and felt neither empathy nor remorse. This was consistent with who I experienced him to be. Immediately after that I became aware of his tangled web that he was now caught in. I was then honest with him in an email and basically told him to F-off. I let him know I saw the man behind the curtain and knew the truth of who he was. In the moment that I sent the email I had a vision: a woman stood at her outdoor clothes line in an open field. The time period was over a century ago. She shook out a large natural colored sheet. As she shook the sheet, my life-long pattern of The Stockholm Syndrome (hyper-empathy and bonding to abusers), shook out with it. Like a snake uncoiling through my body, within a few seconds, I broke that pattern. I was free as a sheet blowing in the wind. The woman who shook the sheet was calm and present. Once I set that boundary with that man and warned him I would no longer protect him, I knew I did what I needed to do. I felt light and let the anger go. I knew his pathology took away his freedom to do any other; he didn't have the wiring to be any other way.

When I did break my silence to a few people, I was seen by a woman as not in forgiveness. She told me many things – one of which was "taking the wounded male down is not the answer." It's how victims are silenced. It's no wonder we silence our anger and push it into our shadow. I'm quite clear I wasn't coming from vindictiveness or had any of the thoughts or feelings going on in my mind or body this woman assumed I had. It's the both/and; I can be free from hate and resentment and speak the truth.

My anger toward that man is welcome again if something else arises. There's no pretending my anger isn't there to make myself feel spiritual. There's wisdom in this appropriate anger. I can then let my anger go when I hear what it wants to tell me.

There's so much crazy going on in the world, it's the healthiest thing I know how to do - to hear myself say what I know to be true. No longer do I doubt my truth in absurdities. I thank healing from abuse for that.

"Enough is enough."

I think about all those years I was silent and let others run roughshod over me as if they knew better than I. My internal voice was, "Are you f*%king kidding me?!"

I feared my anger. But now I know how to have my anger serve as a messenger to me and not to vomit it all over others (except in extreme cases). My anger shows me where I'm not in integrity - split between my internal "No" and external "Yes" - by allowing what's being foisted on me. There's a time for a "No" - when it screams at you on the inside is a sure one. That internal scream may feel like anger.

Now I honor my anger as the gift it is. I feel sorrow for how I ignored her (my anger) or didn't express her in emotional sobriety and hurt others. My anger alerts me to pay attention to some of my highest values of what is right and in truth. It's setting a beautiful fire around me. Love comes in and out, but I have my anger to set the boundaries to protect what deserves to be protected.

The Great Love Affair is romancing this along. When I listen the first time she speaks, my fire doesn't have to get bigger to get my attention. My lioness has shown up, calm but alert, standing as she shifts back and forth under the acacia tree. She wants me to fully see her, love her, and embrace her as the gift she is.

As I edit this chapter on this Thanksgiving Day, I honor those whose land this was before we white people took it. That was neither honored nor protected. I honor and am thankful for my lioness and for how anger - when used in service - helps us love well while practicing elegant and intelligent self-care.

ANGER
REFLECTION

What's your relationship to anger? Are you comfortable with it in yourself or do you feel bad for feeling it when you do?

How do you examine and process your anger?

What would you like to upgrade in how you work with anger?

How quick are you to recognize the first disturbance and not stuff it, intensify it, but acknowledge it as what needs to be honored or protected?

51

Anger and Empathy Must Kiss

"We sometimes think someone's choice to express
anger in an unproductive way is a "will" issue.
Often, it's a "skill" issue. Feeling hopeless and
disconnected from empathy, we then lose the
will to do what serves. But that can change."
Connection * Awareness * Inquiry
- KRISTA VORSE

"Even though I'm not you, I'm not other than you either."
JAMES FINLEY

Mark Goulston teaches that empathy is a sensory experience - it activates the sensory part of our nervous system, which includes our mirror neurons. In contrast, anger is a motor action that's usually a reaction to some perceived hurt or injury by another person. The good news is we can choose to shift ourselves from the motor brain to the sensory brain. Goulston explains further that anger and empathy are like matter and antimatter - they can't exist in the same place at the same time; we have to let one go to let the other in. When we're blaming, we can stop our angry rants when we shift ourselves into an awareness of what the other person is feeling (empathy).

How we work with anger and empathy is foundational. However, we're enormously complex and I hate cookie-cutter approaches to anything. I'm a devoted synthesizer of tools and principles.

Recently I woke up to where I've censored my much-needed fire (anger) by my empathy. I've not honored my anger that was the genius of my emotions wanting to honor my needs and values. It has never been good when I did that. It's a big way I've betrayed myself. I told myself I was fine ignoring it and I was all loving to be long-suffering in those situations. I'm convinced now I was way off the mark to not set boundaries around what didn't feel good to me. I've also lost my way by expressing too much anger at times for sure. But hyper-empathy is also problematic. When something disturbs us, I call it, "Hitting our Whoa Button." We don't want to shut off our Whoa Button automatically by making excuses for the other through hyper-empathy; we don't want to miss what we need to let register in us. We also don't want to lose track of connection and empathy. I was shamed by a "spiritual teacher" – my Necessary Nemesis - that if I felt anger toward him I "wasn't having good will." What a manipulative, cultic bunch of crap.

This is my solution to my problem: Anger and Empathy must kiss.

Feel the anger. Let it drop deep into your belly like a cannonball. It's safe there, grounding you in awareness but it isn't overtaking your brain. Go to silence where awareness and connection to yourself and others will arise. In inquiry, ask yourself, "What is wanted or needed in this situation?"

Empathy will come from there. We're not ranting or blaming but we're not betraying ourselves either. In that stillness, we may hold the clarity, "This is not ok." "What we permit we promote" principle may also be at play. We have our fire to move us. We're in The Infinity Loop of connection, awareness, and inquiry. We're protected in the loop that holds the fire of truth. We're grounded. In that grounding, we're connected to the Ground of Being. In that awareness, we return to our awareness of oneness, and empathy naturally arises from there. "Even though I'm not you, I'm not other than you either." It holds both in the way our brains are able. It's a beautiful thing.

Anger and Empathy Must Kiss
Reflection

Write about a situation where you couldn't feel empathy because of your anger toward someone. What were the consequences?

Write about a situation where you couldn't feel anger (fire) - to register what needed to be honored or protected – by having hyper-empathy. What were the consequences?

In the both/and world of the contemplative mind in The Infinity Loop, how do you see yourself being able to hold both? Journal about the tension and skill needed to not collapse, censor discernment, become enabling or care-taking by hyper-empathy, but also not losing your way by allowing rage and anger to blind you and be an unproductive energy?

52

The Father Wound

"This present moment isn't free of the burdens, memories, and wounds of the past. They must be attended to before you can look around, breathe easily and love the moment you are in right now. A good beginning is to catch yourself when you have a bad memory and say, "I am not that person anymore. For the truth is you are not."

- DEEPAK CHOPRA

I asked my former partner and friend Leo Gorcey, Jr. to describe his experience with The Father Wound. He wrote the book, *Me and the Dead End Kid* about his father's life and their relationship. It's a beautiful, hilarious, and painful story of Leo Jr.'s healing process. Even though he wrote that book in 2003 and experienced a tremendous healing, Leo's aware of how that wound wasn't fully healed and continued to hurt him and others. This is what he had to say about The Father Wound.

(Leo) The Father Wound is about not being enough and living in the shadow. You end up feeling you're not ok. It's passed down from generation to generation. The father's wound takes up all the space and because it does, the son learns to be invisible. It's true to some degree for every man. However, some express their wound with acting bigger and more aggressive. It's either shame or shamelessness and often it's a dance between the two. I've struggled with both not loving myself and disappearing, and taking up all the oxygen in the room.

(Krista) Ironically, narcissistic behavior is often a byproduct when there isn't authentic self-love present. Too little self-love, the wrong amount, or expression of it, can be part of the equation. It can be there's too much love of the separate self. The phrase, "He's just so in love with himself," refers to the grandstanding that may be there to make up for The Father Wound; I believe that defense mechanism of too much self-love, to make up for The Father Wound, can be expressed as being self-centered and narcissistic. I'm not referring to true Narcissists and pathologicals, as this book doesn't address them. When we have authentic self-love, we're more likely to have humility and confidence.

(Leo) Yes, that is so true. In The Father Wound, the son never got the blessing from his father that said he was enough. Many men never heard or experienced that blessing from their father and so they go through life with shame, anger, pain, defensiveness, insecurity, and striving for acceptance from the patriarchal system.

In our situation, Krista, you were in touch with your business instincts, but I was still struggling. Not only was I not able to affirm and allow you to be heard and use your gifts and intelligence more fully, I just wanted to trust the father figures in the company, which were usually driver, authoritative men. These men were often the architects of the culture that needed to be transformed. So, women are hurt by The Father Wound. Not knowing how to transform the pain, we transmit the pain. We run over women by not affirming them when their truth is contrary to the father figure we seek acceptance from, or by being bigger and louder and the authority to them. Intimacy is the biggest threat to us men because that's where we're most vulnerable and so we shut that down too.

We medicate the split with what numbs: anger, ego, distraction, addiction, power. Anger is a strategy to push away the love we need to be healed because we don't think we're enough and worth it. The threat is, "I'm going to let this person get close to me and they're just going to confirm I'm not enough. And I'll be rejected."

It's a miracle any man gets healed or matures in our western culture because there's no rite of passage for us or mentoring. That's why we need wise teachers to help us.

(Krista) And being wise is knowing how to tune into the real need and not just rattling off spiritual jargon, which isn't helpful. Sometimes spiritual teachings are used unskillfully. This can occur toward a man who's feeling his 'not enough-ness.' Byron Katie's and Eckhart Tolle' teachings – about questioning the mind - can be oversimplified and misused. Someone can be told they need to stop believing a story they're telling themselves when what they really need is to go deeper. The pain may be linked to The Father Wound. With someone who will sit, love and guide them through the pain, he can recall when he first felt his 'not enough-ness' and grieve and put balm on that wound. Then he can realize it's not true - that he is enough even though his father didn't give him that message. We need to be sensitive to men as they open up and be aware how often The Father Wound drives men's beliefs and fears about themselves and relationships.

(Leo) That's so needed with the Father Wound. Men also need to do the work on themselves. Blaise Pascal said, "All man's miseries derive from not being able to sit in a quiet room alone." The healing starts with letting everything fall apart – not being able to "hold on in the strongest winds," as you say, Krista. So, instead of loss of control as something bad, we experience it as an opportunity to become whole and free. It starts with the ability to sit with our shame, loss of control, pain and humiliation, and to be loved in the midst of our 'not enough-ness'. When we're loved in our 'not enough-ness', that's what makes us enough. Then we no longer have to focus on proving, promoting or protecting ourselves. We need help with that, and others to sit with us; we can't do it all by ourselves. Others need to love us through that. In coaching, we have someone who will sit with us. But if we don't figure out how to follow up with that and develop a spiritual practice around our awareness, it goes away, we lose it. Once we realize we're enough, we still go out and accomplish a lot of shit but we're not needing to prove anything anymore.

A great coach helps us develop an ongoing practice so we're able to do it for ourselves, and get connected with our True Self that loves and forgives us all the time. Self-forgiveness is the big one.

The core of any effective spiritual practice is one's ability to be a witness to their experience. That's how we become emotionally sober – the ability to not get sucked into the drama of our emotions. It's the addiction to the drama – the stories we tell ourselves. It's what feels like life to us, like substance. However, real life doesn't feel like anything because it doesn't have all the drama. It just has this moment, and in this moment, it has everything.

The paradox that we resist, is the emptiness that's really enough. Instead, we have an attachment that we have to experience reality through our feelings, but that's not reality. Our feelings tell us things, but we step back - "I have my feelings but my feelings don't have me." That's emotional sobriety. When we're emotionally sober, we're ready to grow spiritually. That's our daily practice, witnessing our feelings – that's what contemplation is (allow it, include, love it, let it go). Then what starts to emerge as we stop wrapping ourselves around our feelings, is silence. Silence is where we experience union with Love, in union with our True Self. Our True Self is our Infinite Self, which is all powerful, all loving, all abundant. It has everything we need.

The Father Wound
Reflection

What did you read just now that gave you a more compassionate view of what men are dealing with and why they respond the way they do?

Do you see men in your life that are afraid of falling apart and facing the emptiness? Do you see their burden to keep it all together as men and how society has taught them they are their ego construct? What thoughts come up for you regarding men who have been in your life?

How will you be safer for men to be in a relationship with you, in any capacity, and for them to not feel like they'll discover their biggest fear is true, that they're not enough? Do you agree with the current model of women's directness toward men that ignores the pain underneath their behavior? Do you think it's working? How will you come from more connection, awareness, and inquiry to help men respond differently?

How will you model to men emotional sobriety and your spiritual practice of realizing you're not your ego construct that's easily threatened, but rather something that shows up in your emptiness you face in the silence?

53

Defensive Men to Receptive Men

*"When you're committed to love, growth, and healing,
your weaknesses will transform to become strengths."*
- KRISTA VORSE

The capacity for us to transform is something that will surprise and amaze. Our hearts break open and pour out as we long to be our best selves. Help is on the way. Love is always for us and holding us. Living on the Mystery Side, how sweet it is.

Here I am again with Leo who I met when I was 16 years old and he was 32. That was a long time ago. We have been friends, life-partners, business partners, soulmates, family and co-creators in our art and consulting work. He's the person I'm most aligned in our spiritual path as contemplatives. I value his transparency and insights about men and his own journey growing closer to becoming a receptive man from years as a defensive man.

(Leo) When you're defensive you can't hear. It triggers us and gets us into fight or flight and you physically can't hear. It's called an Amygdala Hijack or **DPA** (**D**iffuse **P**sychological **A**rousal). It's really hard for men because the ego feels threatened and the ego is very attached to its story of not being worthy. So, when it senses anything that threatens its worthiness, it gets defensive and aggressive to protect itself.

Before I'm able to go to receptivity, I have to understand the root cause of defensiveness. The man will say, "It's because I'm being attacked!" But that's not it. It's because of the ego's attachment to the sense of unworthiness, that I feel I have to protect myself as if something someone says will truly diminish my worthiness. We begin when we get to receptivity and realize that nothing anybody says or does will diminish my worth. It's an inside job. From there I decide it's okay to hear another person's pain.

(Krista) A large percentage of people don't know how to work with shame within themselves so if they feel it, they get defensive because it's too threatening. Until we're loved in our shame, we don't know how to deal with it.

(Leo) Right. I don't have to automatically feel shame when I hear another person's pain and think it's always my fault. I can stay in my True Self. I listen without going to defensiveness. That's the first step to understanding. I don't have to fix another's pain but listen to the needs and show up the best way I'm able to support those needs. That's love. In most cases, the person is not feeling loved or supported and if I hear clearly, (be present, open and undefended) because I know they can't diminish me - so I know I'm safe - I'll be receptive and then I will make clear choices about how I can show up for them.

So, the skill is learning how to live in the True Self. Even if I'm not able to get there right away, I have to be able to at least talk about my defenses. Where is that defensiveness coming from? That's where the healing comes. That's the process that builds trust and safety, and it doesn't work all the time, but it's going to work much better than defensiveness.

(Krista) So, the opposite of defensiveness is being open, undefended and immediately present. That's being receptive. In our True Self, we're safe, we're in abundance, we're not in toxic shame. (I use toxic shame here as meaning "uniquely defective and not enough." It's not the healthy shame when we do wrong I'm referring to.) It's the place from which we're able to be most loving. And that's our practice, to get better at living in the True Self.

But we can't always be non-defensive and that's okay too. After Reflection on this, I'll explain in *Lessons in Listening to Myself.*

Defensive Men to Receptive Men Reflection

What was your biggest aha moment about why Leo said men are defensive?

Without stroking men's egos or walking on eggshells, how will you lead men toward listening and being present and not feeling threatened?

How will you live more from the True Self that's secure, so you will model it for men?

How will you show self-compassion versus hatred when you feel hurt and diminished?

54

Lessons in Listening to Myself

"Some have had to work very hard to find their defenses."
- JAMES FINLEY

We want to live in our Abundant Selves where we feel invincible and can take on the world, and being undefended feels easy. But we don't get there because we're told to be undefended. Our tender hearts need us be their guardians. There are times to honor being open and brave and times to honor saying "No" to being cracked open. We feel unsafe and sense something isn't right; we'd have to submit to a violation of boundaries, being labeled, and told what's in our hearts. Assumptions are made about our motives and we get defensive. Our True Self includes our false self. In non-duality, it's transcend and include; we don't pit the false self against the True Self. Our anger can be a God-given gift to alert us when a boundary has been crossed. Even though others may not think a boundary was crossed, they don't know your interior landscape at the time. Or they may operate at a different frequency so they don't get it. And if you get feedback from wise souls who agree with you, then you know you're on track.

Our defensiveness may be tied to our integrity and all we believe is right and good. This isn't the same thing as thinking we are our point of view and getting all defended because our ego is threatened. This is how we see people treating others in unconsciousness and our pushback may be because we're more awake in an area than the group. To shut down the strong emotion in us and just go with the flow is splitting from our integrity.

Sometimes we don't listen to ourselves when we need to guard our hearts because someone has told us that's bad and unspiritual to do. Sometimes it's the most spiritual thing to do. We don't allow our spirits to get crushed, so they can be in service for what we're called to do in the world. May we know when we're to be open and when to shake the dust off our feet and keep on walking to someone who will honor our open hearts.

LESSONS IN LISTENING TO MYSELF
<u>REFLECTION</u>

This is where *Language Beyond Abstractions* comes in. Pat phrases just aren't wise or helpful. Sometimes defending ourselves to protect what is sacred is sound. What comes up for you around listening to yourself and protecting yourself in the face of accusations that you're the one who is wrong for using your right to defend yourself?

Recall a situation where language was used against you to get you to not honor your own values or discernment?

How will you make sure you don't do or allow this to be done to others (cracking them open when they don't feel safe)?

55

Bullying

"The moment we seek to control, we cease to love."
-Henri Nouwen

One of the reasons for our predicament today is the prevalence
of bullying. I've been bullied so much in my life I've struggled to
identify I'm being bullied. After I wrote about bullying, I took a
serious look at it and woke up to relationships in my life that were
contaminated with bullying and were unfixable. We need to be
able to identify it, not enable it, and not bully in return out of fear
and anger. What we need is to be connected to our hearts, connected to the other beyond their bad behavior, and honest in a way
that creates learning and the greatest chance of change. We won't
know until we try.

In inquiry, we ask them if there's another way to communicate
that doesn't feel like bullying. You may ask if there's a way to honor
the disturbance, frustration and hurt, that doesn't shut you down
and contribute to you feeling unsafe.

We all seek to control at times. Some of us do it with our co-
dependency, our concern, our authority, our unconsciousness, our
white privilege, our narcissism. Some do it by bullying.

Some do it in work, in relationships, in families, in community
affairs. Both men and women bully. I've been bullied my entire
life by men, but some of the worst bullying I've received has been
by women. If women have a high degree of aggression, physical
dominance, power to threaten and hurt you, they can be powerful
bullies.

The definition of bullying is:

"Repeated, persistent and aggressive behavior intended to cause fear, distress, or harm to another person's body, emotions, self-esteem or reputation."

"Bullying is the use of force, threat, or coercion to abuse, intimidate, or aggressively dominate others. The behavior is often repeated and habitual. One essential prerequisite is the perception, by the bully or by others, of an imbalance of social or physical power, which distinguishes bullying from conflict."

Because of men's strength, and how it has lived comfortably amidst the patriarchal system that's often passed down from bullying fathers, men find themselves trapped in bullying. Some men who have been bullied by their fathers are paying the toll for it and are mindful to not transmit it to the women in their lives.

Why do people bully? How do we help people stop?

I've asked Leo who wrote in his book, *Me & The Dead End Kid* about how he was bullied by his father and has also bullied women, to share his current thoughts.

(Leo) I think anyone who bullies other people bullies themselves. If you look at men who bully other people, they're hard on themselves. They beat the shit out of themselves. If they make a mistake, they call themselves an asshole. They cut themselves no slack because all weakness is bad. (The exceptions are narcissists and sociopaths. They're insecure, can't see themselves, and don't have the genuine desire to change.) Before it's toward anyone else, it's toward me. "I'm a man of conviction," I would say, to justify my bullying. It's the ego's way of portraying strength to the world. Also, it's me saying I'm not going to be bullied by anyone like I was bullied by my dad; they're more concerned about not being bullied than if they're bullying anyone else. My dad was a bully. His dad was a bully. It gets passed on. It's a survival strategy. It's a story we tell ourselves that always goes back to the ego's attachment that we're not enough. The story is always about: I need to be in control. This is what's safe. I can't be vulnerable. Don't let any disconfirming data in because that will threaten the ego because I believe "I'm my ego." Anything like not having certitude feels like weakness. It feels like vulnerability. I'm going to get hurt.

Scarcity, loss, loss of power, are all the things the false self whines about. It all comes back to what Eckhart Tolle says, - the fear of annihilation, the fear of death. So, a loss of power feels like death to the ego.

People who bully, for the most part, are vastly unconscious of it. They're not intending to hurt people. Underneath is the wound - I'm not enough, the ego's attachment to not being enough. I have to do this, I have to do that. Some successful stuff comes out of it (what people build), but it's not a successful strategy for relationships. Steve Jobs is the perfect example. He was a total bully. An asshole but look what he created. But Woz, the co-creator of the personal computer, told Steve Jobs, "You don't have to be an asshole to be a genius. You can be a genius and a nice guy." But Jobs couldn't do that because of his dualism – it was either/or, not both/and. He was stuck in it. He was convinced he had to be an asshole to get shit done.

The healing is: Any story that can be thought can be unthought, like that story I told myself when I was five years old that I had to be a bully to protect myself. The vast majority of survival strategies that we develop from our stories were started before age eight. When I'm five I can't process all this shit that's happening so I have to create a survival strategy to handle it. That survival strategy is always going to break down at some point in your life. Once I go back and observe the story, I'm able to change the story if it's no longer true. This is where the Byron Katie bit comes in - I'm questioning the story. Once we're able to change the story, (do the Turn-Around), the jig is up. Then you're able to create a new story. I don't need to bully anymore. I'm safe in this world. It's ok. I don't need to protect myself that way or prove anything. There may be times I need to protect myself, but it's going to be conscious and it's not going to be by bullying. I don't need to harm someone to protect myself. I can remove myself from the situation.

The critical piece of the healing is, I have compassion on that part of myself that is that broken little boy, and I love him. Love and self-forgiveness are the healing powers.

It's tricky because there has to be a shift in awareness. That's the key to everything. You have to be able to transcend and step away and see your options of how else to behave. That's where a coach comes in. You can't do it by yourself. Create new brain-tracks, as you say.

For the victims, it's in being able to articulate what's happening and what is causing them to keep going back to the bully. You keep putting yourself in harm's way.

(Krista) There's also the bullying that happens to kids in schools. It's difficult for kids and anyone going through it to see they have options to not put themselves in harm's way. That's being addressed by schools more now, but the kids who bully need an intervention into what causes them to build their ego identity around such cruelty. Research shows how bullying and aggression go way down on playgrounds where meditation and understanding the brain is taught, like in Goldie Hawn's foundation's program, *MindUP*. I believe in the space of meditation, children connect to a life greater than the stories they believe about themselves.

Those who bully must truly desire to change because there may be an addiction to bullying that has formed in them that gives them a powerful psychic charge. It takes an effective approach to open them up to be willing to change. That's one reason I'm so committed to The Infinity Loop.

Bullying happens a lot in private. Victims need to feel safe to speak up and for others to hold the one who bullies accountable to do the necessary work to heal and create a new way to relate; one has to create different patterns of relating. The victims can't be bullied to be quiet. We need to shine the light and come alongside each other in community and mustn't look the other way and normalize when we know of bullying going on. The strength to speak up to power must be found. We need each other to support us in doing this. It takes intention. It also takes wisdom because the one who bullies will feel threatened that their bad behavior is being exposed and take it out more on the person(s) they bully. If we're going to speak up, we need to tune into the situation with discernment and know what serves. The more we intimately share our lives with one another, the safer one will feel to share or even discern themselves that they're being bullied. Our hearts that hurt so badly when we see or experience bullying is our way home.

BULLYING
REFLECTION

Where are you experiencing or have experienced bullying? What was the consequence to you?

How does awareness of the bully's pain underneath the behavior affect your way you look at them? How can you have empathy for them but put your concern for those bullied and make a stand against unacceptable behavior?

How will you call for the bully to get the necessary help out of compassion but without caretaking, minimizing, or ever allowing their behavior?

How will you take your sober inventory to make sure we never bully anymore?

56

Sexual Harassment, Exploitation and Abuse

"The very fact that someone can
manipulate people has to set
off our alarms. It takes humility,
curiosity, and honesty to be
willing to see the truth and stand up for what is love."
- KRISTA VORSE

It saddens me that women don't always support those who have been used. They succumb to the cultic control of male power, charm, and authority. Some care-take these men who act like the victim when they've been exposed for how they exploit women. I've had every trick in the book used against me to shut me up to cover for their cowardice. I brought the inconvenient truth. Wonder Woman would never look the other way or stand with someone because the guy is fun to be around. Sometimes women become the bullies and co-abusers to protect men if the exposer threatens their comfort or attachment to them. But they'll couch what they're doing in spiritual language, as though they're *The Healing Women of All Tantric Bliss*. (That's not a real group – I just made it up.) This feel-good spirituality – what I call "ooey gooey spirituality" – has the belief that either standing by or protecting an abuser is loving and right. This is done without any evidence that these men are committed or capable of changing their behavior - even if these men say the right seductive speeches to garner support. *The Healing Women of All Tantric Bliss* believe they're more spiritual than the women who actually have the courage to tell the truth in the face of all that will come against them for doing so. These women who speak up are well aware those associated with the abuser will be embarrassed. The ones who tell the truth feel that pain in their hearts, but know they're here for more than to protect people from being embarrassed; they heed a higher call. They're aware it's easier to do nothing. Women who speak up are lovers of truth. They want to change the world. They know what's coming – that they'll be judged and told they're doing it wrong and it's not the way to heal the masculine and their wounded feminine. These courageous women will be seen as vindictive, inappropriate, spewing their drama and trauma, lying, crazy, willing participants, and blaming their past pain on the accused. They'll be told it's not helpful to use labels, there are no victims, that they're projecting, this is gossip, and that these conversations should be done in private. Their very wounds will be used against them. They're seen as trying to bring down men who are wounded but are good souls that bring good into the world. Some who speak up may not be healed, transformed, all cleaned up and do it perfectly - that is true. But it's wrong to treat women who have legitimately been abused as though they're the perpetrators. Women who expose a charming abuser are ousted as the abuser's tribe circles the wagons around him. I have told the truth about every one of my abusers – eventually; I know the list well. It's not fun but it's purifying.

We can all fall under the spell of ooey-gooey spirituality. Confused about what is loving and right, we stumble. Struggling to find our footing, we grab what is comfortable. We don't like drama and being woken up from an abuser's cult is both dramatic and traumatic. Also, a women's truth-telling can trigger our own pain we're trying to push down; we think we're ready to have our wound all sewn up. But the truth-teller brings the message: "You still have a bullet in there and that bullet is laced with poison."

Soberly we reflect on the times and ways we didn't speak up and shine the light. We must have a way to feel healthy shame about our complicity, without decompensating because we believe our weakness has the power to name who we are. (*The Red Pouch.*) We can change the world by changing how we choose to humble ourselves and acknowledge we've been duped by these men who we find cute 'n cuddly, witty 'n wonderful. It's up to each and every one of us to wake up, be courageous for each other, and stop looking the other way.

Here are some of James Finley's thoughts on the complexity of the issue.

"Abuse is when a relationship has one person with more power than the another, and the one who has more power sexualizes the relationship and exploits it to their own gratification at the price of the other. In which case, they dehumanize, dishonor, or violate the dignity of the other and show no sense of empathy or caring about that.

In situations like this, there are two things not present. One is force. This isn't a situation where there is physical force - the knife, the gunpoint. And the reason there's no force is because none is needed, because there's no resistance (the second thing not present). And understanding why there's no resistance, we understand why this goes so deep and is so destructive. Because there **is** force - a dark force of another kind. And the person is in a position where it's very personal to them and it gets very scary by just how to cope with this. So, they tend to give external compliance to avoid being attacked or abandoned or face the consequences. And as soon as they do that, then they're in collusion with the secret and there's a base of shame.

What makes it so hard for the person to come out into the open? Why does it take so much courage? It takes so much courage, because one, the price they will pay. That's why anyone in a situation like this needs to have the very prudent courage to bring it to light. And they need someone who's got their back to talk this through and not be naïve about the consequences. So, one is the realities of that. But here's what's bigger: when you come out into the open, the society will side with the perpetrator. And the reason they side with the perpetrator is complicated because society doesn't want to question the father figure, the authority figure. We're all poor, weak human beings. But the person's status in the situation that they're in, doesn't give them the right to exploit, sexualize, or take advantage of anybody. And the more people come out into the open, the more there's a possibility of a tide-shifting here, where it could reach critical mass and more and more people will get the courage to come out. As it comes out into the open, it breaks the secrecy, because it can only continue where's there's collective collusion and secrecy.

The shame is by implication, that if you didn't resist, how can you claim you were abused? And there's the tripping point right there.

One aspect of the spiritual stance is that we have compassion and empathy for those coming forward. We become a part of a societal acceptance and believe in them and help them. It's also help for the perpetrators because they're also tragically broken. They also need help."

Speaking up is how perpetrators are held accountable and potentially helped. But as we know, not all perpetrators are capable of change. Our compassion for these poor men who do this must not cause us to weaken in standing with these women, or cause us to get played by these men. Women are complicit in this. It's time for all of us to change, to change the world.

Sexual Harassment, Exploitation and Abuse Reflection

In what situations have you been sexually exploited in a relationship where the other had more power than you? Emotional abusers have more power.

What insights did you get from James' explanation of why you submitted without physical force?

Is there any situation where you judged a woman for speaking up, because you thought she has no right because there wasn't any force? Do you know when a woman was judged as trying to hurt the man by speaking truth?

We know men who've been accused of leering when they weren't, bumping into woman by accident, etc. Woman have told themselves stories and no one held these women accountable. Do you know a situation where gentle inquiry into a woman's story would have served truth because you don't believe her claims, there's no data, and it's all secretive?

Are there ways you will you feel differently toward women (including yourself) who have been exploited or harassed?

Is there someone you need to question your loyalty and support to, who has been exposed as a sexual abuser, predator, user? Did you use inquiry to dig deep enough?

57

A Tale of Two Men

*"I've been humbled that I don't have special
powers to coach someone who can't see themselves
and won't change. The experts and reality are
right. Now I just show up but let go."*
- KRISTA VORSE

There were two middle-aged men. Both had The Father Wound.
Both transmitted their self-hatred onto those closest to them.
Many never saw those traits, but only the qualities that were more
likable. But they couldn't and wouldn't keep the darkest parts
from their family. How could they? Our families bump up against
us like no other and the irritation of that bump hits the trigger
switch. They felt powerful in those moments when in their anger
and control they didn't have to feel their shame and powerlessness
from the pain they carried from before kindergarten.

But one man, when confronted with how he hurt others,
broke. The losses and being miserable on the deepest level made
him crack. He knew he was imprisoned by emotions that had all
the power. And he stayed cracked. In those cracks, he carried his
weak, tired body to wise, skilled healers who could see past all
his defense mechanisms, his charm, his coping skills that had kept
him from transforming for decades. He faced all the ways he had
hurt others by not wanting to face his own cowardice, selfishness,
and brokenness.

But the other man, was nearly impossible to confront because
his enormous ego and abusive rage terrified others from speaking
up. When he was confronted, he may have cried for himself and

may have tried to convince others through elaborate maneuvers that he was "getting his shit together." However, he couldn't see or feel the pain he caused others, he couldn't even remember doing the things others said he did. He had "a slightly different perspective." He found a support system that supported his image, his illusions, and his like-ability. He made sure there was no way in hell he would have to crack. And so, he didn't.

There were two young men. When one was confronted with how his bullying, lust, and manipulation hurt others, he broke. He wept with a sorrow for his capacity to hurt others. He didn't like that person he was. This young man was so committed to not living in self-deception, he overcame the ongoing temptation to pity himself and tell others how unfair it was. There were lots of ups and downs with the process of transformation, but he became a better man because of it.

The other young man was also confronted. He was more successful at avoiding others who would help him crack open. He spent his energy charming others to keep from speaking truth that could have set him free. He didn't change because he didn't have to. He wasn't in touch with what his soul yearned for. Instead, he went with what his ego yearned for.

We get confused. For that we need compassion. We think letting go, cracking open, surrendering our tricks so we can truly live, isn't better than the life we may be living. However, every time we crack more, every time we allow our hearts to be broken as we yearn to be love, we get to live the better story. It's a tale worth writing ourselves into because we get to be the hero. It's a tale worth leaving behind as our legacy. It's what we call a happy ending.

A TALE OF TWO MEN
REFLECTION

Using your discernment, in what ways will you tell someone who's willing and capable of change and someone whose psychic paycheck for their ego-driven and wound-driven behavior is too great to want to give up?

Great love and great suffering invite us to change. How will you encourage others to choose to take the Transformational Path and do the work? How will you use inquiry to help others become more connected to their hearts, pain, and behavior and aware of their self-deception? How will you create safety for others to look at themselves and not fear the death they must go through to change?

It what situations are boundaries and detaching what is needed?

58

Separateness

"Love is seeing yourself in the other person."
- CARL JUNG

(Leo) "I thought I could be with someone and still have my separateness. That way I could blame all the bad parts on the 'other' and make myself good. I could look good and win that way. But the separateness was an illusion. I was always one with my other. I just couldn't see it. Not 'one' in the way I thought – sexually, physically. But one in the way, Krista, you talk about the Aspens; underneath it all, we're all connected. We're all flawed, both good and bad. All broken. All 'crazy' - meaning we make huge mistakes and seemingly illogical choices when we think we should know better. But we don't. Otherwise, we would. We learn from each other all the time, in every moment. And it's painful and humbling, and perfect, leading us on the path to wholeness, which is always better than being right.

If you have a true I-thou relationship, you can't objectify. It's only when you're separate, superior/inferior and important, that you see the other as a way to feel good about yourself. That's when we're in our false self. That's when we see ourselves as separate. We either see people as a way to get what we want, a way to look good, or in our way. You can't do that when you're one with yourself and one with another person.

Porn is the classic objectification model. It's built on people's illusion of separateness. It shows how desperate we are to try to bridge that separateness. People who are addicted to porn are aching for oneness. The porn industry gives them the hope of that while pandering to their false self. That's why most porn involves the man being separate, superior, important, and objectifying women.

When someone intervenes in that addiction to separateness, the first thing they work on is connection.

And to you, Krista, even though we no longer live together, I see myself more one with you now than ever."

That makes me choke up.

Separateness
Reflection

In what ways do you see how you fall into separateness just like men do? In what ways will you bring more awareness to that in our society?

My awareness about what Leo said about porn addiction and the problem with connection, is how I've seen men use porn to run from connection out of fear of surrender in being present sexually with the woman they love. The vulnerability a man can feel in connecting through intimacy can be terrifying, especially with The Father Wound. What are your thoughts about what Leo said about porn addiction and the problem with connection?

How do you respond in separateness (separate, inferior/superior, important) to men and women who offend you by their ego need to feel separate?

How will you support the awareness of oneness and connection, without allowing anyone to be objectified if you can help it (by speaking up)?

59

I Was Raised to be an Asshole

"I used to feel sad for my broken past of how my
persona was formed around what wasn't whole
and holy. Now I just celebrate my U-Turn."
- KRISTA VORSE

As is the case with all my writing about the patriarchal system, please know it's not all men I'm referring to. We women are so grateful for the men in our worlds who have learned how to love well. And we have compassion for men who are still figuring it out, just like we women are. It seems everywhere we go, people are talking about "the men and women thing."

"I was raised to be an asshole but I'm repenting" is the line Leo said should go on a t-shirt. At 67 years of age (when I wrote this), he's had some time to reflect on the state and struggle of men raised under the shadow of the patriarchal system. He's written about the cost of being raised by his famous actor father (with the same name), a Dead End Kid, and what a son picks up from the front row.

"I was raised to be an asshole but I'm repenting" is a pretty humble and aware thing to say. I applaud him for the witty proclamation and t-shirt idea.

(Leo) I was raised by a chauvinistic, alcoholic, misogynist. It was normalized. It was "implicit bias" (biases we don't even know we have). I had no idea the impact it was having on women, until I started listening, really listening to women, and not being defensive. When I was able to get my ego out of the way and put myself in their place, that was a huge wake-up call and very painful. I had this moment when all I wanted to do was apologize to every woman for my asshole behavior. I've been able to actually feel the pain of my women friends, the things they've been through with the men in their lives. And not because these men want to be hurtful. It's because they don't know any other way. They really, truly believe women are not their equals and there's nothing wrong with the way they treat them. They think there's nothing wrong with having power over women as long as they take care of them. That gives them the right to control them.

One friend told me that when she broke up with her boyfriend of one year, he said, "How can you break up with me after all I've done for you?" He emailed her a bill for what he spent on her during the relationship. Everything he did was with a hook. To him, that was normal. "I take care of you, you belong to me."

(Krista) That isn't a far-fetched story but a common one with variations.

(Leo) As a man, I'm embarrassed to hear this. I'm apologizing for the boyfriend being such an asshole. This is centuries of hardwiring of men.

To fix this, we have to listen. Women are not crazy. They're speaking the truth. We men don't want to hear that our hard-wiring is wrong. We'll fight to defend our ego-driven identities. That may have worked when everything was based on survival but in a scenario where we're evolving to higher awareness levels of love, it's not loving. It's obsolete.

(Krista) How sad that the behavior comes from men's insecurities. I hear these concepts being taught today by chauvinistic men. They may hide it in well-crafted language and say it's based on our deepest gender needs, but it's crazy talk nevertheless.

(Leo) If the idea is to become more loving human beings, then men have to change.

(Krista) For both men and women to change, to transcend our insecurities and hard-wiring that doesn't serve us, we must learn how to live more from our True Selves, our Abundant Selves. The definition of "repenting" is making a U-Turn. Learning to live more from the True Self where we no longer seek to control one another, is the ultimate U-Turn. We don't have to continue to live as Dead End Kids.

I Was Raised to be an Asshole
Reflection

Describe the men in your life that are unaware that they were taught that looking out for women equaled control and being superior?

How will you create more awareness in men through your compassion and strength? How will you stand in The Infinity Loop and create more awareness so you don't behave poorly in return?

What will you do to remind yourself to have compassion for men but not allow it to promote their bad behavior by permitting it? How will you stay connected to your heart and allow it to hurt when you see men lose their way, so you don't lose your way? How will you support new behavior by being consistent in having high standards for yourself and how you're treated and how you respond?

60

One Man's Transformational Road Trip

"I'm hittin' the road and God help me,
I'm not coming back the same."
- Krista Vorse

This is a testament to infinite possibilities. Leo finds his spiritual practice in the Christian mystics so that explains the language. Beyond the language is the truth of a heart that's full of connection, awareness, and inquiry. It's a heart that desires to love, to learn and to lead. It's a model for us and it's from a man who has struggled to do it right. He speaks honestly of his shadow that lives in all of us, that hinders us from leading with true power and beauty. At now age 68, it's a great honor to call this man my spiritual soulmate.

Below is all from Leo, taken from his journal, written during a Spring, 2017 road trip. Leo is utterly beautiful to me in his vulnerable, honest, humble, disclosure of his awareness. I find it a privilege when a man who has the willingness to grow shares his heartache and spiritual practice with me, and allows me to share it with others. Leo has always felt he would not live to be an old man; his words are bittersweet to me and I will cherish them forever. I hope his open-heartedness touches and inspires you in some way. This man has touched and inspired me for many years.

(Leo) Tears are never far off these days when I reflect on the 'bright sadness' of the past year and the many 'treasures and favors' from God that have ensued in the wake of the Great Love and Great Suffering that marks our path to transformation - which has become my deepest desire, replacing all else.

This road trip is about reflecting on and integrating my shadow parts that have unconsciously directed so many of my actions - fear, ego, insecurity, greed, lust, addictions, attachments, illusions of separateness and superiority, needs to control myself and others in unhealthy ways for my own gain, and ways that I've done violence to myself, and therefore projected my shadow onto others, and done violence to them.

I want to know who I really am, warts and all.

And in the process to integrate the "Golden Shadow" - the unmade choices of the positive repressed parts of my life. The needs that have not been lived out adequately.

To see through Love's eyes the perfection of my imperfection. To experience the "absolute irrelevance of my failures and weaknesses in the face of all-pervading grace."

"My deepest me is God and God is my deepest me." - Catherine of Genoa

This time is about deepening my practice of self-awareness in a non-violent, non-judgmental, and transformative way to allow me to love and forgive myself, others and reality for being imperfect, and emptying myself out to make the space to receive the grace and mercy The Beloved desires in every moment to lavish on me in ways that exceed my deepest desires.

I alone have held myself back from this freedom by allowing my psychic space to be filled with a myriad of stories about all that's happened to me, my judgments about others' behaviors and actions toward me pre-occupation with the past and the future, defending, protecting, proving, promoting, and the countless unsustainable survival strategies that have crowded my every waking moment (and even my dreams), and blocked me from experiencing infinite unconditional love, and loving myself, God and others more fully.

This could be a fearful undertaking on one level, but it's necessary for my life experience to align with my deepest truth if I'm to be free from endlessly repeating the patterns of 'resistance to what is' that have marked the past 60 years of my life.

When my "ego was converted" to the Christian tradition 36 years ago, I had no clue what that meant. I thought I 'had it down' because I was a leader, teacher and associate pastor in the charismatic movement for 15 years. I was wrong.

Now my only desire is "to love that which cannot be thought" and live my life in the 'Cloud of Unknowing' (mindfulness and inquiry) as much as possible.

To relocate from my head to my heart. To rest in the love that rests in me.

To think only as much as needed to meet my responsibilities and move to experiencing the Divine Dance and loving service as much as possible.

It'll always be "transcendence and then the laundry," and I, always a beginner.

Still, I desire to deepen my practice and my non-resistance to let go of my comfort to more fully embrace my calling.

To die before I die so I might live in peace, love, and joy now and forever, in oneness with all my fellow beings, God and his creation.

I'm experiencing fear and trepidation each step of the way, and enough insight, inner courage, peace, love and joy to take the next step.

The days since I left Ashland have been strewn all along the way with "treasures and favors" from God. I'm following the trail of bread crumbs to my deepest wound...

"We will run to you..." - Gungor

"In my deepest wound I found you Lord, and you dazzled me!" - Augustine

One Man's Transformational Road Trip
<u>Reflection</u>

What touched your heart from Leo's outpouring of his heart?

In what ways do you see the only hope for all of us, men included, is through the death to our attachments to our egos, our stories, our resistance, and our fleeing from facing ourselves and our shadows?

How is this book your Transformational Road Trip? What would you write?

61

The Shadow

"This shadow-knowledge will become your constant
and most valuable companion on the path if you
always keep turning to it because it keeps you radically
humble whatever happens to you and through you."
- ANDREW HARVEY

Swiss psychiatrist and founder of analytical psychology, Carl Jung, theorized that we all have two sides of our personalities; the known conscious side deals directly with the world around us, and the deeper hidden side that lies below the conscious mind, locked away in the dark cellar of our psyche. He dubbed this part of our consciousness the shadow aspect.

The shadow aspect is essentially composed of bits and pieces of us that we have repressed, discarded or abandoned for being unacceptable. The shadow embodies all of the traits that do not fit in with our views of our ideal self – the persona we wish to present to the world. These rejected characteristics have been deeply buried within to keep them at a safe distance from consciousness so that what the shadow desires are generally unknown to the conscious mind.

Sometimes when we're overly stressed, the shadow aspect makes an appearance. Behaviors that are normally curtailed or avoided because they go against the image that we have built for ourselves, rise to the surface in moments of psychic weakness. After all, they're a part of who we truly are – whether we like it or not.

Jung believed that in order to be whole, you must strive to integrate the conscious with the unconscious, a process he calls individuation. But the process doesn't happen on its own. It requires much self-examination, and a desire to know oneself completely without any of the ego defenses blurring reality. It's part of the process of personal growth; we uncover all of the layers that prevent you from knowing who you really are. It means removing the rose-colored glasses and seeing things in a real way, including those things that are simmering in the dark, way down below. It means coming face to face with your shadow, saying hello, and negotiating some sort of an agreement.

Those who are not at all in touch with their inner selves are the most at risk when dealing with their own shadow aspect. When you don't know your dark side, it becomes your enemy. You have no power over it if you don't see it. There's no negotiating and no compromising. It will stealthily come out of nowhere and interfere with your life. And you will have no understanding of what's happening. Becoming familiar with your darker side will allow you to understand it better, and to deal with it in a more open way. But it's a fine line. There's some risk of succumbing to the shadow, getting lost or being consumed by the dark side.

Once you have seen, acknowledged, and accepted your shadow, you will begin Jung's individuation process. Uniting both sides of your psyche will make you a more integrated and whole person, help you to drop the persona – the mask – and allow you to become and embrace the real you, warts and all. Only then you're able to make a conscious decision to live your life the way you want to live it. Your behaviors will be guided by the clarity of knowing who you really are, all the way through.

But not all shadows are dark. Some people have shadows that Jung calls the Golden Shadow, containing the positive repressed parts of our lives – the unmade choices. And just as the dark parts of the shadow must be integrated to achieve Jung's individuation, so must the positive features of the psyche – the Golden Shadow. For some, rejected pieces of personality are left undeveloped and cast aside at some time in the past for one reason or another, but the subconscious refuses to let them go and continues to cling strongly to them. At various points in our lives, these neglected features call for attention. There is so much positive that's gained when we acknowledge the Golden Shadow when the time is right. When it does call, it's usually related to our higher calling, the thing that puts us straight onto the road to self-actualization.

If there's a feeling of doubt and loneliness, it's usually because we have not been made whole. We have not yet greeted our Golden Shadow. Assimilating one's Golden Shadow means catching up on all of those needs and desires that have not been lived out adequately.

THE SHADOW
REFLECTION

What stuck out to you as helpful to learn or remind yourself of in terms of the shadow and Golden Shadow?

Is there anything you're aware of that may lurk in the shadow, either dark or light?

What practice do you have to help see your shadow?

How will you practice self-inquiry and inquiry to help all of us see our shadow?

62

Supportive Krista Died Tonight

*"Until you make the unconscious conscious, it
will direct your life and you will call it fate."*
CARL JUNG

Our ego needs lead to self-betrayal. When we're driven by our
need to be a certain way because it's how we see ourselves, how our
egos tell us we're good, or how we keep relationships, we lose our
way. We're not able to discern what's needed. That's being in our
false selves.

I'm learning for the first time what it means to "protect my
field" as they say. Two ways I haven't done that: I don't always
honor my truth that says, "That is not what I believe," "That makes
my heart hurt," and by holding onto Supportive Krista that allows
other people's truths to crowd her truth.

Supportive Krista is another one of those that has led me astray.
In my coaching, there's no Supportive Krista. I don't second guess
my instincts and shy away from what emerges in the moment. And
she's supportive. But this Supportive Krista of my personal life was
messed up in the head.

I've been taking my spiritual inventory of how I lost my way
in a relationship because of Supportive Krista. A woman reported
to me over a short period of time a stream of her behavior toward
people she felt anger. In one incident, she reported to me what
she messaged to a female friend of hers in a public group who was
at a delicate time of her life. This was done in pursuit of honesty
and holding someone accountable. It was fueled by hurt and rage
and a reaction to what she perceived as her friend not being in

integrity or being a loyal friend. Internally I gasped and my heart hurt.

Had Coach Krista felt invited to the conversation, she would have stayed connected to her heart, allowed the silence while she acknowledged how her heart was hurting, and gone to inquiry: "What was your intention? Do you think it had the impact you desired? Do you think you'll have any regrets about saying that to her at this moment in her life?" These are some questions I and those closest to me try to ask one another BEFORE we send those messages. It's that slowing down, "What am I not seeing? What's the gap between my intention and the impact going to be? Am I kind of messed up right now because of my own pain that I may be transmitting it to another?" I've sent those messages and regretted them for years. I went back and asked for forgiveness for hurting people. It's a hard thing to face and I wish someone got my head on straight before I did something that was hurtful.

From other encounters with this person I knew Coach Krista wasn't welcome; they only wanted Supportive Krista. Supportive Krista goes against her instincts or isn't aware of them, tries way too hard to be supportive and not judge, shames Krista for even feeling her heart if it's not in agreement with whoever is wanting support at the moment; Supportive Krista betrays herself.

Recently I received (an invisible) Sword of Truth planted in my chest that resonates as my new guidance system. It bounces off what I believe to be true, doesn't judge it, make it bad, or say "Krista's not allowed to feel, believe, or need what rings true for her." If I had my Sword of Truth sooner, I would never have let Supportive Krista run amuck. She was killed by the Sword. Now I'm stuck with the karmic mess from months ago; that woman went after me with the same vein of confrontation that she did to others. What a lesson. It woke me up to see how giving someone the benefit of the doubt instead of practicing more inquiry, actually supports someone else being hurt.

In allowing Supportive Krista to die, there's more space for True Self Krista who is "Here I am, warts and all." She's heart-centered, honest and not thrashed around by wanting to be supportive. She discerns and doesn't need to support. She loves all involved but doesn't need to make anyone feel better about their behavior or point of view. Paradoxically, without Supportive Krista, I'm more supportive of what's truly needed.

We must let go of our old life to get the life that's waiting for us, and we must let go of our old compulsive ways for us to fall and bounce into our True Self. Often suffering will alert us where we lost our way and invite us onto the path that brings life.

May Supportive Krista rest in peace, never to be resurrected. Sometimes long life is over-rated. Living from our hearts and trusting that if we desire to be more connected than separate, and first go to silence before reacting, we'll learn how to speak up in a way that will serve and we don't have to worry that we'll hurt someone (Martha Beck). Living that way is valiant. To live our most courageous life, all that no longer serves must die. We'll be dying until we die. But every time we do, we bounce into greater life. That's the resurrection we want.

Two months after Supportive Krista died, I had another relationship that I got snagged on. The relationship began months before Supportive Krista died, so some patterns were already set in that were making it sticky for me; I was already trying way too hard to be supportive, and supportive of behavior and beliefs that were not in line with my integrity. Therefore, I couldn't be honest in the relationship and it wasn't serving anyone. It felt like I was being used as a support to what I couldn't support. I was about to speak up when the relationship blew up. I hadn't set healthy boundaries.

I took inventory again of what parts of me allowed the relationship to continue down the path it was going. I now had a Sword of Truth pendant that I purchased - a Viking iron sword, forged in the fire - as a reminder of my inner Sword. As it hung around my neck, it didn't take long to get clear what parts of me didn't resonate with my guidance system.

False Humility Krista, Politically Correct Krista, Emotionally Dishonest Krista all would bump up against my Sword and I could always feel how it wasn't the truth. My suffering woke me up. They all died a swift death. Now to keep them in the ground.

I was coaching a client the other day in The Infinity Loop work. It was in the context of speaking up in her workplace that's full of toxic chauvinism. She was wrestling with when to speak up, what to ignore, and how to stop playing into being the scapegoat. She struggled with feeling bad for being bothered by the crazy-making games these two men were playing with her.

She too had False Humility and Emotionally Dishonest identities. She didn't want to appear egotistical if she said the truth in response to their scapegoating. She told one they didn't need to apologize and minimized his incompetent leadership in her Emotional Dishonest identity.

When she did speak up, it wasn't fully in her power because she had stuffed her truth and played into them. Now she looked like the difficult one. The U-Turn for situations like this is to let people know what type of communication works for us. It becomes the perfect excuse to invite a sit-down and explore what happened and how we can learn. It brings things into the light. I gave her some ideas about what she could say. This is after she steps into The Infinity Loop in connection to herself and her desire to connect, her awareness, and bringing awareness to the situation, and using inquiry to improve communication. It promotes accountability without shaming.

We own our power to lead, no matter what the organizational chart says. Others don't have to recognize we're leading. They may never realize we're leading. We normalize everyone being willing to face how they contributed to what's broken, and we don't protect anyone. We're not into CYA (**C**overing **Y**our **A**ss) culture but we won't be silent in untruth and scapegoating.

An Alpha Woman doesn't get back at anybody. By her modeling when she's in error, it becomes an invitation for others to do the same. Humility, honesty, and curiosity become contagious. When we use the power of connection, we bring the other into an awareness that they don't have to protect their egos and positions. Inquiry - we don't know all the data and their process – is modeled. It's a model for all to learn.

When we don't speak up, we play the victim, get to be the judge, the slanderer, and don't have to face how we might have contributed. We don't have to face how we're promoting bad behavior by permitting it. I know how it takes practice and confidence to stand up to power and the unconscious, condescending bullshit we women face. But we keep strengthening the muscles needed to do this. Our tribe helps us along as well. That's why I'll have an online, interactive support group/course and seminars so we can all get masterful at this.

My client was frustrated with herself that she fell into old patterns of relating. I reminded her not to beat herself up but to have self-compassion. We observe ourselves falling into the old pattern and just become aware we did it. Next time we catch ourselves doing it before the end of the interaction. Then in the middle, and then as soon as we begin. One day soon we'll pause, breathe, and drop into connection to our hearts, our guts and the rest of our bodies. Our minds will be clear and calm. We'll be aware before the interaction even begins.

The only way to change behavior is through awareness. We get into our higher brain where change can happen. Once we're aware, we're able to make other choices. Once we do it over and over, it becomes our new way. Just being aware of our lack of awareness puts us into Witness Consciousness (The Watcher). Similar to meditation, once we're aware we're thinking, we're not thinking.

Awareness is a kind of walking meditation. We are the Watcher and the Watcher is aware.

The more we're honest with ourselves because we don't need to see ourselves as humble, cooperative, a team player, unaffected by others, etc., we know ourselves more and operate from that integrity – our internal "No" or "Yes." That integration is needed to be a powerful force for change.

SUPPORTIVE KRISTA DIED TONIGHT
REFLECTION

Was there anything that you read that made you think you may also have a Supportive, False Humility, Politically Correct, Emotionally Dishonest, or other that could use death by the Sword of Truth?

How do those ego constructs make you blind to your behavior (have your shadow run the show)?

In what relationships or situations do those ego needs to see yourself a certain way come out?

What needs to be done to change your way of being to be more in truth and purity and not trying to control?

In what ways do you see these ego constructs as different from who we really are in our honesty and fearless living out loud?

63

Learning to Come from Our 8

*"When we love truth and reality, we embrace
them with a reverence that grounds us deep in
our bellies and hearts. We register truth - and
in that moment - we see differently. We are
present and that grounding makes us wise."*
- KRISTA VORSE

Spring, 2017 I had a powerful dream full of symbolic meaning and a big 'ol tarantula. There are a few significant meanings I've been given as to the message of my hairy spider. One came from someone who was in a dream class. She got excited to look up the meaning and announced, "I think the spider is your totem!"

She then read me the following. We can all learn from the spider totem.

"A spider totem teaches you balance - between past and future, physical and spirit, male and female. She is strength and gentleness combined. She awakens creative sensibilities and reminds you that the past is always interwoven with the future. Tarantulas (and all spiders) are the keepers of the primordial alphabet and can teach you how to write creatively. Her body is shaped like the number **8** and she has **8** legs, which is the symbol of infinite possibilities of creation. Her **8** legs represent the 4 winds of change and the 4 directions of the medicine wheel. Spider's message is that you are an infinite being who will continue to weave patterns of life throughout time. Do not fail to see the eternal plan of creation. Those who weave magic with the written word usually have this totem."

Since the spider has **8** eyes - some they see out of, some they sense with - they have quite a perspective. If we crawled onto the ceiling and looked down on our lives, in the perspective of all of humanity, we would not feel so constricted about our lives. We tap into our hearts and guts from a spacious place, love ourselves, honor our journeys while holding the bigger picture of all that we humans have lost and suffered; it puts things in perspective. As still as a spider, we watch all that transpires down below. Then like the spider, we have Expanded Awareness.

I teach people how to live from their heart and their lower belly (gut). If we put one hand on our heart space and the other on our lower belly, we have each hand in the loops of The Infinity Loop turned on its side; it's the two loops of the number **8**. The spider's symbol of the **8** is for all of us. We weave our words that come from those places within us. I teach language that's woven in connection, awareness, and inquiry; our approach matters. We live in strength and gentleness as we allow ourselves to feel our hearts fully, live from our heart-centered intelligence, and connect with our deepest truth in our lower bellies. Our authentic voice arises from there.

In my late 20s, I had the privilege to work with a voice coach for actors in L.A. She taught us how emotions arise from the breath and we feel it in our bellies. We wait for it to arise and speak from there. I've taught this to hundreds of people in my work to stay connected to their hearts, their empathy, the other, and to ground them. Our true voice resonates with an authority and a power that cannot be denied. It's a type of mindfulness practice because of the present moment awareness and calming of the connection to our breath.

Hippocrates, the father of modern medicine, knew that the gut was central to our health. Now we're getting it. The gut is really, really central. It communicates to the rest of our body.

We know our hearts have an intelligence as well. If we stay connected to our hearts and our guts, let them center us, let the deepest ground of our being come from there, we do well. If we feel our hearts and let the truth emerge from our bellies, we are in connection, awareness, and inquiry, because it will lead us naturally toward inquiry and what we don't already know. And that leads to wisdom. We don't have to feel self-conscious because it's replaced with consciousness. It's fierce because truth and love are fierce. It moves us where we need to go in an elegant and intelligent way.

When we come from our **8,** we're in touch with our guidance system and we weave our lives creatively with our destiny. We weave our lives in love and connection in The Infinity Loop of all that's possible.

Learning to Come from Our 8
Reflection

What practice will you implement that would allow you to live from your **8**?

What's stopping you from doing it more now?

In what ways do you believe coming from our **8** allows us to weave in our strength and gentleness, the magic of infinite possibilities, and tap into a realm bigger than who we are?

In what ways does coming from our **8** connect us with Infinity? How can you remind yourself to crawl onto the ceiling and see your life from the bigger perspective?

64

It's Passing Through

"All great spirituality is about what we do with our pain."
- RICHARD ROHR

April 2017 was the first time I got this image; the front of me appeared normal, but the back of me was completely open and one with the lush, dense green forest that was all around me. It would be a place you would imagine fairies live. My feeling was it was my letting go of my identification of me, the solidness of holding all that has transpired in this body of mine. I felt the letting go, the seeing of life all around me that I was one with. But it's eerie to see yourself with no backside.

Then as I lay in the bathtub in a hotel in Portland last night (May 2017), it triggered a memory. Nearly the entire time I was in Portland, memories were shuffling through my mind; I was having recollections I hadn't previously let settle in me because they were surrounded by trauma with my Necessary Nemesis. I was able to experience them as a witness, and not as something that had the power to name me or diminish me in any way; I was just the observer. The tub memory - something that happened in a tub which was associated with the other memories that had taken over my brain the previous 36 hours - came with more intensity. It was a startling awareness about an incident that was distressing from this vantage point; I wasn't able to see clearly when I was up close and personal with it at the time of its occurrence.

With my disheartening and sickening awareness, deep, physical pain hit my breast bone. It's a specific pain I've only experienced when I was in the cult over 30 years ago, and in a few other situations in certain relationships. It's been diagnosed as anxiety or PTSD but I don't believe that's the whole picture. It may be tied to trauma but I think it's tied to my guidance system. More specifically, I suspect it's tied to where my new Sword of Truth is in my chest. Our inner authority, our guidance system, will do a lot to help us wake up. In all those situations, someone else was violating the sovereign place which belongs only to me. And I was letting them. But I'm willing to die for that truth; splitting from that truth is no life at all. This sensation also may be about feeling my pain and being in solidarity with those who've suffered in this way. It's the sober awareness of the suffering of the whole world. I'm not sure and don't know if I'll ever understand it fully in this life.

Our bodies speak to us, alert us when we're not where we need to be, believing some thoughts that aren't ultimately true, or discerning something; they're trying to get our attention. I'm not yet clear what this pain is about, but it was making me present to what hurts my heart, and well it should. As I lay in the tub, it was as though I was experiencing being in a cross between a Pixar film and a Salvador Dali painting.

My chest hurt so badly like I just woke up from surgery in which my chest cavity was cut open and it's time for another pump of morphine. In that place of pain was a four-inch-wide hole. Again, I had no backside to me and I was again in this forest, but you could also see right through me in this four-inch hole. My front side was more like an inch thin mannequin form, so my sides were non-existent as well. All I could do was breathe deeply and intentionally to let this pain move, and it was moving through the large hole in my chest. I cried, but not for myself and what I went through in the bathtub memory, but out of love and healing for all involved. I witnessed the cast of characters associated with the person involved in my memories, moving through my chest, as I was wishing for their highest and best and healing in their hearts and lives. I had to keep breathing.

I may be dissolving into this love that is rich in life and magic. At least I hope that's what's happening. I want to do what is mine to do, and if that means it's less of me and my identified self, so love and healing flow through me, I'll take it.

I had just listened to Glennon Doyle speak about how our pain is our power, and we need to not run from our pain but be present to it. I think she inspired the vision. My pain, feeling my heart, and my desire to let what hurts transform into healing for others, may be what's happening.

For so many years, what has occurred within the walls of my form, created a way of my being in the world that didn't always allow the flow of life and magic that brought healing. But my deepest yearning of my soul has been to be love and light in the world. My ego's yearning to be separate, superior, and important got in the way, trying desperately to not dissolve into nothing. It's a tough road to hoe when you're trying to get healed after abuse; it gets confusing as to how to dissolve into love when you already feel dissolved by the abuse. I'm finally figuring out how to be sturdy, yet dissolve into love and light.

I don't want to medicate my pain and be told it shouldn't be there. Actually, it should. It's mine and it's beautiful. And Glennon says it's my power.

Today, may my pain be transformed into my power to be a healing conduit, where life and love travel freely through, even if I'm dissolving and I have a hole in my chest that would only be indicative of someone who has died.

I think my vision is showing me that death (to my false self) is surrounded by life and power, to create, heal and transform. I think I'm being wooed to "die before I die," as they say. It's dying to my attachment to my ego-defined-self so I'll operate more from the True Self. I don't think I'm done with this snatched-body-parts-morphing into-less-of-me-vision, and lush green life flowing through me. My intention is to live my life now courageously showing up for what is mine to do, nothing more and nothing less. I think I need to keep dissolving and feeling my pain, letting what needs to flow through it, to be able to do that work.

How would we experience life if we experienced our forms dissolving in this forest where things transform, that's all around us and is one with us? What if our deep pain ripped our hearts open and all those involved could flow in and out in this mysterious realm where healing happens? What if we got out of the way and set an intention to let events transpire that will bring the highest and best for all? I wonder if that's how we'll feel when we die. I don't think death will be a bad thing.

It's Passing Through
Reflection

In what ways does this image of dissolving into love, allowing others to flow through us, with us out of the way, help you surrender to what you can't control, convince, vindicate (seek justice) or make sense of?

In what ways does this land full of fairies and magic woo you to let yourself be dissolved, dis-identified with your persona, and just breathe through the pain, aware a power and mystery greater than yourself is at play?

In what areas of your life would this image serve you as an awareness of surrendering to a death that brings life? What is more alive than a lush, green forest with fairies?

65

The Whole World Lives Inside Us

"I believe this is the fruit of forgiving life,
ourselves, those who have offended us, and God.
We have surrendered to Mystery. It's a good
death. We resurrect into who we truly are."
- Krista Vorse

In *It's Passing Through* I write that I didn't think I was done with my snatched-body-parts-morphing-into-less-of-me-vision. I was correct.

While at a group meditation where I was supposed to focus on something else, I felt led down another path. A vision of the main character (my Necessary Nemesis) that was the catalyst for the four-inch hole in my chest that I refer to in *It's Passing Through*, came into my awareness. The situation I envisioned in regards to this person was "large enough" and had three other people in the image, that I had no choice but be ripped open wide from side to side of my torso and down to my hip crease; I needed that much space for them to pass through.

My spiritual intention is to let others pass through me now and to not let them get caught on me. And for me to not get caught by them. My intention is to remove myself from the story, the outcome, the control, to let Love have Her way - beyond anything I will ever know to be right. I have neither the power nor the wisdom. And so, I surrender.

By letting this person and his way of being in the world that I experienced as extremely painful, pass through me, I was cracked open so wide that it made less of me. In that hole now was one big beautiful yellow ball with a cream glow around it. It was Love and it was the whole world.

In the Transformational Path of dealing with trauma, we're always given gifts. Everything becomes an invitation to do our work, to welcome the Great Love Affair with ourselves, and to allow what threatened to annihilate us, grace us with the capacity to dissolve into Love. This comes after the lessons, the work, the availing of ourselves as we wrestle with the angel and come out changed.

What came to me was, my Necessary Nemesis - who I was seeing in the vision - desperately grasped at addictive strategies to get the love that he felt disconnected from, to live inside of him. When we aren't aware the whole world lives inside of us, we hunger for someone to give us that love; we don't know how to find what lives inside of us.

"The kingdom of God is within you." We don't need the word "God" - or to particularly care for the language - to sense the truth of what that statement is referring to; that kingdom is everything our soul, spirit, and heart wants. That statement needs more press. It's so radical and mysterious, we can't really handle it. It must be false advertising. No matter how you react to the name of Jesus, he said some very cool things. "You must become as a little child to enter the kingdom of God." To enter that realm that is so wildly free, we must be as open as little children.

I've been called a lot of things in my 52 years of mighty flaws. My childlike nature has even been framed to be an undesirable trait. But not to me. Perhaps it's why I see many visions and the veil between the worlds is thin for me; someone who's childlike knows the world is an enchanted place and so they go for the ride that's waiting for them.

In one of the last phone conversations with my aunt, before she died, she shared her compassion for me. "Krista, you've had a very hard life." That's true, but the great mystery is, that hard life has given me a wonderful life. In my desire to end my suffering, I discovered on the Transformational Path that I had a lot more power to think, believe and experience life differently than I thought I did. That power has come to me through the paradoxical way of becoming as a little child.

Even with our pain that rips our insides wide open, we're being prepared for the great reveal; we see that in that place is Love that is there waiting for us to greet.

A message came to me when I realized the hole was aglow and filled up with my favorite color and that it was the whole world: *No matter what happens to you in this life, because you have this Love inside of you, you will always be rich. And it can never be taken from you.* When we realize we have that, it all becomes a wonderful life.

To have the whole world inside of us is also having those that are no longer with us inside of us; it's a way of being with them that is beyond the physical. My aunt who acknowledged my suffering is with me now in a way that defies explanation. And so, I don't.

At age 30 I got what my life purpose was: *To encourage others to embrace Life and to become as a little child that they may enter the kingdom of God.* That was the language I resonated with at the time and is as meaningful to me today. I think to become as a little child is also about not being attached to our thoughts and stories. Our minds that get so addicted to our suffering keep us from entrance.

Whatever it takes to woo us on this Transformational Path to keep going until we get free from what gets stuck in us, and free from what makes our heads spin in the wiring that creates our suffering, is worth it. We have the whole world waiting for us.

The Whole World Lives Inside Us
Reflection

In what ways will you embrace life and become as a little child that you may enter the kingdom of God? In what ways does childlike trust help you to embrace the mystery that we are filled up with the whole world and filled with Love?

How will you use your imagination in your childlike nature, to look down and see your chest to your hip crease is aglow with Love for yourself and the whole world?

How will you bring to your awareness the whole world lives inside of you?

In what ways do you see scarcity is an illusion and that we are never alone when we are connected to that Love? How will you support that connection for yourself?

Part 2: Building the Container
(Connection, Awareness, Inquiry)

66

Remember the Aspen

*"I don't need that thought to feel
separate, superior or important."*
- RICHARD ROHR

The Aspen is believed to be the largest living organism on our planet. Because the roots of the Aspen tree are all connected, a forest of Aspen is one big organism!

When we're not aware of our oneness in this moment, we feel separate and so on edge with our frustration. We're only aware of all the ways we're not *them*. This keeps us in the first glance as Rohr teaches, that's always: competing, comparing, criticizing, conspiring, condemning.

But when we look again, The Second Look (Re-spect), we see our magnificent friends in a new way. When we remember that underneath it all, we're all one, we tap into a power so much larger than ourselves, and an awareness and intelligence that opens the field to a spectacular landscape full of possibilities.

Lots of people don't believe we're one underneath it all, but if we dig deeper, we cannot deny the fact.

"Even though I'm not you, I'm not other than you either."

That's how James Finley likes to describe it.

It's a mystery that can only be experienced when we decide to consider it may be true.

I had the great fortune to live amidst these trees when I lived in the town named after them during some pivotal years of my childhood. Even though my home life was always quaking, there was a strength I felt being near these trees.

Maybe it's because they're a glorious metaphor for we humans - a reminder we can't get enough of. In our frailty, we may feel like Quaking Aspens, but deep down we're grounded in life that's so much bigger than we realize. That life is in our connection to everyone and everything. And that makes us powerful indeed.

When you look out at the world, look again and see if you don't feel a strength through connection to others and a safety in knowing we are one. Remember the Aspen.

REMEMBER THE ASPEN
<u>REFLECTION</u>

"Even though I'm not you, I'm not other than you either."
JAMES FINLEY

How does the metaphor of the Aspen help you be aware of connection to every other being, underneath it all? How does that awareness help you step into The Infinity Loop?

How is remembering the Aspen different than your feeling of being separate, superior, and important? How do the two energies feel different in your heart, body, and mind?

Even though you may be the Quaking Aspen, when you become aware that you're connected to others and the power of Thinking Together, you draw on a strength and collective intelligence that you may not be aware of now. Write about that.

67

Sawubona to Enhance Connection

*"When you look at someone with so much love and
compassion, when you create a safe container to hold
their good, their bad and their ugly, they move more
into The Good, The True and The Beautiful."*
- KRISTA VORSE

Transformed people transform people. Loving well is the most powerful force for growth, healing, and transformation. May we mirror with unconditional love.

Sawubona is a Zulu (South African greeting) used with far more depth and connection than our western "hello" that we often mindlessly greet one another.

Sawubona means "I see you." I see your humanity, your dignity, your respect. I make a place for you in this world.

Shikona is a reply that is used, meaning, "I am here." I am more fully here because you see me.

When we give great Sawubona, we're present and connected with the other in front of us. I teach this in every company I've consulted with. It's always a powerful tool to help us step into more presence, awareness, connection, and energy. It changes people, cultures, and customers.

We need to give great Sawubona to really step into The Infinity Loop.

Some thoughts that are present in Sawubona that lead to the depth of the greeting are:

* Why are we here at the same time?
* What is this moment in time giving us?
* (Giving to the other) What's needed for this moment in life to be enhanced?
* How do I have to be in order for you to be free? You tell me and I will explore that possibility.
* It's a type of agreement we need in order to exercise freedom.
* We can't do it out of self-interest.
* Freedom must be a mutual gift from one human being to another.
* If I limit one person's freedom I limit my own.
* Freedom to be present with another.

If we meditate on these in regards to specific relationships, we may see how to be more present, open-hearted and aware. They're not easy thoughts to digest but Sawubona is a slowing down by nature to actually see someone that allows them to feel seen. When we slow down, we bring to mind some of these inherent intentions into the interaction.

We build connection, empathy, and community by first seeing people. When we see someone truly, we realize we are connected. We see their beauty, their humanity, their divinity. We might just fall in love with everyone we meet.

Giving Sawubona is what releases our powerful neurochemicals to flood our system. When we're connected and aware, we experience that abundance in the present moment. By being present, we lack nothing.

What if we gave great Sawubona to every person we encountered? Not only would we all have happy mirror neurons, but we might just change the world.

Sawubona to Enhance Connection
Reflection

How is Sawubona different than how you're interacting now? How is the slowing down needed for this kind of seeing and awareness of connection?

What will you do differently to give Sawubona?

Which of the nine bullet points on Sawubona stuck out to you? How are they inherent in that kind of presence with another that is beyond a greeting?

How does Sawubona imply we are here for the "we"? How does Sawubona imply we connect and cannot be out of self-interest?

68

The Second Look

"Not taking The Second Look is just our egos
wanting to feel big because we're under the illusion
we're nothing more than our egos. Our True
Selves can take The Second Look all day long."
- KRISTA VORSE

Re-Spect (Re-Look) - The Second Look

The first look is almost always: Critical/Judgmental: compete, compare, conflict, conspire, canceling out all contrary data, finally, condemn.

It results in the initial reaction almost always being a "No." It's stuck in "either/or" model; it's more aware of the boundaries, being separate, superior, important, feeling threatened, defending, holding its ground.

Your world keeps getting smaller. You feel constricted. When you start with "No," you hardly ever get back to "Yes."

We're thinking separately. Not open to being influenced. We're stuck in our own small (negative) story. Work is stressful, emotionally draining, and not fun.

It's knee-jerk, hidden, protecting, suspicious. It's not bad, it just doesn't go far enough.

The Second Look is open, makes space for the other's point of view, open to being influenced, listening, asking questions, suspending judgment. Starts with a "Yes" – (even though "No" may come later as the appropriate response, it comes from a place of awareness and balanced reflection). It's transparent, open and trusting.

Your world gets bigger. More options. Effective solutions come intuitively and more easily. Everyone's talent and contributions are recognized. We expand our capacity to learn. Problems stay solved. We're Thinking Together. We get more done. Work is less drama, more energizing, productive, and more fun!

Be Curious – Inquire the other's Point of View – Be open

1. "What leads you to that conclusion?" "What data can you bring to illustrate that?"
   "What causes you to say that?" "Can you help me understand your thinking?"
2. Explain your reasons for inquiring: "I'm asking you about your assumptions because…"
3. "How did you arrive at this view?" "Are you looking at data I haven't seen?"
   "Have you considered… (other ways of seeing)?"

Question the story I'm telling myself about this person/situation.

1. Is the story I'm telling myself (my assumptions) true? What am I missing?
2. How does my version of the story make me feel? How is my story making me feel separate, superior/inferior, or better/worse about myself? Stressed out? Disturbed? Angry? Negative?
3. What are some other possible stories that would point to contrary data?
4. Would everyone else see it the same way?
5. What would my life be like without this story?

THE SECOND LOOK
REFLECTION

What stuck out to you as the biggest game-changer when you take The Second Look?

What changes do you want to make in your interactions based on The Second Look and all it incorporates?

How can you experience your disturbances which may be valid and wise to register, and take The Second Look that puts you in the bigger mind that can hold it all, gives greater awareness, not separate from respect and honoring one's humanity?

69

Look What Love Has Done

*"When we heed our hearts that want to be free as a
released balloon, our souls sing in the wind forevermore."*
- KRISTA VORSE

I saw your picture today on the internet,
your life, your love, your children.
My heart burst inside me,
with so much love for you.
Your joy is my joy, your children are mine.
We are one and I am free!
We said things that hurt. It wasn't the truth.
Judgments don't have the power to name us,
only Love names us.
But we had forgotten,
and so the space between us.
But when I love you, there is no space.
We are together, connected, free.
I can only say I wanted this more than anything,
to love those who no longer love me.
I got what I wanted.
All the love I feel for you is enough.
Look what Love has done!

I wrote this a few years ago when I realized it had happened to
me; what once brought me pain because of the hurt, was now only
complete joy for the other. There was no awareness that their children weren't mine. They couldn't hurt me because the awareness

of separation was gone - from those I thought caused me the greatest pain. I was wrong. It was me that was doing it to myself because I didn't know we were one. I got so sick of myself and my suffering, freedom from myself became my greatest longing.

When we become free, we no longer believe the lies and we don't fight against the lies that were said against us. Even if they're true, they aren't the Truth, and they don't have the power to name us. Our desire to love becomes our focus.

Look What Love Has Done
Reflection

Love heals our hearts and frees us from the pain that the illusion of separation brings. Have you had an experience like this one or do you long for it with certain relationships?

What needs to happen in you to open yourself up to more of this in your heart?

In what ways is loving others, them not loving us, all we ever need to be free and happy?

In what ways does being Love put us in The Infinity Loop of connection to our greatest source?

We become aware of our connection, and that we don't need thoughts that make us feel separate, superior/inferior, or important. Love comes in and sets us free from our illusion of separateness that creates suffering.

70

If I Look Away

"In Louisville, at the corner of Fourth and Walnut,
in the center of the shopping district, I was suddenly
overwhelmed with the realization that I loved all these
people, that they were mine and I theirs, that we could
not be alien to one another even though we were total
strangers.... There is no way of telling people that
they are all walking around shining like the sun....
It was like waking from a dream of separateness,
of spurious self-isolation in a special world..."
- THOMAS MERTON

If I look away from you,
it's not because I'm dismissing you.
It's because you're so beautiful,
you're shining like the sun;
your light is so glorious,
I'm completely undone.
If I look away from you,
It's not because I find you uninteresting.
It's because I can't contain myself;
I'll lose my composure,
appear as a lunatic,
The lunatic I am,
for Love of course!
For the glorious Love we all are.

When we get used to the contemplative view that takes The Second Look, what we see is a beauty in others that will make our worlds enchanted. My suffering from my sense of separateness drew my heart to the deepest longing to end my judgments of others and see them beyond the first, critical, separate look. When we want to be free from ourselves badly enough, we open the door for grace to come in. Infinite Possibilities await.

IF I LOOK AWAY
REFLECTION

Write about your experience or your longing for an experience where you saw beyond the physical realm to someone's beauty that is blinding? What do you think we're seeing when we see that?

How does the poem serve as a reminder of how when we see others through such Love, we see the Love that created them, sustains them, and is the truth of who they are under it all?

How do we see the beauty that is blinding in others more often?

How does this change us as we step into The Infinity Loop?

71

Awareness

"In Pure Awareness, you are outside of time at
the speed of light, time ceases to exist and you are
everywhere. You can travel through time spiritually."
- MARTHA BECK

Deepak Chopra teaches three levels of awareness. I'll touch on one aspect of it that will serve what we need for awareness. I've taken what he teaches and blended it with others' language and my own.

Constricted Awareness is what happens when our bodies, hearts, and minds constrict because of how we perceive our world in the moment. We feel separate and negative emotions flood us. Deepak says it's like walking into a room with the lights out; because we're not aware and our sight is limited, we bump into the furniture.

When we're able to witness ourselves as the Watcher, our whole bodies, hearts, and minds open up with a spaciousness that sees the bigger view. We see we have options, we breathe deeply and have access to our brains. This, he explains as Expanded Awareness. We walk into the room with the lights on. We don't trip over the furniture. We're more aware of where we are, how we are, and what's around us.

In Pure Awareness, it's like walking into a room and we're able to see all the way through the back wall because we realize the walls are made of glass and we see for miles. That's when we're The Watcher of The Watcher and most aware of ourselves and see reality for what it is. It's a consciousness or what's called Pure Consciousness.

I want to live in that house where the walls are made of glass and I see the beauty of the hills and the valleys with a perspective that makes me calm, clear and compassionate, with full access to what I'm experiencing in my body and brain. If I'm not distracted by my own Constricted Awareness, I show up more for the others in the room.

By becoming aware of the constriction in my body, I take a deep breath and choose to expand my heart and body and observe myself. Now I'm not trapped in that state but include anything I need to pay attention to as I move to the Watcher of my experience in Expanded Awareness.

It's like being on the side of the river in your lounge chair drinking your favorite drink. You watch drama and stress float down the river while you sip your drink. The cool breeze blows over you in the shade as you discern what can float on by and what you need to pay attention to.

In awareness, we learn the art of paying attention to what's worthy of our attention; the disturbance may be there for a reason or it may just need to float on by. We don't have to be disturbed by our disturbance. When we're the Watcher of the Watcher, we sense, discern and love from our greatest capacity. We're in our Alpha brain state as Alpha Women. We're in The Infinity Loop, creating awareness for the other. Infinite possibilities then become available to us.

In Constricted Awareness, our constricted feelings come from our sense of problems and separation. The flow of information and energy in our bodies is hampered. We're stuck in habits and negative emotions that don't send us the messages that serve us. They might be true, but not the spiritual truth of what's true on the deepest level. By honestly acknowledging them and observing them, we can move to Expanded Awareness where energy flows freely. We see the world with more compassion and understanding. We see new possibilities.

Pure Awareness is what happens when we walk through the veil into another realm. We know all is well on the deepest level. We have a perspective that grounds us so deeply, we flow in the Divine emotions of love, kindness, joy, compassion, and equanimity.

If we're constricted, we move out of that state as we learn to observe our state in stillness. We ultimately move toward Essence – Pure Awareness. By owning our feelings, that they belong to us, we allow them to tell us what they want to say or what story's behind them. Compassionately, we realize we no longer need those anymore as we're no longer a threatened child. We're so much bigger than we thought we were.

AWARENESS
REFLECTION

We move out of Constricted Awareness as quickly as possible, by first being aware we're constricted, breathe, witness ourselves, have self-compassion, and unhook from the story that keeps us trapped. Describe what it feels like to you to be in Constricted Awareness. What will you do differently?

What's your experience with Expanded Awareness? How does it feel?

What is your experience or understanding with Pure Awareness where you've moved to a consciousness that is beyond you as The Watcher of The Watcher, watching you?

72

Self-Inquiry that Leads to More Awareness

*"You're either attaching to your thoughts or
inquiring. There's no other choice."*
- Byron Katie

Leo came up with these questions. We're always looking to simplify and make the principles as accessible as possible. On a company leadership retreat, Leo discovered that these questions got the team aware. It allowed them to be the Watcher. Inquiry leads to more awareness.

- What am I thinking?
- What am I feeling?
- What's happening?
- What stories am I telling myself about what's happening?
- Are they true?
- Can I know for sure they are true?
- How are my stories making me feel?
- What are my projections?
- What other explanations are there for what's happening?
- How can I test my assumptions?
- How can I make space for the other?
- What am I not seeing?
- How can I be more curious and shift from judging questions to learning questions?
- How can I improve connection/communication/collaboration?

* How can I contribute to getting more of the intended results everybody wants?
* What do I need from my superiors/co-workers to be successful?
* What's possible?

Self-Inquiry that Leads to More Awareness
Reflection

What questions got your most attention?

In what situations would you incorporate them?

How would this self-inquiry change the interaction?

How will you set yourself up for successful awareness by slowing down, connecting to yourself, and going to silence and self-inquiry before reacting?

73

Creating a Learning Container

*"When your heart is in the People Development
Business, you see everyone through eyes of
compassion. You look for ways to influence
their growth and not be a hindrance."*
- KRISTA VORSE

We know what it's like to be on the receiving end of someone's concern, so-called "inquiry" and advice. We've done it to others. Sometimes it's helpful, but not always. And when it's not, it rips off the thin gauze that was over the raw skin and soul. It suddenly crushes someone's tender heart when they thought they had a welcome respite from grief and trauma. The "helpers" are then shocked and offended that their concern is met with healthy self-protection. Just because we care deeply about someone, doesn't mean we always give them what's most needed.

Because of our concern for another, we can get in Constricted Awareness and not see how reactive, unhelpful and unsupportive we are. We call it a lot of things that sound responsible, but it's our unconsciousness when we project our own fears and assumptions. We haven't dropped into The Infinity Loop that makes us present beyond how we share our opinions and brilliant advice. We don't know how Mystery works in this person's life. We're not connected, aware, or in true inquiry. We're out of The Loop.

I'm a big believer in our sovereignty over ourselves. Coach and author Martha Beck sets the stage for this when she tells those she coaches, "My job is to tell you what I hear and it's your job to tell me where I'm wrong." What a generous way to empower others.

She believes only we know what we experience. Her work helps others find their own North Star.

Being someone who's endured cultic control more times than I'd like to admit, I feel a big "No" rise up when someone crosses that boundary. When I didn't know what to do with the anger, I stayed in the environment of that advice-giving too long and paid a high emotional price. Sometimes the correction comes under the guise of our need to be more open, undefended and spiritual. But we can't always chew the meat and spit out the bones. And those who love us most sometimes can't understand that. Maybe we're not completely healed, maybe we've recently been through serious trauma, and maybe we need to be supported in a way that sets boundaries around what's helpful and what isn't. Just because we're in crisis doesn't mean others get to peek under the gauze to gauge our progress. To have Accountability Partners that look out for us isn't the same as others telling us how to run our lives.

True inquiry – not interrogation, not masked judgments and certitude with a question mark at the end of the sentence – is how we ask questions so both the one who supports and the one who needs support sees what's possible. There's often a flippant judgment to what the one who struggles says feels right to them. If we don't drop into the other's field, we share our wisdom in a type of arrogance. Since arrogance means, "I ask no questions," then we've all been arrogant toward those we care deeply for.

To create a Learning Container for everyone, ask for feedback.
"How are you experiencing what I'm saying?"
"What do you need right now?"
"What would be most supportive for you?"
"Tell me more about your thought process."
To share our beliefs about what makes for a high functioning life to someone in crisis, may make them lower functioning. No one needs "parental" support unless they're young. Ultimately our support of one another leads to the one in need finding the deep

well within themselves that cannot be shaken, no matter what anyone says. And sometimes it's the very shaking that others do to us in their unawareness that causes our fire to rise up to find that center.

After the drop, the destabilization, the self-doubt, we will bounce. If we sit with the fire (that something needs protecting), but not spew it or turn it against ourselves, that fire will gird us up again and confirm our deepest truths. If we keep practicing inquiry, we'll find where we're off.

A Learning Container is respectful. The Second Look sees past what looks like a basket case to someone whose North Star wants to shine. Let them.

CREATING A LEARNING CONTAINER
REFLECTION

Describe a time you've been on the receiving end of this unhelpful help.

Describe a time you've done that unhelpful help to another.

What is your experience with creating a Learning Container this way?

What will you do differently?

74

Inquiry

"We're not our point of view; we're talking about ideas, not our identity. In humility, curiosity, and honesty we move from Debate to Inquiry. When we connect from there, we Think Together!"
- Krista Vorse

True inquiry is rare. And once you teach it to someone, it's difficult to make it stick because of our culture of "Command and Control" and telling others what to do. We think managing is being bossy. We're supposed to manage programs and processes but coach and lead people. We fall into "Selling is Telling" which is advocating our point of view. Inquiry in The Infinity Loop that's based on connection and awareness is utterly transformational and radical. It's radically rare but its time is overdue.

Read through these lists and take note as to what you will begin to incorporate into your life. It will change your world.

Language to Improve Dialogue

Improving Advocacy

- Here's what I think and here's how I got there.
- I assumed that…
- I came to this conclusion because…
- What do you think about what I just said?
- Do you see any flaws in my reasoning?
- What can you add?

* Here's one aspect you might help me think through...
* Do you see it differently?

Improving Inquiry

* What leads you to that conclusion? What data can you bring to illustrate that?
* What causes you to say that?
* Instead of the aggressive "What do you mean?" or "What's your proof?", try:
  o Can you help me understand your thinking?
  o Can you walk me through the process that got you to think (believe) that?
* Explain your reasons for inquiring: "I'm asking you about your assumptions because..."
* Check your understanding by asking "Am I correct that you're saying...?"

Dealing with an Opposing Point of View

* How did you arrive at this view?
* Are you looking at data I haven't seen?
* Have you considered...?
* When you say _____, I'm worried that it means _____. (Be honest)
* I have a hard time seeing that because of this reasoning...

Dealing with an Impasse

* What do we know for a fact?
* What do we sense is true but have no data for yet?
* What don't we know?
* What is unknowable?

- What do we agree on? What do we disagree on?
- Are we starting with two different sets of assumptions?
- What would have to happen to have one of us consider the alternative?
- It feels like we're getting into an impasse and I'm afraid we might walk away without any better understanding. Have you got any ideas that will help us clarify our thinking?
- I don't understand the assumptions underlying our disagreement.

Opening Lines
When views are expressed without reasoning or illustrations:
"You may be right, but I'd like to understand more..."

When the discussion goes off on a tangent:
"I'm unclear how that connects with what we've been saying. Can you say how you see it as relevant?"

When you doubt the relevance of your own thoughts.
"This may not be relevant now. If so, let me know and I'll wait."

Two members pursue a topic at length while others observe.
"I'd like to give my reaction to what you two have said so far, and then see what you and others think."

Several views are advocated at once.
""We now have three ideas on the table (say what they are) I suggest we address them one at a time."

You perceive a negative reaction to others.
"When you said (give illustration) I had the impression you were feeling (the emotion). If so, I'd like to understand what upset you. Is there something I've said or done?"

You perceive a negative reaction to yourself.
"This may be more my problem than yours, but when you said (give an illustration) … I felt…Am I misunderstanding what you said or intended?"

Others appear as though they cannot be influenced.
"Is there anything I can say or do that would convince you otherwise?"

INQUIRY
REFLECTION

What did you learn most from this section?

What do you want to upgrade in terms of how you relate to others through inquiry?

How are you going to bring this tool to the forefront of your mind and your world?

In what ways do you have to incorporate all the lessons of this book to be able to do this as a reflex? What other principles in this book came to mind when reading this section?

75

Coach and Develop Through Questions

"I know that I am intelligent, because
I know that I know nothing."
- SOCRATES

This is one of the main ways by which we create a Learning Container. We're always coaching and developing each other when we live this way.

'Ex Duco', means to 'lead out', as in to lead out of ignorance which is the root of the word 'education'.

The overall purpose of Socratic questioning, is to challenge accuracy and completeness of thinking in a way that acts to move people toward their ultimate goal.

Here are the six types of questions that Socrates asked his pupils, often to their annoyance, but more often to their ultimate delight.

1. Clarifying questions
Get others to think more about what they're thinking about.
Use basic 'tell me more' questions that get them to go deeper.

* Why are you saying that?
* What exactly does this mean?
* How does this relate to what we've been talking about?
* What do we already know about this?
* Can you give me an example?

* Are you saying ... or ...?
* Can you rephrase that, please?

2. Question assumptions

Questioning assumptions makes people think about their unquestioned beliefs on which we found most of our arguments.

* What else could we assume?
* You seem to be assuming ...?
* How did you arrive at those assumptions?
* Please explain why/how ...?
* How can you verify or disprove that assumption?
* What would happen if ...?
* Do you agree or disagree with ...?

3. Question reasons and data

When people are giving reasons for their arguments, question their reasoning rather than assuming it's a given. People often use un-thought-through or weakly-understood data (i.e., anecdotal) to support arguments.

* Why is that happening?
* How do you know this?
* Show me ...?
* Can you give me an example of that?
* What do you think causes ...?
* What is the nature of this?
* Are these reasons good enough?
* Why is ... happening?
* Why? (keep asking it – you'll get to the root by asking it a few times)

* What data is there to support what you're saying?
* On what data are you basing your argument?

4. Question viewpoints and perspectives

Most arguments are given from a position. So, question the position. Show that there are other, equally valid, viewpoints.

* Another way of looking at this is ..., does this seem reasonable?
* What alternative ways of looking at this are there?
* Why it is ... necessary?
* Who benefits from this?
* What is the difference between... and...?
* Why is it better than ...?
* What are the strengths and weaknesses of...?
* How are ... and ... similar?
* What would ... say about it?
* How could you look another way at this?

5. Question implications and consequences

The arguments people give may have logical implications that can be forecast. Do they make sense? Are they desirable?

* Then what would happen?
* What are the consequences of that assumption?
* What are the implications of ...?
* How does ... affect ...?
* How does ... fit with what we learned before?
* Why is ... important?
* What is the best ...? Why?

6. Question questions

Use questions against themselves. Bounce the ball back into the other's court.

* What was the point of asking that question?
* Why do you think I asked this question?
* Am I making sense? Why not?
* What else might I ask?
* What does that mean?

COACH AND DEVELOP THROUGH QUESTIONS
<u>REFLECTIONS</u>

What's your biggest take-away from Socratic Questions? What didn't you know or use before?

How will this change the way you speak up or develop the muscle to speak up, out of curiosity and your desire to make a positive change?

What is the most humbling aspect of these questions in terms of how we're not doing them when it's the smartest and most aware thing to do?

76

The Ladder of Inference
Developed by Chris Argyris

> "Smart people don't learn…because they have
> too much invested in proving what they know
> and avoiding being seen as not knowing."
> - CHRIS ARGYRIS

The Ladder of Inference is a common mental pathway of increasing abstraction, often leading to misguided beliefs.

On the diagram on the next page, start to read from the bottom of the Ladder and go up. See how quickly our brains select data to tell a story that hinders our ability to see the truth of the situation or each other. Until we become aware that we all go up our Ladders, and need tools to get down them, we'll have a certitude about what we very well might be wrong about. We may even call it "intuition," "seeing the meta data," "reading people," but it's not a sound and disciplined way of decision-making. It's been proven how faulty that line of thinking is. Without knowing how our survival brains trip us up, we may react in anger, in offense, and lose our way; our survival was predicated on us seeing what could threaten us. Below this Ladder is the explanation of how it works.

It will rock your world. People who have embraced it, incorporate it into their company or relationship cultures, and are able to see where they're up their Ladders. They're humble and transparent and living out loud. It brings lightness, fun, and humility. We begin to feel safe to be that honest when everyone does it.

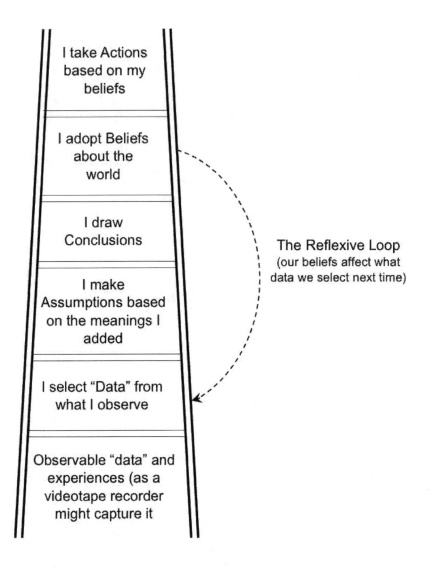

1. Observable "data" and experiences (as video might capture it)
2. I select "data" from what I observe
3. I add meaning (cultural and personal)
4. I make assumptions based on the meanings I added
5. I draw conclusions on those assumptions

6. I adopt beliefs about the world based on those conclusions
7. I take actions based on my beliefs

People jump to conclusions pretty frequently; it's human nature. The more stressed and pressured people feel, the more likely this is going to occur. If you know about The Ladder of Inference, you catch yourself before you over-react or "climb the Ladder" too quickly.

The Ladder of Inference is a model of how people process information. One of the ways we deal with the onslaught of information thrown at us daily is to selectively edit, based on our pre-established beliefs and preconceptions about a lot of things. So, what's the problem? While our beliefs may be our truth, they aren't always "The Truth." Conflict arises when two or more people of differing opinions need their truth to be recognized as "The Truth." In default mode, we don't easily separate our beliefs and opinions with our concept of who we are. As a result, we may take differences of opinion very personally, draw quick conclusions, get offended and shoot off a nasty little retort that makes for distasteful interactions. String a bunch of these interactions together, where everyone is up their Ladder, and you've got a population of chronically offended people storming around alienating one another while giving themselves heart disease. Hardly the fertile ground from which collaboration can spring.

Throughout the course of our day, we make a lot of decisions about what's good, bad, neutral, attractive, unattractive, right, wrong, etc. The new guy in Accounting is very reserved, and we know another reserved person whom we perceive to be a real jerk, so we automatically conclude that the new guy in Accounting is a jerk. Someone in a red sports car nearly runs us down at the crosswalk, so everyone who drives a red car is a self-absorbed SOB who routinely mows people down. You get the picture.

Our skill at reasoning is both essential and gets us in trouble:

1. If we thought about each inference we made, life would pass us by.
2. However, people can and do reach different conclusions. When they view their conclusions as obvious, no one sees a need to say how they reached them.
3. When people disagree, they often hurl conclusions at each other from the tops of their respective Ladders.
4. This makes it hard to resolve differences and to learn from one another.

The Ladder of Inference will help your understanding of how people think and how you interact with people. It will ensure that you are clear in your communication and verifying that people get the correct understanding of the "message." So, for those that aren't familiar with it, this is for you. (For the others, this is a reminder of this tool and the value of using it).

More about how "The Ladder" works:

We live in a world of self-generating beliefs which remain largely untested. We adopt those beliefs because they are based on conclusions, which are inferred from what we observe, plus our past experience. Our ability to achieve the results we truly desire is eroded by our feelings that:

*   Our beliefs are the truth. My truth is "The Truth."
*   The truth is obvious.
*   Our beliefs are based on real data.
*   The data we select are the real data.

For example: I'm standing before the executive team, making a presentation. They all seem engaged and alert, except for Larry, at the end of the table, who seems bored out of his mind. He turns his dark, morose eyes away from me and puts his hand to his mouth. He doesn't ask any questions until I'm almost done, when he breaks in: "I think we should ask for a full report." In this culture, that typically means, "Let's move on." Everyone starts to shuffle their papers and put their notes away. Larry obviously thinks that I'm incompetent -- which is a shame, because these ideas are exactly what his department needs. Now that I think of it, he's never liked my ideas. Clearly, Larry is a power-hungry jerk. By the time I've returned to my seat, I've made a decision: I'm not going to include anything in my report that Larry can use. He wouldn't read it, or, worse still, he'd just use it against me. It's too bad I have an enemy who's so prominent in the company.

In those few seconds before I take my seat, I have climbed up the Ladder of Inference, a common mental pathway of increasing abstraction, often leading to misguided beliefs:

* I start with the observable data: Larry's comment, which is so self-evident that it would show up on a videotape recorder.
* I select some details about Larry's behavior...his glance away from me and apparent yawn. (I didn't notice him listening intently one moment before).
* I add some meanings of my own, based on the culture around me (that Larry wanted me to finish up).
* I move rapidly up to assumptions about Larry's current state (he's bored).
* I conclude that Larry, in general, thinks I'm incompetent. In fact, I now believe that Larry (and probably everyone

whom I associate with Larry) is dangerously opposed to me.

◦ Thus, as I reach the top of the Ladder, I'm plotting against him.

It all seems so reasonable, and it happens so quickly, that I'm not even aware I've done it. Moreover, all the rungs of the Ladder take place in my head. The only parts visible to anyone else are the directly observable data at the bottom, and my own decision to take action at the top. The rest of the trip up the Ladder - where I spend most of my time - is unseen, unquestioned, not considered fit for discussion, and enormously abstract. (These leaps up the Ladder are sometimes called "leaps of abstraction.")

I've probably leaped up that Ladder of Inference many times before. The more I believe that Larry is an evil guy, the more I reinforce my tendency to notice his malevolent behavior in the future. This phenomenon is known as the "Reflexive Loop"... our beliefs influence what data we select next time. And there is a counterpart reflexive loop in Larry's mind...as he reacts to my strangely antagonistic behavior, he's probably jumping up some rungs on his own Ladder. For no apparent reason, before too long, we could find ourselves becoming bitter enemies.

Larry might indeed have been bored by my presentation -- or he might have been eager to read the report on paper. He might think I'm incompetent, he might be shy, or he might be afraid to embarrass me. More likely than not, he has inferred that I think he's incompetent. We can't know, until we find a way to check our conclusions.

Unfortunately, assumptions and conclusions are particularly difficult to test. For instance, suppose I wanted to find out if Larry really thought I was incompetent. I would have to pull him aside and ask him, "Larry, do you think I'm an idiot?" Even if I could find a way to phrase the question, how could I believe the answer? Would

I answer him honestly? No, I'd tell him I thought he was a terrific colleague, while privately thinking worse of him for asking me.

Now imagine me, Larry, and three others as a senior management team, with our untested assumptions and beliefs. When we meet to deal with a concrete problem, the air is filled with misunderstandings, communication breakdowns, and feeble compromises. Thus, while our individual IQs average 140, our team has a collective IQ of 85.

The Ladder of Inference explains why most people don't usually remember where their deepest attitudes came from. The data is long since lost to memory, after years of inferential leaps.

Sometimes I find myself arguing that "The Republicans are so-and-so," and someone asks me why I believe that. My immediate, intuitive answer is, "I don't know. But I've believed it for years." In the meantime, other people are saying, "The Democrats are so-and-so," and they can't tell you why, either. Instead, they may dredge up an old platitude which once was an assumption. Before long, we come to think of our longstanding assumptions as data ("Well, I know the Republicans are such-and-such because they're so-and-so"), but we're several steps removed from the data.

Using the Ladder of Inference

You can't live your life without adding meaning or drawing conclusions. It would be an inefficient, tedious way to live. But you can improve your communications through reflection, and by using the Ladder of Inference in three ways:

* Becoming more aware of your own thinking and reasoning (reflection)
* Making your thinking and reasoning more visible to others (advocacy)
* Inquiring into others' thinking and reasoning (inquiry)

Once Larry and I understand the concepts behind the Ladder of Inference, we have a safe way to stop a conversation in its tracks and ask several questions from the entire Inquiry section:

* What is the observable data behind that statement?
* Does everyone agree on what the data is?
* Can you run me through your reasoning?
* How did we get from that data to these abstract assumptions?
* When you said "[your inference]," did you mean "[my interpretation of it]"?

I can ask for data in an open-ended way: "Larry, what was your reaction to this presentation?" I can test my assumptions: "Larry, are you bored?" Or I can simply test the observable data: "You've been quiet, Larry." To which he might reply: "Yeah, I'm taking notes. I love this stuff."

Remember from *Clarifying The Infinity Loop*, we don't use these tools against each other. Note that I don't say, "Larry, I think you've moved way up the Ladder of Inference. Here's what you need to do to get down." The point of this method is not to nail Larry (or even to diagnose Larry), but to make our thinking processes visible, to see what the differences are in our perceptions and what we have in common. You might say, "I notice I'm moving up The Ladder of Inference, and maybe we all are. What's the data here?" Remember, you have many options from this entire section on Inquiry to choose from, to craft your questions.

This type of conversation is not easy. When a fact seems especially self-evident, be careful. If your manner suggests that it must be equally self-evident to everyone else, you may cut off the chance to test it. A fact, no matter how obvious it seems, it isn't really substantiated until it's verified independently -- by more than one person's observation, or by a technological record (a tape recording or photograph).

Embedded into team practice, the Ladder becomes a very healthy tool. There's something exhilarating about showing other people the links of your reasoning. They may or may not agree with you, but they can see how you got there. And you're often surprised yourself to see how you got there, once you trace out the links.

Take notice of when you're climbing The Ladder of Inference — drawing conclusions and making assumptions — throughout the day. When you conclude someone's a jerk, ask yourself what it is about the person that gives you this opinion. If you find yourself strongly disagreeing with someone else, ask yourself what it is about your own opinion that's so meaningful to you. If you find yourself getting tense and resisting someone else's opinion or request of you, ask yourself what it is about the situation that makes you think you have no choice.

Other good, all-purpose questions in these scenarios are, "Why do I need to be right in this case?" and, "What's the worst that can happen if I just go with the flow right now?" If it's your style, jot your observations down in a notebook.

Just taking notice and questioning ourselves about our assumptions creates some space for the possibility that our belief may not be the only way of seeing something. At the very least, we'll have fewer disagreements and a little less stress.

Here are two more examples of how the "Ladder" works:

* The meeting was called for 9 AM and Joe came in at 9:30. He didn't say why.
* Joe knew exactly when the meeting was to start. He deliberately came in late.
* Joe always comes in late.
* We can't count on Joe. He's unreliable.

See how you can easily jump to conclusions that may or may not be accurate. It's possible that Joe has a valid reason for being late.

It's probable that Joe really hasn't been late to every meeting. It's may be that Joe has too many meetings, or too much on his plate.

It's possible that he doesn't have the right tools to remind him of meetings.

This second example is a common occurrence:

* Beth hasn't responded to my email.
* Beth avoided me when I waved to her.
* Beth must have heard some lie about me.
* I'm incredibly hurt by Beth now.
* Beth isn't a loyal friend after all.

Wow! All of a sudden, Beth is a disposable, disloyal, easily swayed, gossip, that's too cold-hearted to even acknowledge her former friend. I don't realize Beth didn't get the email invite, couldn't see me wave to her because of the way the glare of the sun hit the windshield, and she hasn't reached out lately because she's been emotionally buried under a family crisis.

In either of these cases, you may not have had enough data to work with. You can't live your life without adding meaning or drawing conclusions. But there are ways through improving your communication and your thought process as you climb the Ladder:

* Becoming more aware of your own thinking and reasoning through reflection. "How did I handle the situation?" "Did I reach the right conclusions after the fact?" "Did the person react the way I expected?" "If not, why?"
* Making your thinking and reasoning more visible to others through advocacy. "Here's how I came to that conclusion...", "Here's what I am thinking..."
* Inquiring into others' thinking and reasoning through inquiry. "Do you think I handled the situation well?"

"What would you have done differently and why?" "Would you have reached the same conclusions?"

We filter our dialogue and say what we think they want to hear

* We carry on a private dialogue and a public dialogue.
* We filter our private dialogue, only saying what we assume will be heard, will not upset people, will get us what we want, and so on.
* When everyone keeps important things private, our ability to learn and to make good decisions is reduced.

Dilemma

* If we keep our private dialogue private, we prevent ourselves and others from learning and from making good decisions.
* But if we say what we are thinking or feeling, we may make things worse by upsetting people, making ourselves vulnerable, and so on.

Ways out of the Dilemma

* Be diplomatic or otherwise "pretty up" our private dialogue so it can be made public. There is a place for this, but it is not powerful. People usually see through cosmetic strategies.
* Recognize that how we are thinking and feeling in the first place is itself part of the problem, and learn how to transform our private conversation into something that we can make public.

When we connect to our hearts and one another in The Infinity Loop, we desire to more connected than separate. From there, we can be honest because we're heart-centered, humble and willing to learn. In connection, awareness, and inquiry, we can be honest and we won't be disrespectful or unhelpful. We've taken The Second Look, and with the contemplative heart and mind, won't be shaming or dehumanizing because we're seeing them in their humanity and divinity and are ever aware of what we may not know. We're incorporating everything in this book to be our best selves. Honesty coming from there is a beautiful and much- needed thing.

THE LADDER OF INFERENCE
REFLECTION

What was your biggest learning about how we go up our Ladders?

What is your biggest learning about how to come down off your Ladder?

What is the biggest challenge for you in making this a habitual awareness?

How do you see this tool fitting into The Infinity Loop model?

77

Judger Vs. Learner
(Marilee Adam's work)

"No one can help anyone else from a judger place."
MARILEE ADAMS – *CHANGE YOUR QUESTIONS, CHANGE YOUR LIFE*

We change from a Judger to a Learner when we change our questions. We observe our thoughts, and realize what mindset we're in. We can choose our mindset. We're all recovering judgers!

Learner Mindset – Thoughtful Choices, Solution Focused, WIN-WIN relating.
What happened?
What do I want for both myself and others?
What can I learn?
What assumptions am I making?
What are the facts?
What are they thinking, feeling, wanting?
Am I being responsible?
What's possible?
What are my choices?
What's best to do now?

Judger Mindset – Automatic Reactions, Blame Focused, Win-Lose Relating.
Why am I such a failure?
Why are they so stupid?
Why bother?

Who is at fault?
What's wrong with me?
What's wrong with them?

Judger Vs. Learner
Reflection

What's your biggest growth opportunity to having a Learner Mindset regularly?

What was most helpful about Marilee's work on these two mindsets?

In what ways do you feel empowered that you can change so quickly by changing questions?

78

Four Fields of Conversation

"The intention of Dialogue is to reach new
understanding and, in doing so, to form a totally
new basis from which to think and act."
- BILL ISAACS
DIALOGUE: THE ART OF THINKING TOGETHER

This compilation and the next section on Dialogue came from
Bill Isaacs' work.

With enormous gratitude to Bill Isaacs for his work.

This section will make more sense after you've also read the next
two sections on Dialogue. I recommend you then go back through
this section.

See the Four Fields as four boxes. The first two boxes - Politeness and Debate - are what we often go back and forth between.
We spend most of our time in those two areas. We must decide
to transcend our attachment to our point of view, realizing we
aren't our point of view, to get into box three, Inquiry. This is
now a reflective, learning field. We discover what we don't know.
Once we're able to do that, we will move to the forth field, Generative Flow, where we flow between Inquiry and Advocacy and
Think Together. Box three and four are learning and reflective,
while box one and two are not. In The Infinity Loop, we move to
Inquiry and Generative Flow. The other two fields are necessary
and helpful to uncover issues and create a team spirit and stability.
Politeness has a place, but won't solve the big problems. Neither
will Debate. Usually the best Debater or strongest personality

wins the Debate, whether or not their ideas are the best way to go. This usually needs a facilitator until the skills are learned. When we practice the other principles in this book, we do this process much better.

1. Politeness – Shared monologues

Characterized by Move-Follow sequences. No one opposes or by-stands. Marked by civility (learned ways of thinking and acting): Pleasantries, complaints, what needs 'fixing'. Participants are frustrated but unengaged and unaware of the source. Norms and rules are followed but unexamined. Fear reinforces rule following. Not likely to say what I'm really thinking. What's good for the whole is more important than what's good for the individual.

Goal: Protect participants' images, repress free expression for the good of the whole. Save my face and yours.

Field: Blaming and Non-Reflective

To move to Field 2: "There is no one person to blame – we are all responsible and must discover what to do together." Let go of false hopes of manipulating commitment.

2. Debate/Breakdown – Skillful conversation

Characterized by Move-Oppose sequences. Participants stake out (right and wrong) positions, cling to their perceptions and battle over whose meaning will have more power. Participants seek control. The prospect of endless battling for position is so unappealing that participants retreat back to 'Politeness'. Participants sometimes question if things are okay and view coming together as a mistake. Breakdown is a 'crisis'.

Goal: To skillfully control the discussion and win without upsetting anyone.

Field: Blaming and Non-Reflective.

To move to Field 3: Cool down the exchange and change the meaning of the trauma (crisis). View anger and frustration as fuel for change vs. symptom of failure. Practice 'suspension' – "I am not my view."

3. Inquiry – Reflective Dialogue

Characterized by a 'spirit of curiosity'. Participants are free to explore what is most deeply troubling at a fundamental level – below the surface – and the structures that drive their behavior and actions. No one feels compelled to respond, agree, disagree, or take a position. Dynamics change from participants reporting 3rd person data to reporting 1st person data (my process – personal stories) – transparency.

Goal: To suspend my views and underlying assumptions in order to be free to truly listen to the views of others.

Field: Self -Reflective.

To move to field 4: Move from reporting 'memory' to speaking from our hearts. From personal stories to deeper 'shared meaning'. From speaking our thoughts to valuing our insights.

4. Flow – Generative Dialogue

Characterized by letting go of our isolated identities, fluid creativity and releasing structures that limit the flow of (shared) meaning.

Fosters 'learning' vs. 'knowing'. Opens up new possibilities and options. Consciousness of a larger sense of destiny together and an undivided whole that links all participants. All participants share a 'voice' of equal weight and equal value. Individual insight becomes shared insight, or 'outsight'. Advocacy and Inquiry are balanced.

Goal: Create a container large enough to hold different points of view without attempting to 'pressure' anyone to change their views.

Field: Self-Reflective

FOUR FIELDS OF CONVERSATION
<u>REFLECTION</u>

What did you learn from The Four Fields of Conversation?

What about this tool got your most attention as something you'd like to incorporate or be aware of in your interactions?

In what ways do you feel you've been, or others you know have been afraid of the heat of Debate and gone back to Politeness because you didn't know how to move into Inquiry as a whole?

In what ways are you aware that only Inquiry is going to solve the big problems that keep surfacing? Advocating doesn't bring out what Inquiry does. Write about your awareness of how you've experienced this to be true.

79

Dialogue

> "One must be able to Dialogue to be a leader in
> The Infinity Loop that changes the world."
> - KRISTA VORSE

When I learned Dialogue over a decade ago, it completely changed me, my way of relating in conflict, my way of seeing, and my world. It made so much sense. Dialogue is used by the greatest leaders to try to fix some of our world's biggest problems. Coaches and consultants who facilitate this in relationships and companies, are worth their weight in gold.

Dialogue is a practice that moves us beyond our habitual way of interacting, looking at data, and solving problems. It takes into consideration the problems of our survival brain, where our ego does and does not serve, and the magic of Thinking Together. What emerges in the spaces between our certitude, our dominance, our fears, lies infinite possibilities.

Dialogue is a problem-solving model because of the way it surfaces data and allows truth to come forward. It surfaces assumptions and practices that aren't serving. It creates rules of engagement that provide a structure that creates safety but doesn't stifle truth.

Dialogue is a field we enter into that's based on connection, awareness, and inquiry. Think of it as the Alpha brain and every tool and principle in this book utilized. It's honesty, curiosity, and humility. We remember the Aspen. The future emerges from what we create together that is more elegant and intelligent that what we have now.

80

What is Dialogue?

"The ability to perceive or think differently is
more important than the knowledge gained."
- DAVID BOHM

This came from a conversation with Leo Gorcey.

The definition of Dialogue, <u>dialogos,</u> means, "ideas passing through."
Dia is where we get the word diameter as in "passing across the
circle." Dialogue is ideas passing through.

This will explain further The Four Fields of Conversation.

When we're in Politeness, ideas don't pass through. Ideas are
there but they get filtered and they don't pass through. They get
blocked because, "Oh, I better not say that." "Somebody doesn't
want to hear that." "That's going to piss people off." "I don't want
to sound stupid." So, ideas don't pass through.

In Debate, ideas are killed because we have to decide between
ideas. The word "decide" has the same root word as genocide,
homicide, suicide. It means "to kill every idea but one." So again,
ideas don't pass through. Ideas are blocked because we think we're
our point of view, so we defend, we promote, we argue and then we
have to kill off all the other ideas in the decision-making process,
and all those potentially good ideas are killed off before they get
a chance to be talked about or tested. Only one idea emerges and
if that's the wrong idea, then you have to go through the whole
rigamarole of getting through people's defensiveness to even

acknowledge that they may have even picked the wrong idea, and to try a different idea. But then we're just going to go through the exact same process – ideas not passing through because Politeness and Debate are non-reflective states. There's no reflection, there's no inquiry, no transparency of my thought process or opening my thought process to anybody else's inquiry. It's a closed process. Ideas cannot pass through.

In Dialogue, once you get into Inquiry, ideas pass through. Every idea is presented with the same amount of regard and all the ideas will be put out on the table. Instead of killing a bunch of them, we actually decide to test several of them at the same time, so it's ideas passing through. That's the meaning of Dialogue. We're not blocking them, judging them, killing them, resisting them. All ideas are passing through.

We obviously don't do this on everything or else we'd get nothing done. However, on the big, re-occurring problems that are causing tons of unintended consequences, costing you money, costing you being able to get to your objective and producing the results everybody wants, it's crucial to have ideas passing through. No other way to solve it. If it could be solved in Debate it would have. If it could have been solved in Politeness it would have. It can't. So, you have to move into Inquiry and Generative Flow. You have to get into reflective states of communication and open up the space. In Dialogue, we open up the space.

In Breakdown, which comes from Debate, we mistranslate the message of anger in Breakdown as, "We shouldn't have gone there." "We shouldn't have done that." "We shouldn't have talked about that." "That was a mistake." We then retreat back to Politeness. The reality is, the Breakdown is not a mistake because it surfaces the truth, and in fact, it's the only way we get through to Inquiry. That's why you need a facilitator. Then you get through to Inquiry. Inquiry opens up the space. Debate closes it. Politeness closes it. Inquiry opens it.

Once we get into Inquiry, we're opening up the space around the ideas so, now we're not just talking about ideas, we're talking about our own individual understanding of the ideas. That's why Inquiry often drops down deep into story-telling because now we're not talking just about the ideas, but we're talking about what the ideas stir up in people. We're suspending judgment, suspending our point of view. We're not losing it, not dropping it, not having to give it up, but putting it aside, like pulling down a window shade, suspending it. I'm going to pull it up later – it's still there, but I'm going to suspend it during Inquiry. During Inquiry, what begins to surface through the cracks is understanding, which binds everybody together. Even people of differing ideas can be bound together through understanding, and that's only approached through Inquiry. In Inquiry, I'm asked to now talk about my story about this idea, which flows into us talking about all of our stories. That creates empathy, which creates connection. When we become aware through understanding, that we all want the same thing under it all, that's Thinking Together. Now we go to Generative Flow where we're not impeded by all these blockages and resistances and we're not closed. We're reflective and open. We're transparent. We invite Inquiry into our process so we can discover things we could never have discovered in Politeness or Debate. That's the benefits of it.

In Generative Flow, that's the part where the new ideas are actually being released. This is about what's possible, like what's talked about in The Infinity Loop. We're not all braced to fight each other in these non-reflective states where ideas can't pass through because they're murdered on their way through the gate. When we're in Generative Flow, we're all there together, open to what's possible. That's where the Inquiry comes in and that's where these carefully crafted questions are surfacing data we never had before. Better quality data makes better quality choices, better quality choices make better quality results. In this model, it's in

Generative Flow where ideas are now coming up and then someone's writing them down. You may end up at the end with a page of 20 ideas that were never there before. That's when you go back and prioritize. "Which of these 20 ideas should we test? Let's test these five first because they have the most potential to move the needle." Then you pick out (vote on) which are the five ideas you're going to test and then assign ownership of these ideas, follow through and accountability, time frame, who's going to be accountable, what are the goals, what are the objectives. This process can be done in families, relationships, or any system. These ideas would never have come through Debate and Politeness. They would never have had a chance. They would have been killed at the deciding stage. "We can't do that because..." And instead of one or two people running the show, every single person in the room is participating. These are ideas that may have lived among this group of people for a long time but never had seen the light of day because they were murdered at the gate.

What excites people is innovation. People go from morose to so excited, their eyes light up, their body language is open, they can't wait to get out the door and go do it. That's what Dialogue does. It's infinite possibilities.

DIALOGUE
REFLECTION

What was your biggest aha moment reading Leo's description of Dialogue?

How's Dialogue different from what goes on in your world?

Which principles from The Infinity Loop model came to mind when reading about Dialogue?

What will you do, starting today, to let ideas pass through - not kill them at the gate when someone suggests something in your world? What would it be like in your body, your heart, your connection to another, your awareness, your self-inquiry that could say, "Hmm, I wonder what that would look like? How could that work and be possible? Why do I feel I need to kill that idea as soon as it comes out of that person's mouth? How could I create more spaciousness?"

81

Key Practices of Dialogue
(A compilation of Bill Isaacs's work)

"We haven't really paid much attention to thought as
a process. We have engaged in thoughts, but we have
only paid attention to the content, not to the process."
- DAVID BOHM

1. Find your voice: Say what you really think, not what you've
   been told to think. Be quiet enough to hear yourself. What
   do you really think?

   a. Say what's true regardless of other influences. Suspend
      the voice of judgment that tells you what you ought to
      say. Your authentic voice is not a rehash of the words
      of others. Speaking your voice means feeling the confi-
      dence that what you're thinking is valid and fits.
      "What needs to be expressed right now?"

   b. The magic word "Abracadabra" means: "I create as I
      speak." When you're speaking from your own voice,
      your words are magic. They have the power to trans-
      form your circumstances. Start by asking yourself,
      "What do I want to create?" and "Why do I long to
      create it?"

   c. Learn to be okay with silence. Not everything you feel
      compelled to say needs to be said. Let what is in you
      fully take shape in the silence. The root word for intel-
      ligence means to "gather between the spaces."

2. Listen without Resistance. When you listen without resistance, you're not just listening to your own internal dialogue about what you're hearing or who is saying it.

   a. What am I feeling? Be aware of 'disturbance' and 'resistance'. What's being threatened? What am I holding on to? What are all the different voices here trying to convey? What voices are being marginalized?

   b. What am I thinking? Is what I'm hearing or saying factual? How does it belong? What's happening right now?

   c. Our ability to listen is a present-moment competence that diminishes as we dwell on the past or worry about the future. Prepare yourself to listen by centering yourself in the present.

3. Respect another's point of view. See the legitimacy and power of each person's point of view. You may not like it or agree with it, but give respect while listening.

   a. "I see you (and your view) and hold a space for you."

   b. Recognizing another's legitimacy is the opposite of judging and blaming.

   c. See people for the potential they carry with them. Treat each person as a teacher. What is it this person have to teach you that you don't already know? Treat each person as a mystery you will never fully comprehend. Treat each person as part of the whole – part of 'us'.

   d. Respect is the opposite of seeing people as objects to control.

4. Suspend Judgment. Relinquish your grip on certainty – your assurance that you know exactly what's happening and why it's happening. Let go and open up.

   a. Neither suppress nor advocate, but display views. You are not your view.

   b. Suspend Judgments, including judgments like: "This is the way it is." Suspend 'looking for evidence that you're right'. Don't ignore dis-confirming evidence. Don't impose your view on another in a way that says "You should not be the way you are."

   c. Suspend your grip on certainty. Certainty tends to see others as certain. "They are so opinionated." But you're being opinionated about them being opinionated. This is how we end up doing to others what we abhor in ourselves.

   d. Suspending judgment enables you to hold divisions, dif-ferences, dis-confirming data, and emotional response without intensifying it.
   There is no "They." What "They" are doing to you, is more likely something you are doing to yourself.

   e. Suspending judgment is putting on hold the temptation to 'fix', 'correct', or 'problem-solve', so we can inquire into what we observe. How is this working? What's going on here? How does this problem work?

   f. The opposite of suspending judgment is defending our judgments. We deny any connection to any idea that dis-confirms our own.

5. Suspend judgment by asking questions.

    a. The power of Dialogue is in the cultivation of questions that have no answers. Good questions reflect on what part you're playing in the behavior that's producing the unintended result. Many questions are 'statements' in disguise: "Do you really think Sally deserved that raise?"(Judgment)

    b. Some questions distance the questioner from the conversation, such as questions that imply there is a right answer. These questions keep the questioner's views hidden and inaccessible.

    c. A well-articulated question will likely produce initial silence and tension. Staying with that tension is the doorway to new and fresh possibilities and options for effective actions and results.

    d. Relax your grip on certainty by asking yourself the following questions.
    "Why am I so sure about this?" "Why am I holding on so intensely to this?" "What's the payoff for me for holding on to my position?"
    "What would happen if I let it go?" "What is the risk if I do?" "What might I lose?" "What do I fear I might lose?"

Key Practices of Dialogue
Reflection

Of the five principles, which ones do you feel are your greatest growth opportunities and why?

How will you practice doing these practices and create habits around them?

How do you see these practices as being capable of changing our world?

What's the biggest blocks to practicing Dialogue when needed?

82

Empathy

> "Great anger is more destructive than the sword."
> - INDIAN PROVERB

The more we grow in connection, the more we become self-aware, the more we practice self-inquiry and inquiry into another's point of view, the more we'll grow in our capacity to experience and show empathy. To know and love ourselves in a healthy way, while being humble and curious about what we think we know and react to without question, all will spill out into our worlds and transform them.

When we have what Dr. Dan Siegel calls a "Yes-Brain" state that's mindful and receptive, versus a "No-Brain" state that's reactive and harsh, it allows the other to relax and doesn't trigger a threat-reactive state in them. Fight, flight, freeze, or faint (collapsing), are all a threat-reactive state where one's no longer open to what's going on. This applies to how I talk about working with our anger: we are alert to our anger we feel, but by being mindful, we don't let it take over our brains. We can feel our No - something needs to be honored or protected - and still shift to a "Yes-Brain" state that's open and flexible and where we communicate respectfully. The "Yes-Brain" state turns on what he calls the inter-mind between people. Siegel's work fits well with the tool I'm about to share with you.

Here's one of the tools I use to help clients develop more empathy, or turn on their empathy that is momentarily not activated. It comes from the customer service world, that frankly the customer service world could utilize more often. When I've taught people how to connect with empathy for the other person who attacks them, their lives become much less stressful and their brains and bodies reward them with all the good chemicals that come from love, calm, and connection. They also become successful at their jobs. I've seen and heard this used hundreds of times and it's magical. It's made companies a lot of money and magically transformed relationships I've coached.

If we gave everyone first-class customer service and helped turn on others' empathy, we would change the world. There's a better option besides just getting our voice; our voice can make sweet music for the world.

Develop the reflex to give **EAR.**

Empathize

Apologize

Re-direct

Someone acts rude, unaware, and entitled to us. We feel our anger and either we are shocked and acquiesce to their tantrum and lose sleep over what we should've said to put them in their place, or we set them straight right there. However, rarely will we win and it's certainly not #lovewins. The rude person will most likely not have their empathy turned on toward us or feel appropriate shame. Recall what you read in *Loving Well* chapter: shaming isn't effective in changing the world or influencing another. It's emotionally incompetent and history and the study in social sciences have proven the futility of it.

If we think of that person as a customer that we want to keep, we will care to use more sophisticated communication skills to try to reach them and influence them for the better. We step into The Infinity Loop where we feel safe and strong. We don't have to feel threatened by their reaction, and don't have to threaten them back. We've switched brain states.

The person who's angry with us, our dog, our company, product, or kid, comes at us to defend their point of view and how we've wronged them. They aren't aware of empathy and how they act.

Their focus is to make sure no one stops their speech. When we don't defend our position, or debate them in how they're wrong, we unexpectedly and paradoxically will very often get them to see where they're in the wrong, a contributor to the problem, or at least aware that their behavior isn't kind.

We breathe, take The Second Look to see beyond their behavior we're critical of, to the person with needs underneath - however unskillfully they're communicating in that moment. Set an intention:

How can I bring the most peace to the situation?

How can I step into The Infinity Loop in connection, awareness, and inquiry?

This doesn't work if we say the words but don't feel empathy. There's a magic that happens between us humans, our brains, our hearts, our inter-minds as Siegel calls it, when it's real. The other's brain lights up and usually mirrors back the empathy. You have activated that connection.

Let empathy for them hit you in your belly; if you were them, in their mental model, you see how stressed they'd be. We feel empathy from there. When we speak, we speak in response to that hit in our gut that's our connection to them - *Remember the Aspen*. They're feeling respected, seen, and heard. They probably behave the way they do because they need to feel seen. You do all three parts without pause. When you **E**mpathize, it's real. When you **A**pologize, it's real. When you **R**e-direct, it's real.

Here are two examples of it all put together and then I have examples of each part of it.

> **E**mpathize: I understand how you would be disappointed by this right now.
> **A**pologize: I'm sorry you're struggling and for the pain and loss you're feeling.
> **R**e-direct: However, it would be unwise and unhealthy for me to engage with your sister at this time because of all

that's gone on and how angry I'm feeling. I need to honor it, process it, and establish boundaries around how I'm treated.

Empathize: I feel for you and do see how you would feel that way.
Apologize: I'm sorry for all you went through and how much your heart still hurts.
Re-direct: I wonder if there's another way to look at this though. Knowing what I do about the situation, have you thought about the possibility that there's another explanation for what happened when your parents divorced? Maybe you *were* wanted more than anything in the whole world!

Empathize:
"I would feel that way too if that happened to me."
"I understand how stressful this must be for you."
"I hear how upset you are."
"I've felt like that way too."
"I understand you are concerned and only trying to help."
"I empathize with how angry and frightened you are right now and how hurt you feel."

It's important to stress to you, when we Apologize, we are sorry for their suffering and own our contribution to it if we did, but we are not taking responsibility for being the cause of their pain if we're not. (Unless we're representing a company that was in the wrong.)
Apologize:
"I'm sorry for what you're going through."
"I'm so sorry you have to deal with this."
"I'm so sorry my dog scares your dog."
"I'm sorry for the confusion."
"I'm sorry if I come off unappreciative of your suggestions."

Re-direct:

"Is there somehow we can make this work for us?"

"I'd love to hear more about your process of how you think this should work."

"This isn't helpful for me right now so I need us to change the subject."

"I'm not okay with the way you made fun of me because I didn't know how to use the lighter."

"Is there another way you can communicate with me your frustration?"

The **Re**-direct can be inquiry, a boundary, or how you express your process that's open to feedback (The Ladder). It could be your honest disappointment at what doesn't work, or it may open up a Dialogue that creates learning. Alpha Women are humble, honest, and curious. We want to express our boundaries in connection and understanding around our "No." We need fluffy bread around the meat of the issue to influence the other. We soften our harsh assessments of others so they can metabolize the truth. Approach matters; it's grace and gentleness. That's our "Yes-Brain" state.

Our **Re**-direct may be back to why someone originally ordered a product. Perhaps it's Socratic Questions to get them to illustrate with data their point of view. Since we're obviously not bound by company rules to keep a customer, we focus this tool on being connected, and not in our separate, superior, and important ego state. We **E**mpathize from our own fullness, **A**pologize for their suffering - without our need to own it's our fault if it's not. We immediately **Re**-direct them so we move on to solutions. Now we're in The Infinity Loop and practice all the tools and principles in this book to grow in emotional intelligence while learning how to love well while practicing elegant and intelligent self-care.

The other party will most often adjust their behavior and apologize. Sometimes people's intensity toward us is because they're afraid of being run over themselves and they had to muster up a lot to shoot out what they said. Sometimes they aren't aware, nice, or emotionally intelligent. Some people are in pain in body, mind, and spirit. That's why we're here and come with our golden infinity loop.

We don't become less than them. We get so good at being in The Loop, anything they say, we **Re**-direct to help them examine their own stories and for us to possibly see what we don't see.

"Do you really believe that?"

"I'm so glad we get a chance to talk because your dog humped my dog endlessly last week and I didn't know what to do either. Ha-ha. I'm sure we can find a way to make the dog park work for both of us. What's your dog's name?"

E. "I hear your pain and anger and what you're so upset about.
A. I'm so sorry for how I contributed to it.
R. However, I need to hang up now because the intensity of your rage and accusations aren't helpful or loving to me."

Remember: you create a Learning Container through inquiry. You now speak the truth about what doesn't work for you without being hurtful and unhelpful.

Play around with all the ways this tool works. Let people know you hear and feel their pain, express sorrow for their pain, and then move to what will serve in the **Re**-direct. Giving **E.A.R.** is both strength and gentleness.

EMPATHY
<u>REFLECTION</u>

Where will you utilize **E.A.R.** in your world?

What did you find most insightful or helpful about this approach?

Is there any part of you that disagrees with this? Why don't you think we do this more?

How is empathy the opposite of separate, superior, and important?

Part 3: The Decision

83

The Plane Went Down

"It's both thrilling and unsettling to live in the Cloud
of Unknowing. But anything in our future that feels
secure is more like trying to rest on a cloud; it may
look like a visible mass, but it's just liquid droplets."
- KRISTA VORSE

Living in the Eternal Now is our true home. What joy, lightness,
and playfulness we could experience if we lived there more often.
I want to live in the Now, not in the illusion of a future that I may
never see, nor a past that's just a swirl of atoms around memories.

I met a couple in Spring, 2016. Although I only spent about
20 hours with them, we connected deeply. They believed in me,
encouraged me and wanted to spend more time with me to intro-
duce me to people who we could connect with to make a difference in the world. She was committed to her dream work - what
our dreams tell us and how they guide us. The three of us shared
struggles we've had in our lives. I told them about my cult experience that took place between the ages of 18-20. It moved them to
hear where I've been. She gave me a notebook with a dragonfly
and DREAM stamped into the cover to encourage me to write.
I filled that notebook with notes on Transforming Trauma. That
notebook lay next to me on my bed when I got the call.

The call came from someone who also knew of the couple. She
thought I already knew that their plane went missing the week
prior but search teams were still hoping to find them. She told
me they didn't make it. I wailed. I wailed for the tragic loss but
also because I knew; I knew when the woman told me about a

specific dream she dreamt where she was piloting the plane (she was the pilot) her interpretation and mine were different. When she relayed the dream to me, I felt my intuition in my body. The feeling was in my chest pushing me back and I wanted to scream, "Holy shit! This is how you're going to die!" It seemed so obvious to me what that dream meant. The lyrics to Elton John's song, *Daniel* - about the plane crash that took his brother's life - came to me. I felt sobered, sad, and confused. Then when they were leaving and we stood with them at the tiny airport with their plane, I just knew their plane was going down. 10 1/2 months later it did.

For two days after I got the news, I remained still and quiet most of the time. I felt them with me. I texted the person who told me, "Let's have beautiful lives, full of joy and meaning, in honor of them. Let's go for it." Something happened to me after their deaths. Whatever held me back, was gone. I feel them, like angels, whisper in my ear and lift me up. I sense them beam love, as they took flight to another dimension, free from the constraints of this life. The woman who died may have seen in her dream how her life would end, but she didn't know it. It's all a mystery. But the Mystery is holding us, even when the plane goes down.

I live more courageously today because I met that couple. Because of their capacity to be present, gracious and loving, they saw me. We light up in each other's presence when we're seen, accepted and believed in. One never knows, of course, the number of our days. Today and for the rest of my days, I will go for it; I'll learn what I need to do to show up for my life the most courageous way. I help others navigate through the storms they're in. This couple went down in a storm.

Because of their lives, I want to live mine better. I feel them with me right now, as though we had known each other for decades. Love energizes us to wake up and put our hearts and heads out there to see who else needs to be seen, heard, and encouraged to live their lives more fully.

We'll all go through immense challenges as we navigate the storms we're in and in our commitment to live fully awake and present to the life that wants to be lived through us. Some of us will live a very long time and for others, we'll be gone when it appears we have decades ahead. Whatever the case, I'm going to choose to be 100% alive.

The Plane Went Down
Reflection

What practice do you have to remind yourself, every day, to live 100% alive? What practice do you have to be sober about the brevity of life? What adjustments do you want to make to live more intentionally and courageously?

In what ways do you feel your power to make a difference in someone else's life, just by seeing them, encouraging them, and believing in them?

What does living your life better look like?

What do you need to do to show up for your life?

84

You're Just Right

"You're street smart, wise as a serpent, simple as a
dove. You're nobody's fool, setting boundaries. Down
deeper still, it's this invincible, unshakeable oneness
with this invincible Love that permeates everything
as everything turns out just the way it does."
- James Finley

Marabai Starr, the scholar, author, and spiritual teacher of the
mystics, was asked what message she would give to women today.
She replied, that in spite of the efforts of our mothers and grand-
mothers, women are still living under the message that we're either
"Not enough" or "Too Much." We are neither, she said. "We're
just right."

I remember how he got me – my Necessary Nemesis. We sat
across my dining room table that fateful February night. He found
my Great Wound – shame – "I'm too much," and played it as I wept
so hard I thought there was no end to the pain. He would be the
one to refine me so I wasn't too much.

I would become small, I would abandon my vocation, my
voice, my brain, and discernment. And I would hear how "I'm not
enough" every day, in every way, that would keep me small but
doing more and more in service of what did not serve.

I believe Marabai is right; this message is something we women
live under. Let us recall from *The Father Wound*, men live under
this message as well. We must break free. If we're living under
this, we'll struggle to be seen and heard. Or we'll do it in a way that
doesn't serve.

Let us walk in our "enoughness" and our "not too muchness" in an elegant and intelligent way. May we get bigger when we experience oppression. Bigger in all the right ways for all the right reasons. It's time we realize we're more than we thought we were and have what we need living inside of us.

This book is my amends to myself and others. My hope is that this book will help us live in our "enoughness" and our "not too muchness" better. For the rest of my life, with my life, I desire to make amends for believing these lies, and for all the ways I've lost my way because of those lies, and hurt myself and others as a consequence.

I'm neither "too much" nor "not enough." I'm just right. And so are you.

You're Just Right
<u>Reflection</u>

How were you given the message that you were either "not enough" or "too much" or both?

In what ways are those messages given to women still today?

How will you step into The Infinity Loop, own the truth that "I am enough" and "not too much"? How do you hold that truth in the face of lies and not hate those who are confused?

85

I'm Not Getting Off My Horse

*"You always have two choices: your
commitment versus your fear."*
- SAMMY DAVIS JR.

I wrote this in April 2017, two months prior to when *Wonder
Woman* came out. Now that I've seen the film, I understand more
what this means.

In a session with Ajana, I spoke about my Joan of Arc energy.
The visit before that, as I lay on the table I received an old Sword,
carried by valiant women before me, planted deep in my being. It
is my Sword of Truth. From that moment on, what's true for me
will resonate off that Sword; my new guidance system has been
delivered. When I spoke of how I saw myself on the horse, Ajana
thought it was a Joan of Arc image. She asked if I was able to put
on her armor when needed and then able to take it off and just
be me. I told her, "I'm not Joan of Arc. This is a different Krista.
She's much older, wiser, and no one's getting her off her horse to
burn her at the stake." When those words came out of my mouth,
I knew this was the next big thing in my life.

My life-long struggle to not fully own my power and my intelligence is over. This Krista is on her white horse, in her early 50s,
has a long, wild mane, and is fit with a strong arm that wields
that Sword. Her body is kissed by the sun when I see her in this
open field on this warm, summer day. Her outfit is utterly fabulous: an intricate, sturdy leather vest is wrapped with a leather belt;
her biceps are exposed but leather bands partially cover her fore-
arms; woven braids decorate the shoulders of her silk embroidered,

butter-colored, linen sleeveless dress. The golden thread shimmers in the sunlight. She has a keen eye, sits up tall and strong with a confidence that's fearless. She's a badass and she's magnificent.

This week I've been going through family memorabilia. Seeing my late father's newspaper clippings from ski races touches a curious and deep place in me. I didn't inherit his athletic ability (except his fast reflexes that cause my self-esteem to shoot up every time I drop something and catch it mid-air). But I acknowledge that I've inherited something from that champion that I'll carry with me.

I cannot courageously ski like he did, but I can show up for my life in the most courageous way. I jump off the cliff in trust and head downhill with all my might where nothing will slow me down. I maneuver through the gates I must cut through with skill, strength, grace, and lightness. I train to be fit physically, spiritually, emotionally, and intellectually. I dedicate my heart and life to be the best I can be, with the fierce intention of a champion athlete, to become the vessel for the expression that Life wants lived through me. And so can you.

Now the image of me on my horse is planted in me like my Sword. I feel my strength, my power, my warrior, my heroine. She's fast. I was given this image because I need it; it will serve me so I serve Life and others. It's a miracle; once I was in a dungeon, but now I roam freely with a purpose that will not get me off my horse.

The shifts happen in us first to prepare us for the shifts that will manifest in the material world in our lives. We influence others toward the light as opportunities arise to use our gifts to change our world.

We have something to protect on this earth. We have something worth speaking up for and wielding our Sword as we cry, "Freedom!"

Let nothing and let no one get you off your horse. You are a badass and you are magnificent.

I'M NOT GETTING OFF MY HORSE
REFLECTION

What does it mean in your life to not get off your horse?

What image do you have to bring you into awareness that you're a badass and magnificent?

In what areas will you adjust to being in training as a champion in every area of your life?

What will you do to be the vessel that Life wants to express through you?

86

Magnificence

"As we let our own light shine, we unconsciously
give other people permission to do the same."
- NELSON MANDELA

Five months after I had the vision on my horse - where I saw my
magnificence - I heard author and teacher Andrew Harvey speak
about our Golden Shadow. Our Golden Shadow is our noble parts
we disown in ourselves but celebrate in another. He was asked why
we disown our good parts. After I heard him speak of it as magnificence, I felt again the sacredness and significance of what I saw
for myself and for you. He refers to magnificence in a way that's in
line with my vision. The gist of what Andrew said:

*The Golden Shadow is our magnificence that we project onto
another.* (He made the distinction between *the new-age version of 'magnificence' where we're told we attract anything we
want into our lives like our Malibu mansion, but is just our
depraved narcissism.*)

*The real reason people are terrified of their magnificence is
because it comes with very strong responsibilities. When we're
magnificent, our conscious is clean and we cannot support evil,
darkness or injustice. We're fearless and we speak truth to power.
We've found a way to be fed by streams of sacred passion that gives
us guts to stand up and really call people to task and warn them
what's coming if they don't change, and we risk all the rubbish
that will get held against us for doing that. If we're magnificent, we have to act magnificent to everybody around us. This is*

something we have to do completely and have to honor to really serve and that's exhausting and troubling. Of course, we're scared shitless by it. As we do our spiritual practice, over time we'll get over our fear of being our True Self and we allow the splendor of who we really are to radiate through us. We'll be brave enough because we're grounded enough in sacred practice and humble shadow work to support the flame of our true mission and pay the price as an act of love.

Like I said at the beginning, this work takes courage. We all have the ability and we all are brave. We all are Wonder Woman. We all have the fire. We just need to find it. Here's to being magnificent.

MAGNIFICENCE
<u>REFLECTION</u>

In what ways does the thought of being magnificent inspire you and empower you to up your game to show up magnificently like Andrew describes?

Where could you be more magnificent? What's been holding you back?

Where are you projecting your magnificence onto another, and not owning your own gifting and calling?

87

To Go Forth and Die

"It's in giving our lives away we are transformed into all
our souls yearn for. We give our lives to Love and She
takes care of the rest. She leads us to what is ours to do."
- KRISTA VORSE

The ancient European root of the word 'leadership' is Leith, which
means "to go forth, to cross the threshold, or to die." It was in reference to being in battle. That definition has proven problematic
as it's been seen as winning over another, as in violence. It may also
be experienced as something quite beautiful. We must be willing
to "die" to our old, tired, habitual ways of doing things (reproducing the past) and to our fear of the unknown to go forth – cross
the threshold into the future which will appear as we move into it.
Dying to our small, ego-driven selves must occur so others flourish. It's a spiritual imperative. I have come to believe that one cannot do this work without going forth to die.

To enter into The Infinity Loop, we do indeed go into another
realm that isn't our familiar operating system. We must leave
behind all our old ways that served our egos. To slip through this
cream-colored veil where this magic happens, we can't take anything with us; everything is left behind to gain access. We lose our
control of our image, our ego-defenses, our posturing, our certitude, our getting back at, and all we think will protect, promote,
and prove who we are. When we go to love instead, we have all our
power. We have become Wonder Woman. In this realm, we have
access to what we didn't before - the highest intelligence, awareness, and mastery over ourselves. Love is anything but weak. With

that kind of love, we're free from the fear and scarcity that makes us weak. We fear nothing. We have found our soul and it begins to direct us.

Without us going to that kind of consciousness, we aren't going to make it.

All this fighting in the extreme polarity of our world isn't working. Our suffering is the worthy invitation to let go and enter in. I hope we're all sick and tired of being sick and tired.

May you be wooed to walk through the veil and want it so badly, you leave everything behind.

This is why this book is about spiritual development. Spirituality may mean our inner life, connection, transcendence from our ego identified selves, and our separateness that doesn't want to enter into that loop. We need only to trust that as we let go, we'll be held by a greater force than ourselves. By trusting that there's a greater force than how we control our worlds, we will gain it all. That's The Bounce. We died but would not stay down. We were crushed and oppressed but rose again; not in vindictiveness but in service of what Love wants.

Now that's an adventurous life.

To Go Forth and Die
Reflection

In what ways do you have a new definition of what leadership means? In what ways does going forth and dying appeal to you now?

We must be willing to "die" to our old, tired, habitual ways we do things (reproducing the past) and to our fear of the unknown to go forth – cross the threshold into the future which will appear as we move into it. How's that helpful to trust in The Mystery Side, that the future will appear as we move into it, in the magic of The Eternal Now?

How does this way of being free you from any compulsive thinking to try to figure things out or control them?

How will you experience leadership, no matter what role you're in, as an adventurous life? How will it be more fun to live in this Mystery realm, where connection, awareness and inquiry reign?

88

Sturdy, yet Dissolving

"Knock, and He'll open the door. Vanish, and
He'll make you shine like the sun. Fall, and
He'll rise you to the heavens. Become nothing,
and He'll turn you into everything."
- Rumi

May this image live in you as you go forth as a leader.

You stand there alone in an open field. You've been transported back in time hundreds of years. You're a warrior, a leader, a woman - fierce, loving, and wise. As you turn you're able to see forever in every direction. You're calm and clear. You have steel going through much of your body. You're grounded and sturdy as a redwood tree. And yet, your torso is dissolving and the world can pass through you. You have been ripped open by all of life. And you have let it because you know to be powerful and to accomplish what is yours to do, you must become as nothing; you must dissolve into Essence to move through life that brings life to others.

Now you're ready. No matter what comes at you, you will not collapse. You are something not of this world.

Go forth and shine.

STURDY, YET DISSOLVING
REFLECTION

What will Sturdy, yet Dissolving look like in your life, in your being?

How does seeing yourself, alone, in the intimacy of your own life, in The Great Love Affair, help you to see how powerful, how valiant, how wise and safe you actually are?

To be both grounded and not of this world, Essence takes over as we become as nothing, but also magnificent at the same time. It takes the both/and world to hold it. It's the contemplative mind that holds what needs to change, and the love that sees others through eyes of The Infinity Loop, where anything is possible when we become the change we desire to see. What needs to be surrendered to be that change?

The Infinity Loop
Tribal Movement
to Change the World

If you would like to be updated on all The Infinity Loop Tribal Movements, shoot me an email and I'll put you on the list.

I'll send out tips on living in The Infinity Loop, resources that will help you live this life, and all the Tribal Movements that you can participate in or check out. Online courses, member groups, seminars, retreats, podcasts …

I'd love to hear from you and what you feel you need that will support you in The Infinity Loop.

It's apparent this book begs for ongoing support and deeper work. It's The Infinity Loop Spiritual Practice. So much depends on our development of ourselves to be able to show up for our lives in the most courageous way. A new learning or awareness comes to me and how I wish I knew it just a few weeks prior. The costs of not knowing or being free from ourselves in an area are real. But wisdom comes from our suffering. My heart leaps for joy to be able to share it with you, and have you share your wisdom with me.

Thank you for being on this journey with me through this book. I hope we will connect sometime in some way.

Krista
KristaVorse@gmail.com
KristaVorse.com

Made in the USA
San Bernardino, CA
21 July 2020